Qualitative Research in
EDUCATION

Qualitative Research in EDUCATION
A User's Guide

Marilyn Lichtman
Virginia Tech (Retired)

SAGE Publications
Thousand Oaks ▪ London ▪ New Delhi

For information:

Sage Publications, Inc.
2455 Teller Road
Thousand Oaks, California 91320
E-mail: order@sagepub.com

Sage Publications Ltd.
1 Oliver's Yard
55 City Road
London EC1Y 1SP
United Kingdom

Sage Publications India Pvt. Ltd.
B-42, Panchsheel Enclave
Post Box 4109
New Delhi 110 017 India

Printed in the United States of America on acid-free paper

Library of Congress Cataloging-in-Publication Data

Lichtman, Marilyn.
Qualitative research in education : a user's guide / Marilyn Lichtman.
    p. cm.
Includes bibliographical references and index.
ISBN 0-7619-2935-5 (cloth)—ISBN 1-4129-3734-5 (pbk.)
  1. Education—Research—Handbooks, manuals, etc. I. Title.
LB1028.L436 2006
370.7′2—dc22

2005033277

05 06 07 08 09 10 9 8 7 6 5 4 3 2 1

Acquiring Editor:	Diane McDaniel
Editorial Assistant:	Erica Carroll
Production Editor:	Sanford Robinson
Copy Editor:	Diana Breti
Typesetter:	C&M Digitals (P) Ltd.
Indexer:	Molly Hall
Cover Designer:	Michelle Kenny

CONTENTS

PREFACE

I remember my first education class as an undergraduate. It was during a time when few opportunities were available to women. In my mind, my career path was going to take me into teaching, so I registered for an education class. Its title was "Teaching and Learning." I still remember that class in which we learned 16 principles on the topic of teaching. To this day, I don't know who came up with the principles, but they were considered gospel. "Begin where the learner is; suit methods to the learner; mesh the new with the old." How interesting. They are still important principles. I am sure I did not question them. Why did we learn them? Who decided? Was research a part of this? It was not until much later that I began to think about how education could be guided and informed by conducting research on important topics. In this book, I provide you with a combination of practical and theoretical information that will assist you as you advance in your educational pursuits. But first, here is a little background you might find interesting.

The study of education at the college and university level became popular in the United States during the mid to late 1800s. Universities opened departments of education and separate normal schools were established. Their purpose was to train teachers to work at the elementary or grammar school levels. Courses were of a practical nature. It was not until the 1890s that Josiah Royce asked whether there was science in education. In the next century, especially after World War I, the education community adopted the stance that a scientific approach to the study of education, with an emphasis on quantitative measurement, would take the field to a higher level. Colleges and universities required education students to take courses in research methods and statistics and to read research studies that emphasized experiments and complex statistical analyses. Federal government funding of educational research was directed at studies with a scientific underpinning. Journals published articles based on quantitative research. This point of view permeated the educational community, and even as I write this today, in 2005, many colleges of education firmly believe that the scientific method has the highest status and should be the one used for research.

However, in spite of their best intentions, many educators found they were still unclear about some basic questions: What are the best practices for teaching reading? How should classroom discipline be managed? How should teachers work with disadvantaged youth? How could teachers working with adults provide appropriate training? There was a large chasm between the teachers in the schools and the researchers and professors in the universities whose mission was to educate school teachers.

Several factors led colleges and departments of education to begin to look at the value of the **scientific approach**[1] to the study of education. Some thought that adoption of the scientific method did not make sense when so many variables were outside of the control of the researcher. Lagemann (2000) speaks of a misguided attempt to be scientific. In addition, many teachers found statistical modeling and experimental research foreign to their own experience and difficult to grasp and implement. Teachers began to take ownership of research conducted in schools, and the teacher researcher and **action research** movements moved the central focus from universities to the schools. Finally, more women and minorities entered the educational research community and brought new ways of thinking and a different sensibility to the endeavor.

I do not want to mislead you, however. Many education schools still expect you to be well versed in the scientific method. But since you are reading this book, you are in a program where alternative ways of answering questions are considered.

THE EARLY DAYS

Although anthropologists and sociologists have used qualitative methods for about 100 years, researchers in the field of education adopted methods drawn from the natural sciences and psychology. You can read this history in detail, with many interesting photographs, in the first chapter of Bogdan and Biklen's book (1992) on the foundations of educational research. These approaches tended to be quantitative in nature and involved hypothesis testing and generalizations. It was not until the 1980s that anthropologists began to work in educational arenas to any great extent (Spradley, 1979). Lincoln and Guba (1985) suggested studies be conducted in natural settings rather than in laboratories. They referred to this as **naturalistic inquiry**. But, the primary mode of conducting educational research remained experimental in nature. Students were expected to become conversant in behavioral science and statistics. Most research courses and programs were dominated by the scientific method.

Qualitative research is a relatively new field in educational research. It was not until the 1990s that scholars, publishers, journals, and government agencies began to think about qualitative research. *The Handbook of Qualitative Research* (1994) led the way. The University of Georgia had its first Qualitative Interest Group (QUIG) conference in 1992 and continues to this day as a leader in the field. *The Qualitative Report* issued its first paper journal in 1990 and went online in 1994. Free online distribution made the information accessible worldwide.

Just as qualitative research in education has witnessed a phenomenal growth, so, too, have changes in approaches to research been seen in other disciplines and in other parts of the world. Psychology, often the last bastion of the scientific approach, has seen increased interest in the field. The American Psychological Association issued *Qualitative Research in Psychology* (Camic, Rhodes, & Yardley, 2003), a series of edited papers expanding perspectives in methodology and design. *Forum Qualitative Social Research* publishes articles and reviews reflecting this more open perspective from a Western European point of view. See my review of the proceedings of a conference on Qualitative Psychology (Lichtman, 2005). Parker (2003) and Harré (2004) suggest that psychologists might even consider that it is qualitative research that is scientific.

There are several reasons for the increased interest in qualitative research beginning in the 1990s. First, the opening up of the educational research field to women and people of color led to alternative sensibilities and alternative voices. No longer were quantitative studies (developed by white European men) the only choice in research methods; other ways of knowing might be considered just as legitimate. Second, there was a growing dissatisfaction with educational research findings based on quantitative studies alone. Educational research findings were often vague, subject to many problems in implementation, poorly disseminated, and often irrelevant. The public school community made decisions based on many factors other than research results. Third, teachers demanded a larger role in design and conduct of research and were drawn more to action research projects. Finally, publishers broadened the base of their offerings, and methods drawn from many disciplines were disseminated to a much greater extent than previously.

In these early days, most of us were not really sure what qualitative research was. Was it ethnography? Yes, said some. Was it having findings emerge from the data using a grounded theory approach? Yes, said some. Was it **phenomenology** or **hermeneutics**? Yes, said some. Was it an approach, a method, a philosophy, a science? All of the above and more, said some.

As for universities, there were few courses in qualitative research in the early 1990s. Many educational research departments offered none or devoted one lecture in a survey of methods to qualitative research. Faculty who taught qualitative research either came from the discipline of anthropology or were self-taught. I recall feeling very much like an outsider in my own department of educational research when I decided I wanted to learn about this field. One colleague described what he knew about qualitative research as fitting on the nail of his little finger. Others denigrated the field. It was seen as a field for those who were not objective, who were soft, or, worse yet, who were incapable of doing "the really hard stuff" that involved statistics. Since many research faculty, as well as other education faculty, had little or no training or experience, they often did not know how to react to what they read. They looked for research that fit the mold of quantitative research. When it didn't, they were unsure what to ask for and what to expect.

Publishers of qualitative research textbooks were very few in the early 1990s. Most books that were issued were devoted to a particular discipline. For example, Glaser and Strauss's *The Discovery of Grounded Theory* appeared in 1967, but this book dealt with only a small portion of the field. Bogdan and Biklen's *Qualitative Research for Education* appeared first in 1982, but it was written from an ethnographer's point of view.

Journals that either published articles written from a qualitative perspective or were devoted primarily to qualitative articles were rare in the early 1990s. Many of these journals struggled with establishing appropriate criteria for judging qualitative work and locating reviewers who were appropriately trained.

Professional associations, such as The American Educational Research Association, barely recognized the field of qualitative research. A few special interest groups existed in the early 1990s and a few presentations were given. For the most part, however, they were relegated to a minor role.

Communication between and among qualitative researchers both in education and in the larger social science arena was rare in the early 1990s. There were few avenues for researchers to find each other, to share ideas, and to discuss common issues.

As for teaching, I found it very difficult to find appropriate materials in the early 1990s. I searched journals for articles that were on target and combined them in textbook format, issued by our bookstore. The Internet was not readily available to most students or faculty, so it was difficult to get access to new material and make it available to students.

In those early days, if you were interested in teaching about or doing qualitative research you were often criticized. Quality was nonexistent, thought some. This couldn't be science since you did not test hypotheses. This couldn't be science since it wasn't objective. This couldn't be science since only a few were studied.

LATE 1990S AND BEYOND

In less than 10 years, this field has exploded. The *Handbook of Qualitative Research,* first issued in 1994, was completely restructured and a second edition was published in 2000; a third edition was published in 2005. Additional online journals came into being. *Forum Qualitative Social Research (FQS)* was established in 1999. Based in Berlin, it is a multilingual online journal for qualitative research. It includes articles, reviews, debates, interviews, and special topics. QUIG and *The Qualitative Report* expanded greatly. Listservs devoted to discussions of qualitative topics were developed, such as QUALRS-L@LISTSERV.UGA .EDU. Sophisticated qualitative research software was developed with a Listserv available to provide assistance (qsr.news@qsr.com.au).

Qualitative research became an umbrella under which many different types of information were included. It used a **feminist perspective**. It became **postmodern**. It became structural. It used case studies, action research, or mixed methods. It included various ways of gathering data. Sophisticated computer software packages were developed. Many disciplines adopted qualitative research ideas.

Some sought a compromise position by using by quantitative and qualitative methods in the same research study. Bergman (2005) spells out the central issues. Beginning about the mid 1980s, much of the writing suggested that as a researcher you should choose either one or the other approach, since their philosophical underpinnings were incompatible with each other. Some 25 years later, he suggests that there are a "wealth of possibilities in relation to data collection and data analysis techniques" (Abstract, p. 1). I'll discuss this in greater detail in a subsequent chapter. (See also Creswell, 2003.)

Qualitative courses were offered at many universities and in many different departments. Online teaching became available. More dissertations and theses were written and accepted. More faculty became interested in the field.

The publishing field exploded. Journals devoted specifically to qualitative research were issued. It became very difficult to capture the essence of the field. The Internet entered the scene, so information became instantly available. Researchers beyond the United States and Great Britain began to make contributions.

Professional associations, government agencies, and universities acknowledged the field and broadened the scope of the scientific community.

The marginalized voices began to make contributions that previously had no arena. People of color and women addressed issues of power and disenfranchisement.

CURRENT CHALLENGES

Today the field is booming. New books, new Web sites, new journals, new conferences, and new faces appear almost daily. I find it difficult to keep up with all that is out there. But lest you think that all is rosy, I want to highlight a few challenges that this field faces.

Preparation of Students and Faculty. While many new courses are being offered, much still needs to be done. Faculty who teach in the field need ways to stay current; faculty who work in other fields need to be educated as well. Issues that appear to be put to rest still emerge. Just this week as I write, a spate of e-mail discussions appeared on a qualitative Listserv regarding the use of first person in writing. Many students speak of having difficulty pleasing their advisers, who find the use of first person arrogant or too informal. Students suggest to others that they need to jump through appropriate hoops to receive their degrees and that they should not make this their battlefield. Of course, many other areas are still subject to question and debate.

Criteria for Evaluation. I think this is an area that remains challenging and conflicted. I do not believe we need to find parallel criteria to those used in quantitative research. At the same time, however, the field needs to stake a legitimate place in the scholarly community. The debate continues as to how qualitative research should be evaluated.

Rigidity, Structure, and Conservatism. I worry that as we become fixed and rigid, we move toward a conservative nature. Those opportunities for other voices to be heard, for other means of sharing what we learn, and for creativity and new ideas to emerge may be stifled in the interest of wide acceptance. Once we become mainstream, do we lose what we have been looking for?

Managing Information Overload. It is not just the domain of qualitative research that faces this problem. We are constantly bombarded with information in the field. Some of it conflicts with other ideas. It reminds me of the dilemma we face about our health. Should we drink a glass of wine at dinner? Should it be red or white? Should we eat carbs or not? Is being slightly over the optimum weight good for you?

How Do We Balance Acceptance of Various Alternatives With a Sense of Scholarship and Rigor? Should there be rigor at all? How can we dispel the idea that anything goes? Can we say that some ways of gathering material are better than others? Can we say that some writing is more convincing than others? There is still a debate about what constitutes scientific rigor. Maxwell (2004) suggests that qualitative research can offer a "legitimate scientific approach to causal explanation" (p. 3).

These are all ideas to think about as you begin to learn how to be a qualitative researcher.

STRUCTURE OF THIS BOOK

I have divided this book into three parts. In Part 1—Traditions and Influences—I provide a blend of history, traditions, influences, and specifics. My intention is to put you immediately into the setting. Many readers of this book have heard about qualitative research and find themselves attracted to it. You may like the fact that it usually does not involve numbers or statistics. You may like the idea of personal stories, or you may be taking such a class to fulfill a requirement. By blending history and tradition with some practical ideas, I hope to provide you with a framework to continue your studies. Chapter 1 identifies 10 critical elements that are part of the new paradigms of qualitative research. It also addresses such issues as objectivity and the researcher's role. I conclude this and every chapter with group and individual activities. Chapter 2 builds on the first chapter and provides additional insight into the field. In Chapter 3, I look at the past and toward the future to give you a sense of the field and how it has changed. I believe that one of the best ways to become a qualitative researcher is to become actively engaged in doing. As such, Chapter 4 provides some suggestions about learning to be a qualitative researcher. I end Part 1 with Chapter 5, in which I provide you with details about how different traditions inform the field. This last chapter is very challenging. You may find that you will need to read it more than once.

Part 2—Gathering, Organizing, and Analyzing—is designed to provide you with practical information on doing qualitative research. Although there are many traditions on which qualitative researchers may base their work, when it comes to methods, there is much agreement. Chapter 6 is concrete and based on my many years of experience working with students. After I ask and answer 20 questions about qualitative research, I provide you with a detailed example I have used in my classes, and I include examples from student writing. Chapter 7 introduces you to some new ideas about doing a literature review and offers some steps in doing such a review. Chapter 8 and Chapter 9 deal with learning about others. In Chapter 8 I focus on qualitative interviewing and focus groups. In Chapter 9 I examine other ways of learning about others, including observations, document reviews, using images, and gaining information online.

Part 3—Putting it All Together—also contains five chapters. In this section, I intend to take you from collecting data and analyzing it to thinking about how you can draw meaning from what you have gathered and subsequently how to say it, what others will say about it, and what you learn about yourself. I deal with drawing meaning from your data in Chapter 10. Chapter 11 addresses issues of communication: how to write and present a qualitative study. Chapter 12 addresses how qualitative research is judged by others and by ourselves. In Chapter 13, I look at reflections about the self; I also share my personal journey. Part I concludes with an epilogue in which I discuss keeping abreast of an evolving field.

The Appendix is a checklist you can use when doing qualitative or focus group interviews.

At www.sagepub.com/www.sagepub.com/lichtman, you will find a resource titled "Teaching Qualitative Research Online." This resource presents a detailed online interchange that occurred in one of my classes. The material is about phenomenology, but the process can be adapted to any topic.

BECOMING A SAVVY LEARNER

I have tried to provide you with tools to facilitate your learning this complex material. The quotations that are presented as you begin each chapter help you see other influences and ways of thinking. I suggest you do a quick read of each chapter before you begin to study it. In this way, you will have an overall view before you get bogged down in details. The images presented at the beginning of each chapter provide a visual alternative introduction for what is to come. The group and individual activities that come at the conclusion of each chapter have been used in my classes over the years; most students find them helpful. I hope you will have a chance to use some of them. I suggest that you keep a journal of your thoughts and ideas about becoming a qualitative researcher throughout the time you study this material. It should be your personal journal, but in keeping with my philosophy of self-reflection, I hope you will share it with your peers and your professors.

You will be faced with much material that is new to you. You will need to decide what is important and what you accept. Since qualitative research has no right answers, this puts you in a state of flux. I know that some students like to be told what to learn and memorize. This book is not intended to be used that way. I want you to begin to think about what research is, what qualitative research is for the field and for yourself, and how you might make contributions as you pursue your personal goals.

NOTE

1. I introduce many terms in boldface and provide definitions in the Glossary. I hope this assists you as you continue reading and learning.

ACKNOWLEDGMENTS

I began this project in 2002 when Art Pomponio from Sage called me to explore my interest in writing a text aimed at education students taking a first course in qualitative research. He had read my review of a textbook and was interested in some of my ideas. At that time I was teaching a graduate class at Virginia Tech that combined online teaching with face-to-face teaching. I was exploring several strategies for presenting material online to students. After several phone discussions and an outline submitted to Sage, Art offered me a contract to write a textbook that targeted the education field. I developed an extensive outline and wrote several chapters. You may wonder why it took so long to bring this project to fruition. My husband, Martin Gerstein, became ill and died in May, 2003; it took me almost a year to get myself back together to return to the book.

To my students. I want to thank all my students who, over many years, taught me perhaps as much as I taught them. We challenged each other to think outside the box. We valued each other's creativity. We questioned each other's ways of thinking and of knowing. To all of you, a special thanks. It is always a risk to provide a list of names since it is so easy to leave someone out, but a special word of thanks to Gohar Farahani, Paul Glass, Donna Joy, Judy Smith, Warren Snyder, Satomi Izumi Taylor, Leanne Wells, and Frank Wong. To Mary Repass—your support and encouragement mean a lot to me.

To colleagues. To Ron Chenail. We began our discussions about qualitative research almost two decades ago. Your continued help and ideas always challenge me to think about this topic in new ways. To Günter Mey and Katja Mruck. Your openness and support have broadened my knowledge base extensively and I value your friendship. To my colleagues at Virginia Tech, both in Blacksburg and Falls Church, thanks for all the good years together. To Diane McDaniel from Sage, who took over editorial work from Art. Your feedback and organizational ability are wonderful. To Erica Carroll from Sage. I appreciate so much your attention to the myriad details involved in making this book happen. To Diana Breti, copy editor, and Sanford Robinson, production editor, you have made bringing this book to fruition all the easier by your insightful comments. To all my friends and colleagues at The Corcoran Gallery of Art. I continue to be amazed as I find connections between the art world and the world of qualitative research. Also, I would like to thank the peer reviewers of this project for their helpful feedback and suggestions: Alberto M. Bursztyn, Brooklyn College and The Graduate Center; Sharon Anderson Dannels, The George Washington University; Douglas Fisher, San Diego State University; S. Kim MacGregor, Louisiana State University; Stephen A. Sivo, University of Central Florida; Charles Tesconi, American University; and James R. Valadez, California Lutheran University.

To my family. To my daughters, Ellen and Judy. Thanks for being my sounding board and providing me with challenges and ideas and for listening to my gripes. To my son, David, I always know I can count on you for anything. To my brother, Lee, thanks for reading and editing. I should have asked you sooner. To Jim, my son-in-law. Our talks about art continue to get me to think about things in different ways. To the rest of my family—Claire, Margaret, Anath, Michael, and Lilah—thanks for being there. I couldn't have done this without all your support. To my extended family, Judy Barokas, Louise Appell, Joan Blitman, and Shari and Curly Johnson. I value your thinking and ideas greatly. And finally, to my late husband and best friend, Marty. I know you are proud of this effort. I love you all.

—*Marilyn Lichtman*

PART 1

Traditions and Influences

I have organized this book in three parts. In Part 1, I introduce you to the very exciting field of qualitative research. Chapter 1 provides an introduction. Chapter 2 includes an overview of the field. Chapter 3 presents insights from the past. Learning how to be a qualitative researcher is covered in Chapter 4. Chapter 5 examines major traditions and approaches. If this is your first course in qualitative research, you probably have little knowledge or experience. These five chapters combine and interweave both practical experience and traditions. You might find it interesting that the field has grown so rapidly over the past 20 years. Many voices have shaped the field. Ultimately it is hoped that the knowledge gained from this kind of research can inform educators of both children and adults to provide a more meaningful educational experience for all.

My intention is to provide a balance of knowledge about the past and knowledge of various traditions that have shaped the field with practical experience. I believe that active participation will help you internalize some of the more abstract ideas you will face.

Each chapter concludes with a group activity and an individual activity. I have used many of these activities in my own teaching. I urge you to try some of them to fix the information in your mind.

CHAPTER 1

Introduction

Anyone who isn't confused here doesn't really understand what's going on.

—Anonymous

As a doctoral student who had returned to academic life much later in life than most students, I wanted to pursue a dissertation topic that was relevant to me and to develop a research project where I could bring my personal experiences and explore a subject that was intriguing. After all, I realized that writing a dissertation is a project that was going to consume months of my life and if I was to dedicate this time to active research and creating a product that would be useful in the future, it should be a subject for which I had a passion and a desire to learn more.

—Mary Repass

No doubt many of you who read these pages currently work in schools, have done so in the past, or are contemplating doing so. Others of you may work with adults in training settings or basic education classes. Much of your professional experience targets the here and now.

As you think about those with whom you work, you might have asked yourself these questions: How do I get my students to apply themselves, to pay attention, to enjoy learning? Why is it that some students seem to learn more quickly than others? What ways should I use to motivate students to learn? How can I account for individual differences among my students? How can I understand those students who are so different from me? How is my class similar or different from others around me? What about students who have had few home experiences that foster learning? Why can I reach some students, but not others?

As you think about teachers, you might have considered other kinds of questions. What is it like to be a teacher? Why do so many who are initially attracted to teaching decide to leave the profession? What could schools do to retain talented teachers? What could schools do to help teachers who are having difficulties but think they still want to remain in the profession? Or you might find yourself interested in looking at special groups of individuals in the educational field. What challenges do women face as they seek to move up the ladder? How do minority teachers express their views and share elements of their **culture**? Or you might consider how adults navigate in online learning environments. I suspect you can add to this list yourself by thinking about the problems and challenges you face every day while working in the educational arena.

Now why do I pose these questions and what do they have to do with qualitative research? I put forth these examples of questions because they are important to consider but are not often addressed from a **research** perspective. Many approaches to research typically involve conducting a survey of a large group to answer questions that have to do with how many graduate from school, how many pass the state standards, or how much money is spent for books in the library. Other research approaches might be in the form of an experiment where one method of teaching is compared with another and evaluated in terms of how well students perform on standardized tests. While this information may be valuable, it does not provide answers to the kinds of questions I posed earlier. This is where qualitative research fits in. Qualitative research approaches fit these kinds of questions quite well.

Many of you are unfamiliar with qualitative research. You may have heard the term but do not really know what it means. In this book, I introduce you to many aspects of qualitative research. I talk about various traditions from which qualitative researchers have drawn. I provide specific ideas about how to do **qualitative interviewing** and observing. I consider the complicated issue of how to organize and make sense of the data that you collect. I introduce you to current thinking about how to evaluate a qualitative research study. Throughout this book I provide you with many examples that will help you as you embark on this very interesting journey of thinking about conducting research in a new way.

You might find it helpful to know a little history of how the field developed. When preparation for a degree in education expanded beyond the study of how to teach, many institutions of higher learning added a research component. These institutions were faced with a challenge: What were appropriate ways for educators to conduct research? The answer appeared straightforward. They would adopt research methods associated with the scientific world. By using such methods, they reasoned, the field of education would be elevated to a high level.

I think you might find it helpful if I review some of the basic tenets of the approach generally referred to as the scientific method. One very important characteristic of the scientific method is that the data and the methods of analysis are quantitative in nature. The scientific method relies heavily on numbers and statistics. Different terms are often used to describe the scientific method. In this book, I have used them interchangeably. I might talk about the scientific method, quantitative methods, experimental research, traditional paradigms, foundationalist paradigms, **positivism,** or traditional research paradigms. While there are subtle differences among the terms, for your purposes those differences are not critical since my focus here is to consider alternate approaches to conducting research.

Traditional research paradigms made certain assumptions about the world. They assumed that there was an objective reality that researchers should try to uncover as they conducted their research. Further, they assumed that the role of the researcher was to be neutral; his purpose was to discover the objective reality. These paradigms are called positivist, a term associated with Comte, who wrote in the first half of the 19th century. In his development of the field of **sociology**, he suggested we should look for observable facts and apply methods of the natural sciences to the social sciences. This positivist tradition dominated the way research was done in education for many years.

However, it became evident that capturing a reality that was "out there" was difficult, if not impossible, to achieve. As a consequence, **postpositivist** ideas took hold. A postpositivist point of view held that researchers should strive to capture reality by using multiple methods. In such a way, reality would be approximated. Traditional ways of doing research (positivism and postpositivism) dominated the field of research in education until the 1980s. For a variety of reasons that I discuss in detail in Chapter 3, alternative approaches to conducting research began to surface. Much of the influence came from the field of **anthropology**. We began to see ethnographies about schools in the education field. Those doing ethnographies called themselves qualitative researchers—no doubt to distinguish themselves from those doing traditional **quantitative research**. Most of these individuals tried to meet some of the criteria of quantitative research and adopted methods that relied on validity, high structure, and computer analysis to count and tabulate data. Some even said that qualitative research "attempted to do good positivist research with less rigorous methods and procedures" (Denzin & Lincoln, 2000, p. 9).

But it became clear to other qualitative researchers that striving to be positivists or postpositivists and accepting the assumptions of these perspectives were not what they wanted to do or to be. New generations of qualitative researchers adopted a **poststructural** or **postmodern** point of view. In their view, a positivist or postpositivist stance was no longer the only acceptable way to conduct research. Multiple realities constructed by the researcher replaced the traditional single approximation of an objective reality. This group of people also rejected the traditional criteria associated with judging quantitative research. They were concerned that a traditional view of **science** kept the voices of many silenced. Instead of objectivity and validity, they were interested in personal responsibility, multiple voices, and verisimilitude.

I think what is often confusing about this field is that no longer does one point of view predominate. You will still find some qualitative researchers in the 21st century who do associate qualitative research with seeking approximations of reality. They design studies that are highly structured, giving the sense that they want to be objective. They look at ways to control bias or use inter-rater checks to seek a common interpretation of reality. But you will find many others who adopt alternate stances to postpositivism. In this book, I look at many alternative paradigms of research, not just those connected with positivism or postpositivism.

Qualitative research means many things to many people. Some people think of qualitative research in terms of the way they see the world. While quantitative researchers think about the world as having an objective reality, many qualitative researchers speak about a world view where reality is constructed by the researcher. As such, there is no single reality that exists independent of the researcher. Rather, multiple realities are constructed by the researcher. For example, in postmodern thinking, subjectivism and constructivism are two terms that are often used to describe how people see the world. Crotty (2003) suggests a subjective stance: We see the world through our own construction of it. You can understand this more clearly if you think about the idea that "the subject is the meaning maker, and whatever meaning is imposed may come from a seemingly endless source of experiences" (Faux, 2005, ¶ 5).

Lincoln and Guba (2000) use the term **constructivism** when they write about how the world is viewed. Similar to Crotty's writing, their writing suggests that realities are socially constructed. It should be clear to you that the researcher's role in qualitative research is critical since he or she makes sense of or constructs a view of the world.

Others associate qualitative research with methodologies rather than views of the world. They consider how to conduct qualitative interviews or observations. They explore how to analyze data and look for **themes**. Still others associate qualitative research with the various research traditions or paradigms that inform their work. They look for a tradition that will provide a theoretical basis for their thinking. They might decide to do a case study or an ethnography, for example.

All these ideas are important. How is a world view determined or constructed? What methodologies are used to learn about the world? What traditions serve as a theoretical basis for the research? What is critical for you to know is that there is no "right" way to think about qualitative research. It is a way of knowing and a way of doing.

New ideas abound in the 21st century. You might find yourself reading about **postmodernism**, or about **queer theory**, or **postfeminism**. You might encounter research that is presented in dance, in poetry, or the theater. No doubt by the time you read this book, there will be ideas that I have not even thought of. The field is changing so rapidly that Lincoln and Guba (2000) remark that "in the half dozen years [since the earlier edition] . . . substantial change has occurred in the landscape of social scientific inquiry" (p. 163).

How can I help you make sense of all of these myriad ideas? What information can you read that will help you as a newcomer understand this field? In this chapter, I have identified 10 critical elements that apply to much of the research that is called qualitative. I identify these elements below and ask that you think about each one. In subsequent chapters, I will discuss in greater depth methodologies, traditions, and philosophy. I hope you will find this journey challenging, stimulating, and fun.

SOME BASIC COMPARISONS BETWEEN QUANTITATIVE AND QUALITATIVE RESEARCH

I think it might help you to understand these two different philosophical and methodological ways of knowing if I make some basic comparisons. I do this to assist your understanding; however, I want you to recognize that the lines between the two are not completely fixed and overlap is often possible. In fact, one accommodation to the overlap is to look at what is known as the mixed methods approach. At this point in your learning, however, I will draw some major distinctions. I will approach this by looking at assumptions that each makes. In this table I compare and contrast these two ways of thinking about and doing research from both a theoretical and practical perspective. You will see that this is an overview to aid you in trying to make sense of the field. Of necessity, I have had to oversimplify some of the ideas. In the next section, I focus on qualitative research specifically and explore critical elements. Although there are many different types and kinds of qualitative research, most include those elements.

Theoretical	*Qualitative*	*Quantitative*	*Comments*
Nature of Reality	Multiple realities. Reality is constructed by the observer.	Single reality. In a well-designed study, a reasonable approximation of reality can be observed.	These two ideas are not as far apart as they seem. Most qualitative researchers do not take the position that any reality is a reasonable one. Many quantitative researchers acknowledge the influence of the observer, even while trying to limit it.
Objectivity/ Subjectivity Dichotomy	Subjectivity based on role of researcher is expected. Objectivity is inconsistent with the idea of a constructed reality.	Objectivity is critical in a scientific approach to acquiring knowledge.	Quantitative researchers acknowledge difficulties in reaching objectivity. Many qualitative researchers still hold on to the objectivity stance.
Role of Researcher	Researcher is central to any study. Interpretations are based on researcher's experience and background.	Researcher tries to remain outside of the system, keeping biases to a minimum.	In fact, both acknowledge that researcher cannot stay outside the system. Double blind experiments are designed to do this, but other factors may compromise things.
Generalizability, Cause and Effect	Not interested in cause and effect or generalizing, but want people to apply to own situations.	Goal to apply to other situations.	Quantitative researchers more successful in cause/effect than in generalizing, since samples are often limited.
Ways of Knowing	Multiple ways of knowing. We can learn about something in many ways.	Best way of knowing is through the process of science.	But science is not so pristine.

Now I want you to think about some of the practical distinctions.

Practical	*Qualitative*	*Quantitative*	*Comments*
Purpose	Understand and interpret social interactions.	Test hypotheses. Look at cause and effect. Prediction.	In general, most qualitative research is not interested in hypothesis testing and most quantitative research is. However, survey research using quantitative techniques describes without testing hypotheses.

(Continued)

(Continued)

Practical	Qualitative	Quantitative	Comments
Group Studied	Tends to be smaller, non-random. Researchers may get involved in lives of those studied.	Tends to be larger, randomly selected. Anonymity important.	Many quantitative researchers not able to randomly select.
Variables	Study of the whole rather than specific variables.	A few variables studied.	But qualitative researchers sometimes use numbers and quantitative researchers conduct interviews.
Type of Data Collected	Emphasis is on words. Increasing interest in visual data.	Emphasis is on numbers.	While both might use computers, statistical programs are more widely accepted.
Type of Data Analysis	Coding and themes. Some use computers.	Statistical analysis. Computers.	These distinctions are fairly clear.
Writing Style	Less formal, more personal.	Scientific and impersonal.	Informal style of qualitative may suggest less value to traditionalists.

TEN CRITICAL ELEMENTS OF QUALITATIVE RESEARCH

1. *Description, Understanding, and Interpretation.* In general, the main purpose of qualitative research—whatever kind—is to provide an in-depth description and understanding of the human experience. It is about humans. Qualitative research has as its purpose a description and understanding of human phenomena, human interaction, or human discourse. When we speak about phenomena we often think of lived experiences of humans. When we speak about human interaction we often think of how humans interact with each other, especially in terms of their culture. When we speak about human discourse we think of humans communicating with each other or communicating ideas. Sometimes a study of phenomena, interaction, and discourse are intertwined.

Qualitative researchers tend to ask "why" questions and questions that lead to a particular meaning (Hollway & Jefferson, 2000). Since qualitative researchers are interested in meaning and interpretation, they typically do not deal with hypotheses. Quantitative research is designed to test hypotheses. But no type of qualitative research is designed to test hypotheses or to generalize beyond the particular group at hand.[1]

While early efforts at qualitative research might have stopped at description, it is now more generally accepted that a qualitative researcher adds understanding and interpretation to the description. You may know of some early work that sets forth things that happen to a particular group, group member, or subculture. Wolcott (1973) gives a detailed account of a principal after following him for a year. His emphasis is a descriptive account rather than an interpretation.

But many believe that it is the role of the researcher to bring understanding, interpretation, and meaning to mere description. An example might help you to see this more clearly. Angrosino (1994) writes a very moving account of a mentally handicapped adult with whom he spends a considerable amount of time. Vonnie Lee's life history/biography is more than an account of his life. The details of his life are only minor to Angrosino's interpretation of the meaning Vonnie Lee attaches to certain events—in this case a bus ride—and the metaphorical interpretations are the author's most important contributions, rather than his description of Vonnie Lee. Good qualitative work clearly distinguishes between what the respondent said and the research analyst's interpretation or account of it.

You will see as you become familiar with qualitative research that most writers focus on description and interpretation. However, some **feminist researchers** and some **postmodernists** take on a political stance as well and have an agenda that places the researcher in an activist posture. These researchers often become quite involved with the individuals they study and try to improve their human condition. Some even contribute a portion of their royalties to those they studied.

2. *Dynamic.* In general, qualitative research is thought to be fluid and ever-changing. As such, it doesn't follow one particular way of doing things. There are many traditions that inform qualitative research. Often qualitative researchers choose to go about posing new kinds of questions and exploring new ways of answering them.

Here are some examples that will help you see how dynamic qualitative research has become. In the past, ethnographers (one way of doing qualitative research) traveled to countries and cultures different from their own. They immersed themselves in the culture for an extended time period and attempted to try to understand the culture. You may have read of Margaret Mead's trip to Samoa or Oscar Lewis's visit with five families in Mexico. Some sociologists (the Chicago School) tended to study immigrants and their life experiences. Today some ethnographers take field trips with their students. Wallace (2003) conducted field work with his students in Guatemala. Others define culture in quite novel ways and immerse themselves in the culture of the Internet. For example, Markham (1998) studied themes of life in cyberspace.

Qualitative researchers often conduct interviews in which the participants tell their own stories and do not follow a predetermined format or set of questions. Rubin and Rubin (1995) speak about interviewees, **informants**, or conversational partners rather than subjects or sample. They suggest that qualitative interviewing is "a way of finding out what others feel and think about their worlds" (p. 1). They comment that qualitative interviewing is "*flexible, iterative,* and *continuous*" (p. 43) rather than "prepared in stone" (p. 43). I know that this dynamic nature of qualitative interviewing is a critical element in the development of a successful qualitative study.

Qualitative researchers do not always know who they plan to study or what they plan to study. Qualitative researchers feel free to modify protocols as they progress through the ever-changing landscape of those they study. They sometimes rely on some of their participants to identify others who might be studied by using a **snowball sampling** technique (Atkinson & Flint, 2001), or they might ask key informants to nominate others who can be studied. Qualitative researchers do not always begin with a detailed and concrete plan for how they will conduct their research. They may find that the questions they investigate evolve as they begin to gather and analyze their data. In keeping with the dynamic nature of qualitative research, you will discover that "qualitative research characteristically does not use standardized procedures—and this is a main reason for the low reputation qualitative research in some social disciplinary 'communities.' Doing qualitative research makes the impact of the researcher far more obvious than in its quantitative counterpart" (Breuer, Mruck, & Roth, 2002, ¶ 3).

3. *No Single Way of Doing Something.* There is not just one way of doing qualitative research. When qualitative research began to take hold in education, many equated qualitative research with ethnography and saw extensive field work as the way (and for some the only way) to conduct research. Bogdan and Biklen's (1992) work makes this quite clear. While its title is *Qualitative Research for Education,* its content is limited to a discussion of ethnography and related methods. Others identify **symbolic interactionism**[2] with qualitative research (Blumer, 1969). Others equate qualitative research with **grounded theory** (Glaser & Strauss, 1967; Strauss & Corbin, 1990). Others see qualitative research as being **case studies** (e.g., Merriam, 1988; Yin, 2002). You will read more about some of these approaches in Chapter 5.

I think the fact that there is no specific or better way of conducting qualitative research is one of the reasons students sometimes have difficulty understanding what qualitative research is. They want it to be a single thing. Tell me how to do it, they say. After all, if I do scientific research and conduct an experiment I know what makes a true experiment (Campbell & Stanley, 1963). I know what difficulties there are in conducting an experiment in a real-world setting and how to approximate a true experiment (Cook & Campbell, 1979; Trochim, 2001). I know how to conduct a survey (Dillman, 1978). Why can't I have the "right" or "best" way to conduct qualitative research? As consumers and conductors of research, we are so often wedded to our old positivistic or postpositivistic paradigms, and we know that old ways are hard to discard.

Of course, we are all aware that there is no one way to do something; there is no right way to do something; there is no one best way of doing something. You might come to appreciate this idea if you move out of the discipline of research and into the field of art. What is the way art should be? It used to be the church that set the standard for good art. There was only one way. But then some artists tried new ideas. People laughed at Impressionists like Monet, and now their work is appreciated by so many. People jeered the Cubists (Picasso and Braque), and yet they are seen as opening the doors to so many other ways of making art. People said modern art was not art, and now much of it commands millions of dollars. So I urge you to keep your minds open as you explore alternative ways of doing research.

"Multiple realities" is an expression I touched on earlier. Can you accept that there is no single reality that exists independent of your interpretation? I am not talking about the philosophical question of whether a branch dropping from a tree in the forest makes a sound. I am talking about social interactions among humans or thoughts individuals have about a topic or the inner workings of a unit in a small company. There are potentially several ways of interpreting what you see or hear. As the researcher, you do the interpretation. Of course, your interpretation will carry more weight if it is supported by the data you gather, the manner in which you organize the data, and the vehicle you use to present it. For more information on credibility and legitimacy of your research, read Chapter 12.

4. *Inductive Thinking.* A traditional approach to research follows a **deductive** approach. Deductive thinking or reasoning works from the general to the specific. In contrast, qualitative research deals with specifics and moves to the general. You can think of this as going from the bottom up, moving from the specific to the general, using observations to generate hypotheses, if indeed there are any hypotheses. Qualitative research moves from the concrete to the abstract. Researchers begin with data and use those data to gain an understanding of phenomena and interactions. They do not test hypotheses as is typical in experimental research. Since qualitative research employs an **inductive** way of thinking, I have followed an inductive way of writing and presenting the material in this book. I suggest that you begin with collecting data by initiating some kind of research project. This inductive approach is in contrast to a deductive approach to doing research. In the latter type, you would do a considerable amount of advanced planning and write a proposal for research rather than actually conduct research.

5. *Holistic.* Qualitative research involves the study of a situation or thing in its entirety rather than identification of specific variables. Gunzenhauser (personal communication, 2005) speaks about the particular, contextual, and holistic characteristics of qualitative research. Qualitative research relies on studying the whole of things. It does not identify specific variables or look for relationships among those variables. You can think of it this way: Qualitative researchers want to study how something is and get to understand it. They are not interested in breaking down components into separate variables. Many of you who have studied scientific methods of research are used to looking at how one variable is caused by another one, or how several variables are related to each other. This approach is used in order to test hypotheses. But in qualitative research, we are not interested in testing hypotheses. In fact, as I said earlier, most qualitative research traditions aim for description, understanding, and interpretation and not examinations of cause and effect. Let's look at an example. Sharon has been working with young females who have returned to complete a high school education after having a baby. She meets with them once a week in the evening at a local high school. While Sharon feels she knows something about their basic skills in reading and math, she does not understand other aspects of these students' lives. She decides to try to determine what life is like for these students. She knows she is not interested in looking at various factors that might predict their poor performance; she feels she knows some of this already. Rather, she wants to know what they are like as individuals. How is their life now, and how do they think it will be when they complete high school? I think this is an ideal situation to do a qualitative study from a feminist perspective. The students are available, she has access to them, and she hopes to empower them to take charge of their lives in a more meaningful manner.

6. *Variety of Data in Natural Settings.* Qualitative research typically involves a study of things as they exist, rather than contriving artificial situations or experiments. So a qualitative researcher might be interested in looking at a particular classroom rather than having a teacher change her classroom in some way to see how something she does might have an effect on how the students learn. I recall a former student of mine who was interested in studying how kindergarten students develop formal and informal rules of conduct. She observed a class each day for several months. She also joined the class occasionally and participated in some of their activities. In these ways she was able to learn how children established rules. She did not ask the teacher to change the way she was doing anything.

Natural settings are preferred when talking to people or observing them. Interviews can be conducted in the home or office of the participant, or by phone, or in cyberspace. Observations can be conducted in classrooms, in homes, in the school yard, or at a parent-teacher meeting. I had a student who observed a chat room of middle school girls online (Robbins, 2001). I have interviewed people in school libraries, at fast food restaurants, online, and even in a custodian's closet.

Natural settings also are desirable when collecting other types of data. Such data might include photographs, videos, or pictures created by the participants or of the environment in which the participants live or work. I have seen family portraits used as data. I have seen drawings made by young children as data. Other forms of data are notes taken by the researcher, either at the time of an observation or as soon thereafter as possible.

Here is an example of the use of a variety of data in a natural setting. Don was interested in studying teenagers away from their school setting. He decided that an excellent place to do this was at a local mall. He gathered his notebook and digital camera and set out for the mall. Of course, he had been there many times before and knew that teens often congregated at the food court. He got a soda and settled down at a table near some teenagers. Since these teenagers were in a public place, he did not need to ask their permission. But he needed to be cautious about being observed himself, and he decided that he would be direct if anyone asked him what he was doing. He sat for about an hour and watched and listened. He took notes and used his camera. These data obtained in natural settings form the basis for Don's study.

7. *Role of Researcher.* The researcher plays a pivotal role in the qualitative research process. It is through his or her eyes and ears that data are collected, information is gathered, settings are viewed, and realities are constructed. Further, the qualitative researcher is responsible for analyzing the data through an iterative process that moves back and forth between data collected and data that are analyzed. And finally, it is the qualitative researcher who interprets and makes sense of the data (Coffey & Atkinson, 1996). Quantitative researchers are more likely to select a statistic that is appropriate to the **hypothesis** being tested. Their role in the actual analysis is therefore limited. Of course, how they interpret the statistical data and how they organize and display it are critical.

I know I have said this before, but it is important to remember that the researcher is the primary instrument of data collection and analysis. Unlike an experimental study where scientific scales or measuring instruments are often used, when doing qualitative research it is up to the researcher to decide what information to gather. All information is filtered through the researcher's eyes and ears. It is influenced by his or her experience, knowledge, skill, and background. Most qualitative researchers acknowledge the dilemma of trying to be unbiased and objective. In fact, postmodernists, interpretists, constructivists, and feminists acknowledge that the elusive objectivity often sought in research modes that are traditional or scientific is inappropriate in the qualitative research arena. They have come to believe that what exists out in the world can be understood as it is mediated through the one doing the observing. I want to be very clear about this idea. There is no "getting it right" since there could be many "rights." Descriptions, understandings, and interpretations are based on the data you collect and your ability to organize and integrate them to make a meaningful whole.

Bias and qualitative research is a topic that challenges both students and their professors. One view is that bias can be eliminated or at least controlled by careful work, triangulation, and multiple sources. I do not believe this is true. Bias is a concept that is related to

foundationalist, traditional, or postpositivist thinking. The position I take here is that striving for objectivity by reducing bias is not important for much of qualitative research. I think that some are reluctant to adopt a qualitative research approach because they think the researcher is biased. Well, of course, the researcher has views on the topic. After all, she probably would not be investigating a particular topic if she had not thought about the topic. There is no single or simple answer to this dilemma. I think the following viewpoint is instructive.

> The (social) sciences usually try to create the impression that the results of their research have *objective* character. In this view, scientific results are—or at least should be—independent from the person who produced the knowledge, e.g., from the single researcher. According to this perspective objectivity is what makes the difference between valid scientific knowledge and other outcomes of human endeavors and mind. On the one hand, there are many efforts to justify this perspective on **epistemological** [boldface added] and philosophical grounds. On the other hand, various practices are used to support and produce this idea of **objectivity** [boldface added] (a rather well-known and mundane example is the rhetorical strategy of avoiding the use of the first person pronouns in scientific texts). In their everyday scientific life almost all (experienced) researchers nevertheless "know" about the impact of personal and situational influences on their research work and its results. "Officially" and in publications these influences are usually covered up—they are treated as defaults that are to be avoided. (Breuer, Mruck, & Roth, 2002, ¶ 1)

What we learn is that researchers know that they influence the research and results. But other researchers, those who still hold on to a positivist or postpositivist position about objectivity, maintaining distance, and the need to reduce bias that Breuer and his colleagues cite above, try to identify ways to reduce the "subjectivity" of the qualitative researcher. There are several stances taken. Some qualitative researchers who see themselves as phenomenologists use a technique they call **bracketing**. I will talk more about this later, but for now think of it as trying to identify your own views on the topic and then putting them aside. Other qualitative researchers take the view that they can verify their interpretations by having others look at the data and go through the same process. They refer to this process as member checks or inter-rater reliability. Other qualitative researchers take the view that if they collect data from multiple sources they can have a more accurate picture of things and thus remain less biased. They refer to this as triangulation. You can see here that you are beginning to question some of your basic assumptions about doing research. Can we really take an objective stance? Should we want to? Why should we want to?

8. *In-Depth Study.* Another critical element of qualitative research involves looking deeply at a few things rather than looking at the surface of many things. An important aspect of the investigation is to look at the whole rather than isolating variables in a reductionistic manner. If we want to understand something fully, we need to look at it much more completely. Some have said it is like opening up an artichoke and looking at the layers upon layers until you reach the core. And like the artichoke, there are often gems hidden down deep inside, but there is a struggle along the way to get there.

So much of qualitative research involves studying and looking at a few individuals, sometimes just one. The study of Jermaine (Hébert, 2001) illustrates this principle well. Hébert and his colleague spent a considerable amount of time in Jermaine's environment and collected documents, talked to others, and learned about him. Angrosino (1994) studied Vonnie Lee and Wolcott (1973) studied a single principal. More often, however, qualitative researchers study some individuals or groups who have similar characteristics. Glass (2001)) studied families of autistic children. Repass (2002) studied professional women preparing to retire.

Others tend to study small groups as they interact with each other in a particular setting. Some of these groups may be highly structured and others loosely structured. Kidder (1989) studied a fifth-grade class. What is important for you to understand is that the number of individuals you study is not critical. Rather, it is the nature of the study and the degree to which you explore complex in-depth phenomena that distinguishes qualitative research.

9. *Words, Themes, and Writing.* Qualitative research is also characterized by words rather than numbers. Quite often direct quotes from the participants are included to illustrate a certain point. Details are often included about those studied or the setting in which a study is conducted. Those who studied cultures, the ethnographers, took the position that **thick description** (Geertz, 1973; Ryle, 1949) is desirable in order to see underlying meanings and understandings. The idea of thick description has been adopted by many different kinds of qualitative researchers. You will often read details about the setting in which a study was conducted, how the participants looked, or even the non-verbal gestures used by respondents.

I suspect that almost any piece of qualitative research that you read will have used either interviews, observations, or both as a major source of data. Words or visuals constitute the kind of data collected. But most of you think of data in the form of numbers, not words. As you begin to think about any kind of qualitative research, try to remember that data do not have to be numbers. They can be words. And increasingly, with the use of technology, data can be visual representations as well. Let's try an example. Diane was studying women principals and how they dealt with issues of power. She interviewed 10 principals. She also observed them in their offices, at faculty meetings, and at school board meetings. In addition, she reviewed their written memos to faculty. It should be clear that she obtained her data through interviews, through observation, and through reviewing written material. The kind of data she collected were thoughts about interacting with superiors and subordinates, the observations she made of how the principals interacted with these two groups at meetings, general observations of the physical surroundings in which they worked, and review of written material provided by the principals. As you read the information in later chapters, you will find some differences in the kind of data that are collected by the various traditions. For example, ethnographers tend to spend more time immersed in the cultural environment while phenomenologists are more likely to talk at length to participants. Contemporary ethnographers often study online culture and so the data they collect may come from e-mails or chat rooms.

Themes are developed from the data. All of the traditions and approaches eventually lead to your taking the large amount of data you collect and making sense of it. Grounded theory uses a structured approach to data analysis and offers specific steps to follow in order to organize and synthesize your data. Most of the other approaches are very general in terms of how you make meaning from your data. Computer software programs facilitate organizing, searching, combining, processing, and locating data. Unlike a statistical package, however, your input and decision making is critical for qualitative software.

Qualitative research is also characterized by a style of writing that is less technical and formal than is used in more traditional research. Additionally, qualitative researchers often write in the first person (Hamill, 1999; Intrator, 2000) or active voice. Such active voice often leads to greater trust and accountability and is more forceful. Intrator (2000) suggests that writers include ways to get the audience to trust the author as well as ways to show how description and interpretation are intertwined.

Rather than writing a report or an account as a vehicle for disseminating information, some avant-garde researchers take the output of qualitative research to a different level. They publish poetry (Weems, 2003), look at contemporary photographs or videos of significant events (Ratcliff, 2003; Robertson, 2003), or perform a dance (Blumenfeld-Jones, 1995).

10. *Not Linear.* We often think of traditional research as following a certain order. You might begin with a research question, conduct a review of the literature, gather data, do an analysis, and write your conclusions. The order is relatively fixed. In contrast, qualitative research can be viewed as having multiple beginning points. You could start with an interest in a particular type of individual. You could begin with an observation about how an event affects certain individuals. You could begin with an interest in something you read. In addition, while quantitative research follows the sequence of data collection followed by data analysis, qualitative research takes a somewhat different approach. In qualitative research the process moves back and forth between data gathering/collection and data analysis rather than in a linear fashion from data collection to data analysis. Imagine that you are weaving back and forth between gathering data and analyzing data. This is in contrast to what you would do if you were conducting an experimental study. Here is an illustration of how Glass (2001) may have progressed through his study of families of autistic children. He identified a number of families who fit the criteria of having an autistic child. He scheduled his first appointment and visited the family in their home for one afternoon. Following his visit he transcribed the interview he conducted with the mother, recorded his observations of the family, and began his journal. All data were entered into a database using his word processing program. He subsequently imported these files into **NVivo** (a computer software program) and began initial **coding**. He knew the **codes** were tentative and served as guidelines. Next, he scheduled a visit with a second family. He refined his questions to these new family members based on his initial coding and his own thinking about what he had learned so far. He went back to his journal and his observational record. He also returned to importing his data into the software program, processed the second set of materials, and reviewed everything. This back and forth nature of the process is what I mean by iterative and nonlinear.

ADDITIONAL ISSUES

In addition to the 10 critical elements I have outlined above, I want to expose you to some other important and basic considerations. I don't want to confuse you with too much technical language, but you need to be aware of important current issues. I want you to understand that what you read here may have changed between the time I write and the time you read. I have drawn much of my material from Lincoln and Guba (2000). They address a variety of issues. I include those I find to be critical, but you can read details of their thinking in their chapter in the *Handbook of Qualitative Research*.

Objectivity as Fiction. If you have received any training in research methods, you will have been exposed to the idea that research should be designed in such a manner as to yield objective and scientific evidence. This is a tenet of positivist research.[3] In order to accomplish this, the positivists suggest that the researcher needs to remain outside of the system and strive to be objective. However, the postpositivist movement acknowledged that it is not possible for the researcher to be separate from the system or society he is studying. Rather, objective reality is approximated rather than achieved. The underlying assumption, however, is that if we had the correct tools, we could characterize our reality objectively.

Some of the subsets of qualitative research, such as **interpretivism**, **constructivism**, and **critical theory,** accept that reality is virtual and is shaped by various forces. Further, findings are value-laden rather than value-free. In postmodernism and poststructuralism, inquiry is value-determined. Given these changes, I want you to begin to think about research in a new way, one that acknowledges the role of the researcher and his or her own belief system. It is not meant to be considered bad; rather, it is just another way of thinking about how we gain knowledge and what knowledge is. So, for now, try to open your mind to the idea that designing a study to provide data that is objective and true is not part of your goal. And you are to disabuse yourself of the need to be sorry that you are not quite sufficiently objective.

No Right Answer. If you conduct an experiment and analyze your data statistically, you will be able to test a hypothesis and make probability statements based on your analysis. Anyone who uses the same statistical analysis will reach the same result and conclusion. We are very used to thinking about "getting it right." But if we assume that there is no objective reality, but rather multiple realities constructed by the researcher, there are many possible interpretations. This is not bad. This is just the way it is. Sometimes I find students wanting to seek my approval that they have the right answer. Now, I believe that there are a variety of possible interpretations of the same data. Some might be more plausible than others. But who is to say which one is better? As students, you may find this way of thinking somewhat antithetical to what you already know.

Critical Role of the Researcher. Given what I have said above, you must know by now that the researcher's role is critical to qualitative research. She is the one who asks the questions. She is the one who conducts the analyses. She is the one who decides who to study and what to study. The researcher is the conduit through which information is gathered and filtered. It is imperative, then, that the researcher has experience and understanding about the problem, the issues, and the procedures.

Role of Those Studied. Traditional research often refers to those studied as **subjects**. More recently the term **participants** has been used. But whatever term is used, quantitative researchers tend to treat those they study as anonymous objects to be measured and observed. In qualitative research we talk about participants, informants, or **co-researchers**. As such, those studied become the experts on the topic. Some qualitative researchers think of them as co-investigators.

*The Nature of Reality (**Ontology**).* Although Lincoln and Guba (2000) no longer include this term as one of the key issues, I think you will encounter it quite often. Ontology is concerned with what is real or the nature of reality. Alternative paradigms take different views of what is real. A traditional scientific paradigm (positivist) would accept an objective reality. A postpositivist view would accept that reality can only be reached in an imperfect manner but nevertheless would anticipate a researcher striving to reach it. Those espousing a critical theory paradigm consider historical realism, while those who see themselves as constructivists speak of relativism and constructed realities. Paradigms that are participatory speak of realities that are created by both the participants and the researcher. So the nature of reality means different things to qualitative researchers.

Values and Ethics (Axiology).[4] You can think about the values held by the researcher and the extent to which it is possible or desirable to keep those values from influencing aspects of the research study. I would suggest that it is neither possible nor desirable to do so. I find some qualitative researchers apologizing for their beliefs and talking about how they try to keep their beliefs out of a study. Both qualitative researchers and quantitative researchers operate within a certain belief system; however, quantitative researchers strive for a position that is value-free rather than value-laden. A second issue regarding values relates to the role of the research subjects. As participants, what level of involvement can and should they have in the research and how do you protect them? I want you to think about these ideas. For the moment, suspend your judgment about the issue. However, be aware that it influences much that is new in qualitative research.

How can various paradigms accommodate each other? Lincoln and Guba (2000) suggest that certain paradigms can accommodate each other, but that there are fundamental differences between positivist and other models and that "the axioms are contradictory and mutually exclusive" (p 174). I think some examples might help you to understand this idea. If you accept a traditional scientific approach to research, you are looking for a single correct answer. It might be a statistical test that helps you decide whether or not to reject a null hypothesis. In traditional thinking, you either reject or fail to reject a hypothesis. While you might have a choice of which statistical test to use, you would accept the finding of the analysis. In contrast, in a number of qualitative paradigms, you are looking for a way to understand and interpret the meaning of human interaction or human views. The information you receive, filtered through your own lens, is subject to a multitude of interpretations. There is no single interpretation that is better than another. You are not necessarily better at interpretation than someone else. Your faculty mentor is no better than you. Using a computer program does not make your interpretation more correct. So because some paradigms look for a single right answer while others do not, some paradigms cannot accommodate the assumptions taken by others. But others see a way to handle quantitative and qualitative paradigms in the same study. Creswell (2003) and Tashakkori and Teddlie (2003) speak about a **mixed methods** approach, which uses elements from both qualitative and quantitative research. You can read about some of the practical applications at the Web site of the 2004 American Educational Research Association conference (http://convention.allacademic.com/aera2004/).

What role does action play in research? Trained as a traditional researcher, you would take the position that action is not part of your responsibility. You do the work; someone else uses it. I am reminded of the current controversy regarding the 9/11 Commission. When their report was submitted in July, 2004, they were officially disbanded. But they received funding to open an office that will deal with getting the word out and having the government make policy changes. In a way, they have taken on a new role for themselves, but who better to do so? This same kind of issue about action presents another distinction between traditional positivist and postpositivist thinking and newer paradigms. Since action suggests subjectivity, these thinkers reject it out of hand. I can recall so many government offices with so many reports on bookcases gathering dust. Newer participatory models seek action.

> Action has become a major controversy that limns the ongoing debates among practitioners of the various paradigms. . . . The mandate for social action, especially action designed and created by and for research participants with the aid and cooperation of researchers, can be most sharply delineated between positivist/postpositivist and new-paradigm inquirers. (Lincoln & Guba, 2000, p. 175)

I suspect these are ideas new to many of you. I do not believe that you are required to do something with each piece of research you do, but perhaps you can at least think about why you are doing what you are doing and what you hope to do with the information.

Issues About Who Is in Control. Suffice it to say that traditional inquiry places control in the hands of the researcher. However, control issues are intertwined with voice, reflexivity, and textual representation in some new paradigms. I agree with Lincoln and Guba (2000) when they say that "nowhere can the conversation about paradigm differences be more fertile than in the extended controversy about validity" (p. 178). You will read about this topic in greater detail in a later chapter. At this point I want you to be aware of the issues. What are the criteria for judging the worth of something? Who should set the criteria? Should there be any? How do the criteria differ or compare to those for traditional research? Is one way better than another? These are all issues being debated even as I write this book. There are three additional issues: **voice**, **reflexivity**, and postmodern textual representation. Researchers who adopted new paradigms became aware of how critical it was to have informants speak in their own voice. Most of you are familiar with reading quotes from participants. Some of the newer avenues for voice are in the form of plays or town meetings. Reflexivity can be many things about the self. You are the researcher as well as the learner. You might change the experience or be changed by it. Ultimately you come to know yourself. How we represent what we learn and know is also at issue.

Self-Reflection. Qualitative researchers often include a section on **self-reflection.** How have my own background, concerns, and interests affected the project at its various stages? How might somebody else have gone about it? For example, what questions might he or she have asked? How might he or she have interpreted these passages differently? How have I changed as a consequence of learning about others? This self-reflection can be carried out to varying degrees. You may use it to assure yourself as a quality control indicator for a particular interview. Or you may wish to modify parts of your write-up in light of it. You may even wish to document this self-reflection as a section in the written report, that is, as an account of your own part in the construction of the project and its results.

Breuer et al. (2002) devote two issues of an online journal to the topic of subjectivity and reflexivity. Such issues as the construction of a narratory self (Day, 2002), or the way in which a hermeneutic procedure for interpreting narratives helps us understand real psychological meanings (Ratner, 2002), or the postmodern view that subjectivity is assumed and appreciated (Russell & Kelly, 2002) point to the view that not only do subjectivity and reflexivity exist in qualitative research, but they should be there.

Challenge of Doing Qualitative Research. I have heard some people say that doing qualitative research is appealing because you don't have to deal with numbers, statistics, and tables. But often I believe the lack of rules, the vast amounts of data to process, and the tasks of writing are baffling to some. If you are uncomfortable with ambiguity, have difficulty putting words on paper, and need high structure, you might find qualitative research frustrating.

You no doubt might also find yourself keeping a journal, engaging in self-reflection, writing extensive notes, taking videos or photographs, filling your kitchen table with note cards and colored pencils, learning how to store and retrieve information on your personal computer, learning how to access chat rooms and download conversations, writing drafts of your project, meeting with your faculty advisers, commiserating with fellow students, ignoring your family and social life, feeling the joys and hardships of your participants, and traveling on a journey of growth, frustration, and accomplishment.

SUMMARY

I hope that you have been stimulated to think about doing some research on a topic of interest to you. That is where researchers usually start. They might have questions about the workings of a school. They might be interested in families and how they handle a child with a disability. They might be interested in adult training models. They might want to explore online learning communities. They might be interested in exploring women's changing role in the school system. This is a journey that is challenging, exciting, and fun.

GROUP ACTIVITY

This activity is normally done in the first or second week of class. You may not know the other students. Each student should select a partner. Then you should choose one idea from the Ten Critical Elements listed above and discuss how this element might be contrasted with an element from traditional research. You should then write a one-paragraph summary of your ideas and present it to the entire class.

Instructor's Note: This works for a class of about 20 students. If the class is larger, form triads. If the class is smaller, each pair could choose more than one element.

INDIVIDUAL ACTIVITY

Begin your journal. Purchase a small notebook that you can take with you to class and other places. Alternatively, create a new file on your computer that you will use for your journal. The advantage of a notebook is that you can write anytime. The advantage of the computer is that your ideas are already loaded into the computer and you will be able to share with others.

Instructor's Note: One activity I have used throughout a semester class is to have journal entries from each student imported into a computer software program such as NVivo and then used those data to practice coding, forming nodes, and identifying themes.

NOTES

1. One exception is a type of qualitative research called **grounded theory,** in which hypotheses may emerge from the study.

2. Symbolic interaction refers to the nature of the interaction between humans. Interpretation of the interaction is based on the meaning attached to actions. With humans, actions are mediated through symbols.

3. Rusu-Toderean (n.d.) provides a detailed background of the various movements, beginning with Comte's positivism up to the positivism of the 1950s and 1960s that dominated social science research.

4. Axiology comes from the Greek word *axios* meaning worth.

CHAPTER 2

An Overview of the Field

The definition of artistic quality proposed here is work which is both ambitious and original, is technically competent, connects to people, and leaves them challenged or rewarded in some lasting way.

—Arts Council of Ireland

I was a bit naïve when I started my doctoral degree journey. I thought the most difficult part would be to complete the course work rather than the dissertation. I was wrong. As a full-time researcher for more than 20 years, I thought I had the skills to accomplish the task. However, the process was long. It took one and a half years to complete my dissertation. The process taught me a systematic way of thinking about the research question, having a focus, deciding on a research method, and sticking to it. Also, I learned that different audiences (in this case committee members) may perceive the same research question differently depending on their backgrounds and expertise. Consequently, the research direction(s) might be impacted by that perception. Therefore, I learned that clear communication to the audience about the purpose of the research is vital.

—Gohar Farahani

I want to convey a general understanding of what qualitative research is all about. You should be able to see that the field is multi-dimensional and fluid. You should be able to see that certain kinds of questions are more amenable to being answered by qualitative research methods than are other types. You should be able to see that it relies heavily on the voices of humans. You should be able to see that it uses an inductive approach moving from the specific to the general. You should be able to see that novice researchers are sometimes frustrated and challenged but at the same time exhilarated. You should be able to see that you can learn how to do this kind of research. And finally, you should be able to see that you are about to embark on a challenging and exciting way of thinking about answering important questions. The path is no doubt different from one you have followed previously, and therein is the challenge.

DEFINITIONS

I find myself struggling to provide you with a definition that is meaningful, inclusive, and yet conveys the diversity within the broad term of qualitative research. Among the first to write about the field extensively were Lincoln and Guba (1985). By the time the first *Handbook of Qualitative Research* was issued (Denzin & Lincoln, 1994), definitions included "multi-method in focus," "interpretive," and "naturalistic approach to subject matter."

But it is evident that there is no clear agreement. Some speak of a lack of a coherent definition (Olson, 1995) or one that is difficult to get (Simmons-Mackie & Damico, 2003). Many people contrast it with quantitative research and define it by what it is not, I suspect because for so long we have relied on quantitative research paradigms and believe that many know what elements are included. Some take a very narrow view, while others give it a broad brush. For your purposes, I would like you to consider this definition:

Qualitative research is an umbrella term. It is a way of knowing that assumes that the researcher gathers, organizes, and interprets information (usually in words or in pictures) with his or her eyes and ears as filters. It is a way of doing that often involves **in-depth interviews** and/or **observations** of humans in natural and social settings. It can be contrasted with quantitative research, which relies heavily on hypothesis testing, cause and effect, and statistical analyses. Some would have us believe that procedures are systematic and analytical, but I do not think this holds true in many cases.

Perhaps some examples will help you to get a clearer picture of what qualitative research is. Mary, a student in her early thirties, was particularly interested in young children. Throughout her life she had been a "loner" with few friends. She wondered about other children who seemed like herself. Mary decided she wanted to study the informal ways young children form friendships or find themselves outside of the mainstream. Since she volunteered in a preschool, she asked permission to observe several classes. She developed a schedule that involved her spending at least four hours per week in the school. She decided it would be wise to observe at different times of the day. Initially, she did not know quite what she was look-ing for. She decided to look both at students who always seemed to be part of a group and those who stayed by themselves. She thought she knew what was meant by friendship and by being an outsider, but decided not to review the literature at this point. Rather, she made an explicit list in her journal of what friendship meant to her and what she remembered about forming friendships (or not) when she was younger. During the course of the three months of her study, she took extensive notes. Sometimes she took photographs or videos. She also decided that she would speak to the teacher and aides about their ideas of friendship. In a few cases, she decided to approach some of the children individually. Eventually she recorded all information into a database. She began her analysis by coding the notes she had made. For example, if one student always hung around with another student, she coded that. If one student offered to assist another student, she coded that. If one student was always alone, she coded that. At this point, she decided to examine what others had written about friendships among young children. I have just given you a bare outline of the study, but I hope you get the idea. The study built on Mary's personal interests and her professional experience. If you wanted to give this type of study a label, you might call it classroom ethnography.

Steven was also interested in the topic of friendship. He was a retired military enlisted man. He had decided to return to school and to explore working with seniors. His area of expertise and interest was the elderly. He gained access to a seniors' home and received permission to conduct extensive interviews with those residents who were willing to participate. He, too, began by making explicit his own view of friendship. Writing in his journal, Steven found himself thinking back over the years. Who had his friends been? How long had the friendships lasted? What kind of person did he choose? Who chose him? He was a little confused with so many questions. His general design involved extensive interviews with several residents of the home. He was concerned that the residents might not be able to maintain interest for too long, so he planned to conduct at least two interviews with each of 10 residents. Since Steven had some knowledge of qualitative computer software, he began by putting his notes into the computer. He also transcribed each interview after completion. He began initial coding. He found himself working back and forth between coding and questioning. In this way, he refined his questions, picked up missing information from some residents, and got a better feel for his data. This type of study relied heavily on in-depth interviews and might be labeled a case study of friendships as seen by seniors.

A third example shows yet another way to consider the topic of friendship. Alice was especially interested in teenage girls. She volunteered at an after school program that served many girls. She had begun to notice certain cliques forming and decided she wanted to investigate the nature of these cliques; how the girls formed friendships within the cliques; and how others were invited into, or excluded from, the cliques. Alice had some experience conducting focus groups, so her main avenue to gain information was focus groups. She also decided that she wanted to use the computer chat rooms that the girls had formed. Alice also added video clips of club meetings and informal gatherings to her database.

In these three examples, you can see that each investigator approached the topic of friendship somewhat differently. Each made use of professional contacts to obtain access to certain groups. Each tried to narrow the scope of the investigation by looking at a particular type or class of individual (e.g., young children, seniors, teenagers). Each chose data collection methods with which they were comfortable and which afforded them rich data. One relied on computers to assist in data analysis. Some performed a study that fit a particular type of qualitative research (e.g., ethnography) while others operated from a more eclectic mode. Let's return to the definition from above:

> It is a way of knowing that assumes that the researcher gathers, organizes, and interprets information (usually in words or in pictures) with his or her eyes and ears as a filter. It is a way of doing that often involves in-depth interviews and/or observations of humans in natural and social settings. It can be contrasted with quantitative research, which relies heavily on hypothesis testing, cause and effect, and statistical analyses.

Each type of study meets the criteria outlined in the definition. As you read examples of other studies, you should decide to what extent other studies meet the criteria.

WHAT IS SCIENCE?

"Once I was a positivist. I thought sociology could become a true science, and I was eager to make it more scientific. I thought 'the more you quantify, the better.' I thought: enough with social philosophy, down with abstract theorization. Let us go to the facts! . . . I thought I knew what science was about" (Bertaux, 1981, p. 29). I just reread these words that I had not looked at for a long time. Bertaux is a French sociologist. He is a proponent of life history. I first encountered his writing in the early 1990s, but I recently discovered he is still an active researcher and he spoke in 2004 in Denmark at the Life History and Biography Network conference held at Roskilde University. When I read his comments, I thought I was talking.

Most traditionalists argue that the only proper or real **scientific research** is quantitative research. Qualitative research, then, is judged against the criteria we use to judge quantitative research. I discuss this in greater detail in Chapter 12. However, I want you to think about these issues in a different way. Suppose that qualitative research is seen as science (Harré, 2004; Parker, 2003). According to Parker's interpretation of Harré, laboratory experiments are actually pre-scientific, and quantitative researchers need to account for "the reflexive capacity of human beings, the meaningful nature of the data they produce, and the way that claims are made about individuals from aggregated descriptions of behaviour from particular populations" (p. 4). Parker continues forcefully as he discusses questions about quality.

Now, Parker does not answer these questions. He poses them for you to consider.

It is crucial to the enterprise of scientific work generally and qualitative research in particular, that the way we go about it is open to debate. We note here some questions for which there are no clear answers and much disagreement.

1. *What counts as good?* (a) It corresponds to the norms of established scientific study. (b) It will improve the lives of those who participated. (c) It is intrinsically interesting and will provoke and satisfy those who are curious about the questions posed.

2. *Who should it be for?* (a) It should be directly accessible to ordinary people outside psychology. (b) It should contribute to the accumulating body of knowledge for the use of other researchers. (c) Those who participated should gain something from it in exchange for their time.

3. *What counts as analysis?* (a) A careful redescription using some categories from a particular framework. (b) The discovery of something that can be empirically confirmed as true. (c) The emergence of a new meaning that was entirely unexpected.

4. *What is the role of theory?* (a) Mystification by those versed in jargon at the expense of those who participated. (b) A necessary antidote to the commonsense and often mistaken explanations for human behaviour. (c) The space for thinking afresh about something. (Parker, 2003, p. 5)

You need to understand that the questions Parker proposes are quite different from traditional ideas. I offer them to you so that you can begin to really think about the activities in which you are involved. I don't mean to imply that there are right or wrong answers. That would be presumptuous. Nor are there right or wrong questions. As you continue with your learning, keep in mind that things are not always as they seem or as they once were.

MULTIDIMENSIONAL

There are many ways you can think about doing qualitative research. You can think about what sort of *research approach* or tradition (Creswell, 1997) you might use. When thinking this way, researchers often select a research design to follow. They may choose to follow a **phenomenological** approach in which they study the lived experiences of individuals with the primary goal of describing the experience (Husserl, 1917/1981). Influenced by feminist and humanist perspectives, more recent attempts at phenomenology look at the role of the researcher as "an interested and subjective actor" (Lester, 1999) rather than as an impartial and unbiased observer. Often phenomenological studies consider very serious topics such as the finality of death (San Filippo, 1992), the drive to be thinner (Santopinto, 1989), or the experiences of women undergoing biopsy (Lindwall, von Post, & Bergbom, 2003).

Some researchers choose an **ethnographic** approach. Those who choose to conduct ethnographies are interested in sociocultural phenomena and how humans interact within a culture or subculture. Early on, those doing qualitative research in education often conducted ethnographies by visiting classrooms. Genzuk (2003) suggests that ethnographers of today study "schooling, public health, rural and urban development, consumers and consumer goods, any human arena." In related approaches, some researchers conduct auto-ethnographies, in which an individual examines himself or herself in terms of beliefs, values, and traditions of a subculture. In an early work when she was a graduate student, Ellis (1995) offers a memoir about an intense personal relationship as a beginning of her writings in the auto-ethnographic arena. Some auto-ethnographers (also called video-ethnographers) use photography rather than text as a means of telling a story (Goldman, 2004).

Some rely on doing **case studies** of a particular event or setting or of particular people. Teachers' lives have been studied extensively (Goodson, 1992). Information technology within a university setting (Tellis, 1997) and the dynamics of resilience in elementary schools (Nettles & Robinson, 1998) are illustrations of case studies.

Some researchers have considered using a **mixed methods** approach rather than relying on purely qualitative research. A mixed method approach combines elements from both qualitative and quantitative models. The idea has become quite popular in the 2000s. Both Creswell (2003) and Tashakkori and Teddlie (2003) write about this idea and provide examples. For many reasons, researchers might find it appealing to use such an approach. Creswell suggests we need to make certain that we pay attention to priority, implementation, integration, and theoretical perspective. Since quantitative methods have a much longer history in education, it might be easy to give them priority. Creswell cautions against this. Katsulis (2003) suggests that using mixed methods might expand our understanding from each method. She suggests that the whole is greater than the sum of its parts but cautions that extensive data collection and intensive data analysis will be needed. While I can see that in certain situations it might be valuable to combine elements from both qualitative and quantitative research designs, I think it is critical that novice researchers get a clearer sense of the central questions of their research and select one or the other type of design as primary.

You can also think about *who* is studied. Sometimes qualitative researchers are interested in exploring individuals who are disadvantaged, or homeless, or deviant, or in trouble. In a very early qualitative dissertation, Liebow (1967) studied men who were unemployed and living on a street corner in Washington, D.C. Several decades later, Liebow (1993) studied women who

Figure 2.1

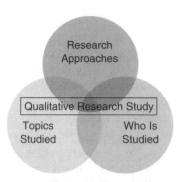

lived in a homeless shelter. Some do ethnographies on specific groups of individuals. Correll (1995) studied a lesbian online "bar." Although you would expect that who is studied follows from the general question, in my experience researchers sometimes decide they want to study individuals with whom they identify. Repass (2002), thinking about retiring herself, studied professional women as they planned their retirement. Glass (2001), a parent of a child with autism, studied families with an autistic child. Snyder (2003), a consultant to the military, studied a military organization's adoption of an innovative technique.

You can also think about *what topics* are being studied. Qualitative researchers have studied surviving a heart attack, and living with AIDS, and experiences of female school superintendents. They have asked questions about forming friendships, about successful minority students, about reading programs that work. The topics are very often close to their own hearts. In keeping with the newer participatory paradigms of qualitative research, some have chosen areas in which they could intervene and make social change.

Whether a researcher begins with a topic, a research approach, or participants to be studied, the ideas tend to become intermingled, as depicted in Figure 2.1.

What is evident is that there is no single idea of what qualitative research is or which approach to take. One person might equate qualitative research with case study. Another might say it is doing ethnography. Another might say it involves extensive interviewing. Another might speak of a rich, thick description. Others might speak of a theoretical viewpoint or a research paradigm. I will try in the chapters that follow to help you see the field from various perspectives.

TRADITIONS, APPROACHES, AND BEYOND: AN OVERVIEW

It might clarify your thinking to have a brief overview of several approaches or traditions that are associated with qualitative research. I see qualitative research as an umbrella term that includes many ideas. Imagine that it looks something like Figure 2.2.

Sometimes researchers choose a particular tradition or orientation to guide their research. I think that at times they are guided to do this by their mentors. You might choose not to use

Figure 2.2

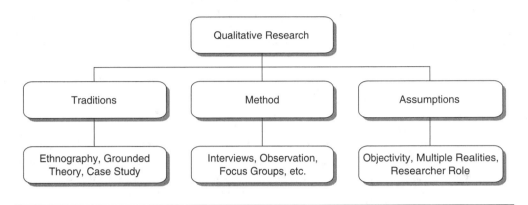

any tradition but rather rely on a generic approach. I am not always sure that researchers know why they select a particular orientation. In fact, since it is quite common to rely on one or more of the myriad approaches to qualitative research methodology, I think it will be helpful for you to learn about some of them. Additional information about some of these approaches is included in Chapter 5.

Ethnography. The purpose of ethnography is to describe the culture and social interactions of a particular group, setting, or subgroup. It involves extensive immersion in a particular setting (e.g., a school, classroom, playing field, lunchroom, bus, nurses' station, or airport). Offshoots of the ethnographic method that you may come across are auto-ethnography, photo-ethnography, and micro-ethnography. In some cases, researchers conduct studies that are ethnographic in nature but do not involve extensive interactions or immersion. The ethnographic tradition, long a mainstay of anthropologists, has been widely used in education, especially since the 1990s.

Grounded Theory. The purpose of grounded theory is to generate theory that is grounded in or emerges from the field. In addition to immersion in a particular setting, people also do grounded theory by studying how individuals react to a phenomenon (Creswell, 1997). Those doing grounded theory are also interested in the actions, interactions, and social process of people. This tradition arises from the 1960s (Glaser & Strauss, 1967) and has become widely used in education and nursing research.

Phenomenology. The purpose of phenomenology is to describe and understand the essence of lived experiences of individuals who have experienced a particular phenomenon. This tradition is closely tied to existential philosophy. Originally proposed by Husserl (1917/1981) and predominant in Europe in the 1930s, it has been reinterpreted by a variety of writers and extended to the United States. In the last few years, with the wide availability of the Internet, phenomenology has become prominent in diverse areas of the world. In the 1990s, nursing researchers and educators were among the first to make use of phenomenological approaches. Hermeneutics is closely associated with phenomenology; its purpose is to interpret text. It originally was associated with interpretation of the Bible.

Case Study. The purpose of case study is to study in-depth a particular case or several cases. You may be familiar with case studies in psychology or counseling; doing case study research is somewhat similar. But instead of a focus on one individual, a case often is identified as a particular program, or project, or setting. It is up to the researcher to identify the case and set limits or boundaries. I often find that case study research may be combined with other approaches. So, you might encounter a case study of a nursing program using grounded theory. As with several other traditions, this came to education in the late 1980s.

Feminist Theory, Contemporary Feminist Thought, and Feminist Methods. The purpose is to use a feminist perspective in conducting research. Although not exactly a research approach or tradition, **feminist theory** is a movement that arose in the 1980s. In part, it was a reaction to the disparate power, politics, and equality between those conducting the research (typically white men) and those who were being studied (often women, minorities, or those with disabilities). Feminist theory is also related to postmodernism, postcolonialism and post-Freudian psychoanalysis. This movement and more contemporary feminist approaches have a stronghold in Canada and Australia as well as in the United States. Geiger (1986) argues that feminism depends on women's point of view, and the meaning of their life experiences and histories provides important insights.

Generic Approach. The purpose of a generic approach is to use qualitative methodologies to collect and analyze data (Lichtman, 2004). Users do not ascribe to any one of the approaches mentioned above; they often select elements from many of them. The use of a generic approach has gained fairly wide acceptance in the last decade.

Narrative Analysis, Biography, Autobiography, Narrative Storytelling Analysis, Life History. The purpose is to tell a story through the use of the written or spoken word. Often an epiphany is interpreted from the story. Denzin (1989) describes several steps: collect an objective set of experiences, either chronologically or in life stages; gather actual stories; organize stories into pivotal events or epiphanies; search for meaning in the stories; look for larger structures to help explain the meaning in the stories. Goodson (1992) writes about teachers' life histories. I have grouped these oral traditions together since they rely so heavily on narrative and stories. Narrative analysis is a general term that incorporates first-person accounts in story form, biography, autobiography, life history, oral history, autoethnography, pathography, discourse analysis (Lemke, 2003) or life narratives. Although life histories as a technique (developed in the Chicago school) was popular from the 1920s, the technique came under fire when the debate between statistics and case studies became more intense and participant observation took on a greater predominance compared to life histories. But there has been increased use of biographical methods and life histories since the late 1980s (Bertaux & Delacroix, 2000; Chamberlayne, Bornat, & Wengraf, 2000; Creswell, 1997; Denzin, 1989).

Postmodernism and Critical Theory/Research. These approaches represent more of a philosophy and intellectual movement than a research method or theory.[1] According to Lemke (2003), postmodernism derives from *poststructuralism* and *deconstructionism,* which were initially criticisms of the *structuralist movement* of the 1960s. Critical theory derives from neo-Marxism and feminist theory, extended to include postcolonial theory and queer theory.

Perhaps the most characteristic tenet of postmodern critical work is that everything that European philosophy and science has held to be fundamentally true at an abstract or programmatic level is in fact a contingent, historically specific cultural construction, which has often served the covert function of empowering members of a dominant social caste at the expense of Others.[2]

Critical qualitative research or critical theory is related to postmodern research. Its purpose is to change the social context. Tripp (1992) argues that socially critical research in education is informed by principles of social justice.[3] Other key concepts associated with critical theory are sexuality and gender. You can see how closely related these ideas are to feminist theory.

Post-Postmodernism. The purpose of post-postmodernism is to react to "postmodernism's monstrous balloon of misconceptions" (Steinberg, 2000). Postmodern research, a trend popularized in the 1990s, challenges other forms of research. This is an outgrowth of the challenge to the modern world offered by the postmodern movement (Imel, 1998). I see this as primarily a philosophical movement and beyond the scope of our thinking here. You will find that the newest challenge is post-postmodernism. Many of the contributors to this movement are associated with phenomenology and hermeneutics.

Diekelmann (2002) points out that "postmodern discourses share a commitment to egalitarianism and emancipation through deconstruction of the subject as opposed to recognition of its social and historical dimensions. The metanarrative, or grand stories of the culture, are considered discursive regimes of power and are deconstructed to reveal new thinking and possibilities" (¶ 1).

Mixed Methods. The purpose is to intertwine both qualitative and quantitative methods in a single study. A researcher who uses a mixed method approach usually combines elements from both quantitative and qualitative methodologies. Many students are drawn to mixed methods since they learn that many professors like the more structured approach of statistics but acknowledge that data from observations or interviews yields rich information. Creswell (2003), in his book *Research Design: Qualitative, Quantitative and Mixed Methods Approaches,* provides some details on how to conduct a mixed methods study. You can also read Tashakkori and Teddlie (2003) on the same topic.

QUALITATIVE QUESTIONS

Some questions seem to fit so well into the qualitative domain. Others fit neatly into a quantitative approach. Still others seem to fit into some combined niche. Qualitative questions address meaning or understanding or interpretation. Qualitative questions address sociological, psychological, or political aspects. Qualitative questions are those that focus on human beings and how they interact in social settings or how they see themselves or aspects of their environment. Qualitative questions tend to ask why and how rather than what and how many. Qualitative questions tend to be general and broad.

Take a look at the topics of some recent research conducted in the field.

- Exploring online teaching
- Planning for retirement: A perspective from professional women
- Questions and issues of Alzheimer's family caregivers
- Gender, power, and the television remote control
- What is it like to be an occupational therapist practicing in a rural area?
- Voices from the margins
- Mentoring pregnant adolescents
- Exploring the personal in qualitative research
- Personal narratives of elite college athletes: Stories of career-ending injuries
- Always single and single again women
- Change from teachers' perspectives: A model of personal change
- The triangulation of researcher interpretations of interview data: Cross-gender friendships
- School, family, and community context of African American children in South Carolina
- Marks on paper: Exploring literacy through theatre

You can see that these kinds of questions are quite different from those that ask you to look at the relationship between two variables, or ask you to test hypotheses, or ask you to make generalizations.

CONDUCTING A SIMPLE QUALITATIVE STUDY

By now you might be ready to begin to think about how you would plan a qualitative research study. Here is one way you might want to get started. Identify a co-researcher. This should be someone from your class. It is not necessary that you are interested in the same topic or that you have the same major. In fact, I suspect you might learn more from someone who is quite different from yourself. Here are some helpful steps that you can follow.

Meet with your partner and brainstorm topics or questions of interest. Spend about 45 minutes doing this. Initially you should not reject any idea. After the allotted time, select two or three topics on which you can agree. Each of you should write down the topics before you discuss them. In my experience, people sometimes have difficulty distinguishing between "the" research question and research questions. The research question might be "How are friendships among seniors maintained?" The research questions might be "What does friendship mean to you?" "How did you initiate a new friendship?" "Do you distinguish between friendships with men and with women?" "How important are the friendships to your overall well-being?" By now I hope you get the picture. I also want you to understand that the question you start with might not exactly be the one you end up with. As you begin to turn up new information, you might modify or adapt your question.

Your next step is to consider from whom you might gather information on the topic. At this point it is easier if you can avoid obtaining permission through Institutional Review Boards since that is often time-consuming and counterproductive. One thing you might consider is to study adults—co-workers, relatives, or friends. Usually they are willing to be studied and you can work out a time to meet with them.

Your next step is to explore the kind of information you might want to collect. Do you want to conduct interviews? Will people be willing to write their thoughts to you in e-mails in answer to your questions? E-mails will save an enormous amount of time that you otherwise would have to spend doing transcriptions. Can you get people to bring in items from home on the topic (e.g., photos, notes, albums, records)?

You have now identified three important preliminary steps: what question you want to answer, from whom the answers will come, how you will gather the information. You are now ready to get going.

You will need to clear things with your professor, make a calendar, divide up the work, and do some practice. Having a plan for keeping track of things is also a very good idea. I can't imagine doing this kind of research without a computer, so I would suggest you create a new folder with several files on your computer. You can name the folder My Class Project. You will have several files in your folder. One file should be reserved for your personal thoughts, notes, and reflections on the process. Another file should be used for the data you collect. If the data are e-mails, you will need a system to import the e-mails and keep track of dates, and so on. If the data are interviews, you will need to transcribe and create a new file for each interview. So the work doesn't seem so tedious, I suggest you transcribe some information each day you are working on the project. Do not wait until after all your data are in. Remember that qualitative research is not a linear process. You need to go back and forth in your design. You will also need a plan to share files with your partner. And so you don't make the mistake that so many people make, keep a copy of all files saved on an external drive just in case your computer crashes.

Notice that I have said nothing about conducting a literature review. At this point, I don't think you should be looking into the literature, but you do need to clarify your own thoughts on the topic. Something that has worked very well for me is to make explicit your own views on the topic by writing them down. Both you and your partner should do this before you talk about the topic with each other. After you finish your own ideas, share with your partner.

There are now additional steps that you need to take to complete your first qualitative research project. You will need to perform some kind of analysis of the data you have collected. In its simplest form, this might involve reviewing the material you have, generating some codes, and eventually identifying some themes. At this point, unless you have a lot of experience, I suggest you do everything without using a computer program. Since you are not using a computer program, you will need a simple system. Using color coding and different fonts can be done very easily with most word processing programs. Here is an example of how you might begin. Suppose your data is about friendship. Read one complete interview. Think about the different ideas that are mentioned. Now reread the interview. You will probably notice that two ideas that are mentioned are "forming friendships" and "keeping/maintaining friendships." Choose one color to represent "forming friendships." Every time you see something mentioned on the topic, highlight the phrase and color code it blue. Do the same thing for keeping/maintaining friendships, only this time you will use the color green. You will notice that sometimes the text does not contain the term "forming friendships." Instead, the participant might have given a specific example of making a new friend. That would still be color coded blue. Coding and searching for themes can be done on your own or in conjunction with your partner. I have found that doing it alone and then meeting with your partner helps you to think more clearly about what is important to you and then to justify it to someone else. You are now ready for the meat of your project. You've identified a question, gotten some data, and made a stab at analyzing the data. Now you have to determine what this all means. I suggest that you identify three to five central ideas that you have learned about the topic. You are ready to write up what you have learned. I would limit your write-up to five to seven pages. You can write alone or with a partner. In either case, both of you need to practice writing. Use first person and make your writing accessible. Make liberal use of quotes from those you studied. Include an illustration or two. Make some hyperlinks in your paper. And finally, if you want to look at the literature now, go ahead. Find three or four examples that relate to what you studied. Remember, this is supposed to be practice; it is not meant to be comprehensive.

Another activity you might enjoy doing is to take the data you have and try to write it up in an entirely different way than the first way you wrote. Can you create a poem or play? How about writing your interpretation and interspersing that of your partner? That works well also. Think about what you found and how you might communicate it to an audience. Try to write two papers that are different in style and format and contrast with traditional scholarly writing.

VOICES OF HUMANS

So much of qualitative research depends on what people have to say. After all, we come to understand people by listening to them, watching them interact, and thinking about the meaning beyond, beneath, and around the words. No matter what approach you take or what group you study or what topic you consider, you will gather some information that is represented by what your respondents tell you. This might be supplemented with pictures, observations, artifacts, videos, or notes, but you cannot get away from the fact that to learn about people you have to listen to them.

I know that when students start going out and listening to others, they sometimes feel unprepared. They don't quite know how to do it. I will discuss these issues in a later chapter on qualitative interviewing, but for now I want to tell you about some techniques that work very well for me and for my students.

One of the best techniques to get people started during an interview is to ask them to tell a story about something that happened to them last week (at school, at work, at home, on the street). In this way, you can delve immediately into something specific, concrete, and meaningful to the person doing the talking. While it may not be quite what you, the interviewer, had in mind, you will be very surprised at how it sets the stage for what is to come. It takes the speaker and the listener right into the nitty gritty of their lives. And, after all, isn't that a part of what qualitative research is about? You'll find that it is very easy for people to talk about themselves. You need to set the stage, be accepting and open to what they have to say, and be nonjudgmental. This is not always easy, but it comes with practice, I assure you.

You don't have to stay in the immediate present for individuals to open up to you. Sometimes stories can be from the past. I recall many years ago I asked my father-in-law to come and speak to my classroom of teachers about his early days in school. At that time, he was well into his nineties; he had attended school in New York City as a young child. He was very reluctant, at first, to come to my class; I suspect he was afraid that he would not do the right thing. However, when I arrived at his home to transport him to my class, I found him all dressed up in a shirt, tie, and sport coat. I knew he was ready. When he got to my class, I began interviewing him about his earliest memories of school. He spoke about first grade.

Initially he said he didn't know what I wanted him to say. I replied that I wanted him to say what he knew and remembered. He said that perhaps he wasn't doing the right thing. I assured him he was. What things he remembered. The most meaningful event was being sent to the "rat cellar" by the janitor if you somehow behaved inappropriately. I asked him if he had ever been sent there. He replied, "Just once." He smiled and my class burst into laughter. Well, I opened up a flood of memories and learned much about schooling in the early 1900s, about my father-in-law, about how young people react to those generations removed from them, and about myself. I was fortunate that I had the foresight to tape record this interview because he is no longer here to tell these stories.

I use these illustrations to help you see what qualitative research is and can be. Qualitative research has as one of its central goals to describe and understand human behavior. Qualitative research relies heavily on words. Qualitative research seeks to capture voices of individuals as they are. These examples reveal how much individuals have to say if the stage is set for them to speak. It takes skill and practice to interview someone. Neophyte researchers are often nervous when they begin conducting qualitative interviews. Talisha sums this up quite well in her journal:

Journal Entry 09/18

I thought the interview process was going to be a lot easier than it actually was. I felt unprepared and unorganized because I did not have any set questions in front of me to ask. I was surprised because I am usually someone that enjoys carrying on conversations and I found it difficult to "go with the flow." There was one point in the interview when I had to turn off the recorder to gather my thoughts and come up with another question.

I also felt pressured to meet the 30–45 minute suggested interview time. Before I could ask a question, the interviewee had already answered the question in a previous response. So, it was really hard for me to come up with other questions.

After conducting this interview, I realized why I prefer having set questions. In my opinion, it helps the interview to flow smoother.

If you experience these same feelings, you should know that they are very common. Like learning any new skill, you get better with practice.

AN INDUCTIVE APPROACH

You have heard the term inductive approach often throughout your school experience. But what does it really mean? Here are some thoughts that might help you sort through your own ideas. An inductive approach moves from the specific to the general and builds to a conclusion. In such an approach, one thing leads to another, a kind of scaffolding. You begin by gathering a good amount of data. You then go through your data to see if you can find many examples of a particular thing (a concept or theme). Of course, you might find some statements that do not support the theme. As you collect and simultaneously look at your data, you begin to move to more general statements or ideas based on the specifics found in your data. Think about moving from the concrete to the abstract.

GENERAL IDEAS ABOUT THE FIELD

Before you get involved in historical background, or learning the complexities of phenomenology or how to do axial coding in grounded theory, I think you need to address the basic questions of what the field is about.

Here is an illustration taken from an interview by a student on the topic "what life is like as a graduate student."

Paul: Tell me about a recent experience you've had at Tech.

Pablo: There are many. One of them is the recent statistics course I am taking at Tech. In the case of here, compared to what I had in Venezuela, I feel like it is really kind of easy. You can see how the teacher is trying to help you, kind of all the time. It is completely different. The teachers are more concerned with demonstrations, or not even thinking that you need to understand stuff. It's like they want to screw you, instead of helping you. Something like that.

Well, you might ask what you can learn about Pablo from this story and what else you would like to know. Can you see how appealing it is to let people talk to you in their own words? One thing you can definitely say about qualitative research is that it is about listening, thinking, and making meaning from what you hear and what you see.

Let me restate so you get my meaning. Research is a process by which and through which we seek answers to questions. The kinds of questions and the way we seek answers are up to the researcher. If our questions have to do with the relationships between money spent in a school system and student performance, we would not want to conduct qualitative research. We could get much more reliable answers to this question by conducting a simple survey. If our questions have to do with examining the effectiveness of two kinds of reading programs, we would not want to conduct qualitative research. We could get much more reliable answers to this question by designing an experiment and seeing which program yielded higher test scores. But suppose the questions posed have to do with looking at how rules are developed by the children in kindergarten, or experiences of families who have suffered a death of a child, or how school atmosphere and style are exhibited in a small rural school, or how leaders develop, or what it is like to plan for retirement. A survey or an experiment won't provide very insightful answers to these questions. This is where qualitative research comes in. We have different kinds of questions. They do not ask us to look for relationships among variables. They do not ask us to test hypotheses. They ask us to think about the whole, about the ways humans interact. Now we have to look for ways to answer them.

As a novice researcher, you might say, "Well, why don't I just go and talk to the people and see what they have to say?" You can probably imagine that you need a plan and way to conduct your research that follows a particular methodology. There are a number of methodologies to choose from. Sometimes it will be very clear to you which methodology you will want to follow. Other times it seems as though you choose elements from more than one methodology. That is all right as well. And other times you may want to combine elements of qualitative and quantitative methodologies. Sometimes you are not quite sure whether you are using any specific methodology at all.

You might ask, what makes a piece of research qualitative? How do you know? In general, research that involves looking at things in their natural settings, or talking to individuals about a particular topic, or investigating individuals who have experienced a particular phenomenon is qualitative.

Once you have clearly formulated your questions, you need to decide how to go about answering them. You might decide to conduct ethnography, where you immerse yourself in the culture of a particular classroom. Or you might conduct interviews with the intention of trying to have some theory emerge from your data. Or you might want to study one or several cases representing a particular phenomenon. All of these approaches represent different models of conducting research.

What do you think the field is about? It may be too early in your exploration to have formulated clear ideas to answer this question, but many students new to the field of qualitative research have some terms they identify with the field. They know about doing interviews, case studies, small samples, and looking at a natural setting. They are usually very attracted to what they read and identify with much of the style of writing used in qualitative research. They question how they can be objective and unbiased in conducting qualitative research. They express concern that the research doesn't appear to be very scientific and wonder if it is legitimate. They may have heard from some professors that qualitative research takes too long or is not real research. However, the academic and research communities have come to accept alternative ways of conducting research. No longer is experimental research the only or best way to answer questions.

You can sort out your own ideas about qualitative research by reading, thinking, and talking with others. Be open to new ideas. Be willing to step outside of the box. Be prepared for ambiguity. You are on a fascinating adventure.

SUMMARY

I began this chapter by defining the term qualitative research. I identified several components of qualitative research. I addressed the idea that it is multidimensional and fluid. As such, it is not a single thing, nor do people agree on what it is. It could be a paradigm, a way of asking questions, or a philosophy. I think that whatever it is today, it will probably be something different tomorrow. I also believe that hearing the voice of those you are studying is critical. I think traditional research, by its very nature, is sterile and impersonal. Qualitative research is quite the opposite. Who you are studying is important; they are not just anonymous subjects. The questions that you ask are critical. This is a field that is ever-changing and challenging.

GROUP ACTIVITY

Purpose: To get you to think about the topic before you become too involved in jargon and reading what others have to say.

Activity: You can complete these statements on a note card.

1. Qualitative research is . . .

2. One of the things I know about qualitative research is . . .

3. I think qualitative research appeals to me because . . .

Pass your comments to another person in class.

Instructor's Note: You can either write the statements on chart paper or have others read and comment on the statements.

Evaluation: You can determine how ready and open you are to new ideas. You can also keep your statements and use at the end of the course to see how your views have changed.

INDIVIDUAL ACTIVITY

Purpose: To help you come to terms with multiple definitions and meanings of qualitative research.

Activity: Refine your earlier statements in light of the group discussion.

Evaluation: You might have some difficulty with venturing into unknown territory and have a need for the one single definition or statement.

Instructor's Note: You can identify students who need additional support to explore their own ideas and be willing to step into unknown territory.

You should continue writing in your journal. This week's entry might answer this question: How can I deal with my comfort level as I am exposed to new ideas?

NOTES

1. Postmodernist is the term used to refer to sociopolitical analysts known as the Frankfurt School, including Adorno, Marcuse, and Habermas. Freire has taken the movement into education in his work with oppressed minorities. See also Michael Apple and Henry Giroux.

2. It dismantles the most foundational procedures and assumptions whereby prior European philosophical traditions sought to establish universal truths or principles. It is fundamentally a revolutionary political movement, argued in intellectual terms. For a rather casual introduction to some of these issues, see Lemke, 1994.

3. Tripp continues, "It involves strategic pedagogic action on the part of classroom teachers, aimed at emancipation from overt and covert forms of domination. In practical terms, it is not simply a matter of challenging the existing practices of the system, but of seeking to understand what makes the system be the way it is, and challenging that, whilst remaining conscious that one's own sense of justice and equality are themselves open to question" (Tripp, 1992). According to Tripp, there are a number of methodological principles associated with the theory. They include participation by mutually supporting groups, consciousness that influences the way we teach and conduct research, and meaning which suggests that knowledge is not "subjectively neutral objectively verified facts." Rather, it is socially constructed facts that are artificial and held differently by different groups.

CHAPTER 3

Insights From the Past

A work of art must balance three elements: Does it understand the past? Does it elucidate the present? Does it reflect a personal vision?

—Jake Biddington

It was also very helpful to work closely with the school system where I planned to do the research. In the end, we formed an excellent match for doing qualitative research. The school system has a very comprehensive mentoring program for beginning teachers. They had substantial survey data, given annually to all mentors and beginning teachers, which documents the value of this program. However, there had been no inquiry into how the mentor/mentee relationships are operating at the local school level. This helped to solidify the research questions.

—Judy Smith

In this chapter I set the stage for the field of qualitative research. I begin with a discussion of educational research in general. Then I include a history of how the field of qualitative research developed. Emphasis is on the last century and in particular on the burgeoning growth and changes in the field since the 1980s. I conclude with speculations on the future of qualitative research in various fields.

The education of teachers in the United States began with teacher training and normal schools designed to teach young women how to work with children of elementary school age. They received training in psychology and pedagogy. Universities were not involved in teacher training until around the turn of the last century. It was only when graduate programs began to be developed in the 1920s that educators recognized the need to conduct research about education and to train future educators in methods of conducting research.

From the scientific movement and testing that began in the 1920s, educational research adopted a stance that was scientific, objective, and rigorous. Breuer et al. (2002) remind us that "the (social) sciences usually try to create the impression that the results of their research have *objective* character" (¶ 1). There was little room for other disciplines that seemed to be "soft" or "subjective." Thus, anthropology, sociology (unless it was statistical), phenomenology, or other approaches to answering questions were seen as somewhat lesser. These would not be approaches that could be used to answer important questions in education or to provide us with pure factual information. At least until the 1980s, it was accepted practice to conduct educational research using the scientific method. Experimental designs and statistics were emphasized. Hypothesis testing was expected. Objectivity and rigor were considered critical. The field was dominated by men who valued the approach of the natural scientists.

You might be interested to know that other fields also have a hierarchy. For example, for many years, most European artists and their audiences valued historical or mythological paintings as the highest form of art followed by portraits, genre paintings, landscapes, and still lifes. It was not until the center of the artistic community moved from Europe to New York and abstract painters took hold that this hierarchy was called into question. One reason that such a hierarchy was established is that it was thought that a historical or mythological painting was more complex and thus more difficult to accomplish. Its scope and size were usually larger than other types of paintings.

By the 1980s, the scientific method was no longer considered to be the only way to conduct research. Other voices began to be heard. Women were crying out for an opportunity to influence what was studied and what methods were being used. Anthropologists, phenomenologists, and others wanted their views heard.

I can remember back in my graduate school days (in the mid-1960s) I was a firm believer in a traditionalist viewpoint. I did not question why; I seemed to just follow along. I never really thought about issues raised by some that the field was dominated by European white men. What did I know? I was learning but not really questioning. It seemed like a status thing to me. If we could get the "real" or "true" data, we could find the answers. This view was fueled by the increasing availability of computer programs and advanced statistical techniques. More numbers, better answers. We felt so good about things. I have to say that I bought into this completely. Now I ask myself what I was thinking about. But then it was really different. In the sections that follow, I discuss these changes in greater depth.

EDUCATIONAL RESEARCH PRIOR TO THE 1980s

Imagine that it is one hundred years ago. You are working in the schools as a teacher. At that time teachers were trained in teacher training or normal schools. The first state-supported normal school opened in Massachusetts in 1839. Since women were excluded from preparatory schools, this was the only form of advanced education they could receive. The psychology of child development was emphasized, and the curriculum did not include anything about research. By the turn of the last century, many normal schools had become four-year teachers colleges. The first graduate program was established at New York University in 1887, and Teachers College at Columbia University opened its doors the following year. So it is not surprising that research was not a topic of much interest. It was not until the late 1920s, when the scientific movement became popular, that universities recognized that the discipline of education could be enhanced with more rigorous and systematic study. One of the first institutions to do so was Teachers College at Columbia University.

I suspect that there was not too much discussion about what kind of research approach to use since the scientific movement favored by the natural sciences was seen as the highest form of research. Educators were quick to follow in the footsteps of those disciplines that were considered more rigorous. Thus, they were strongly influenced by psychology and the testing movement, which, too, had adopted the scientific method.

I think it is interesting that in these early years there was quite a bit of collaboration between school administrators and professors. Topics of interest generally came from needs and concerns of the schools. As I researched this early literature, I came across one topic that both groups found important. Given that there were so many small high schools, the question on the minds of some was the adequacy of education offered by these small high schools. Administrators, principals, and teachers were concerned that students were not receiving proper training to enter college. One idea was to offer students correspondence courses through universities. You might find yourself asking this question that these educators posed: Do students who take correspondence courses learn at the same level as those exposed to regular classes? If the answer was yes, then educators could avoid closing small schools without jeopardizing students.

In 1926, Rufi wrote his dissertation on the inadequacy of the small high school. Influenced by his findings, Wooden and Mort (1929) conducted a study on the question of supervised correspondence study for high school pupils. Wooden was a superintendent of schools and Mort was a professor of education at Columbia. This is one of the earliest published research studies in education. Wooden and Mort took a real problem that had surfaced in other research and attempted to conduct a systematic investigation. By today's standards, one might not say that their study constituted experimental research since it is basically a description of how a small high school can make course material available to its students. But I think this study is important for two reasons. It demonstrates that school and university people can work together on problems of common interest. Second, it shows that decisions in education can be based on systematic investigation and study.

Very little of this early research was experimental in nature, although Crump (1928) wrote about correspondence and class extension work in Oklahoma for his doctoral research at Teachers College. He concluded that there were no significant differences between those studying in regular classrooms and those who studied by correspondence. This is one of the earliest experimental research studies conducted in the United States. On a national scale, one of the first major educational studies was begun in 1930. It involved 30 secondary schools and 300 colleges. Known as the Eight Year Study, it was designed to examine how high schools prepared students for college. It was led by Ralph Tyler, who was considered one of the strongest advocates of the scientific study of education. Unfortunately, World War II minimized the impact of the study. Tyler (who received his Ph.D. in educational psychology) returned from Ohio State to the University of Chicago where he became head of the Department of Education and then the Division of Social Sciences. The University of Chicago also had strong influences in research in the sociology department. This type of research was more similar to qualitative research than Tyler's experimental work. Known as the Chicago School, these researchers emphasized going out into the field and collecting data about life in the city. Because there were so many immigrants to the United States during the early years of the 20th century, these researchers became vitally interested in studying their behaviors.

They also relied on in-depth interviews and life histories to collect data. I know firsthand about various immigrant groups, such as the Polish, because I grew up in Chicago.[1] Chicago was one of the great cities with immigrant populations who lived in virtual ghettos throughout the city. To this day, you can find many ethnic restaurants reflecting these groups.

I suspect that you will find other studies addressing problems facing the schools in this early time period. But you need to remember that very few educators were trained to design and conduct research. The majority of the professors were trained as psychologists or measurement specialists. I want to stress how important the scientific movement and scientific thinking were to this newly emerging discipline of education. Educators adopted the method of science as a method that was suitable to the study of education. After all, this method had been used by psychologists such as B. F. Skinner, who contributed so much to our thinking about teaching and learning. Although Skinner studied rats and pigeons, his conclusions were widely applied to teaching. He was a behaviorist and believed that children could be conditioned to learn a certain way through operant conditioning.[2] You may not be aware that one of Skinner's first books on how organisms behaved became the model for experimental research. As recently as 2001, Bissell suggested that the theoretical constructs and experimental results presented by Skinner had a critical influence on education and teaching. Today almost no undergraduate student in education is exposed to research design and practice. Many graduate students receive a research methods course, but overwhelmingly the emphasis is on traditional research paradigms. Increasingly, these courses are expanding to include work in qualitative research methods.

I planned to provide you the names of those leaders and innovators who became synonymous with educational research. This turned into a much more difficult task than I had envisioned. I finally came to accept the fact that although I wanted to tell you who the father of educational research was, I was not able to find anyone who was clearly acknowledged as such. As I said earlier, I think that is because much of research was intertwined with testing and psychology. If you are interested, you can read about the father of modern testing, of the testing movement, of creativity, and of educational psychology.[3]

I think it would be fair to conclude that the discipline of educational research developed after universities became involved in advanced training of those going into education. Psychology and the testing movement played a pivotal role in guiding what should be studied and how it should be studied. The field was completely dominated by men and the scientific movement was the preferred, if not the only, mode of investigation. As more universities developed doctoral programs in education, this view permeated approaches to the conduct and training of research. Few women studied research methods or made contributions to the field.[4]

You cannot ignore the impact of World War II. Thousands of men inducted into the military needed to be tested, and test development became highly specialized. Educators addressed these issues. By the 1950s, the era of Sputnik, American educators moved even more rapidly into a scientific stance. Federal funding for research in the 1960s also encouraged and stressed scientific approaches to the field of research. The widespread use of computers by the 1970s enabled advanced statistical analyses to be conducted, which also reinforced this scientific bent. So you should not be surprised that there was little room for a discipline that seemed antithetical to what so many believed.

Applying ethnographic methods to the study of educational topics has existed for a long time. In my experience, however, these studies were conducted by anthropologists trained as ethnographers who found their way to a study of education rather than by educational researchers who were steeped in the traditions of the scientific method. In many universities, educational ethnographers were not in departments of educational research whose domain was statistics and experimental design. Yon (2003) reviews the growth of educational ethnography as a subset of anthropology. In particular, he speaks about a movement toward reflexivity.

I do not think there is a single event that we could point to that led to an opening up of research methods to move beyond the positivism and postpositivism that pervaded the field. But it is clear that things were brewing. Qualitative research as a field or separate discipline did not exist in education until the mid 1980s. The Qualitative Interest Group (QUIG) at the University of Georgia was one of the first groups devoted primarily to qualitative research. Its inception in 1985 and its sponsorship of an Annual Conference (the first one in 1988) support the timeline I describe. In addition to QUIG, Qualitative Research for the Human Sciences, a Listserv operating on the Internet (QUALRS-L), began in 1991. (See QUIG archives for details on this and related history.) As I mentioned, prior to that time educational research was guided by research from the natural sciences. Students learned experimental design and statistics. Faculty wrote articles that were of an experimental nature. Sometimes surveys were conducted, but since they were not about hypothesis testing and generalizing, they were not seen to be as high quality as those that were experimental. Students across the country were trained to conduct scientific experiments and to think about hypothesis testing and generalization. The professional organizations, like the American Educational Research Association (founded in 1916), did not have a special interest group that was interested in qualitative research. Little was available in terms of textbooks or printed material. Most publishers were not interested in publishing books about qualitative research.

I do not mean to suggest that there was no research that could be characterized as qualitative prior to the 1980s. Ethnographies became popular. Some researchers came to the field of education from an anthropological background and began to conduct ethnographies in schools and classrooms. Often these individuals were not part of departments of educational research and were seen by some as outside of "real" research. These early ethnographies were typically designed to address issues of credibility and respectability. Although the ethnographies were often on topics of interest to educators, few were specifically about education.[5] Ethnographers tended to study whole cultures and immerse themselves in the topic for extended time periods. As an adaptation and recognition of the difficulties of conducting such ethnographies, some researchers adopted a case study approach. Thus by looking at a smaller part of an entire culture, an ethnographic stance could be adopted yet made manageable. Denny (1978) suggests that the case study in education was growing in popularity.

While Bogdan and Biklen (1992) agree that the dominant paradigm was hypothesis testing and measurement, they acknowledge that prior to 1980 there were other traditions that influenced the development of research methods in education. Denzin and Lincoln (2000) characterize the time period from the early 1900s until the end of World War II as a traditional period. They say that those individuals who were conducting qualitative research wrote "objective" accounts and were practicing in a positivist mode. In spite of these modest attempts to introduce alternative research approaches, they did not catch on to any great extent, and the field continued to be dominated by the traditional paradigm.[6]

Denzin and Lincoln (2000) speak about how the "modernist ethnographer and sociological participant observer attempted rigorous qualitative studies of important social processes" (p. 14). Bogdan and Biklen (1992) suggest that although not in a central position, these methods that are labeled qualitative could no longer be labeled fringe efforts. And Denzin and

Lincoln speak of the golden age of rigorous qualitative analysis. As I see it, qualitative research until the late 1980s was striving to fit into a traditional, quantitative paradigm. I am not sure that they actually recognized that they were trying to put a square peg into a round hole. I would disagree with the view offered by some that qualitative approaches mushroomed in education. Eisner and Peshkin (1990) echo my sentiments: "To conduct experiments and surveys was to be scientific; to do otherwise . . . was to be soft-, wrong- or muddle-headed" (p. 1). In my own experience, those who were involved in qualitative research were often discounted and seen as soft or aberrant. I remember one colleague who asked me whether I had lost my mind when I said I was interested in research methods that were qualitative.

THE 1980s TO 2000

By the 1980s, many more people were being trained as educational researchers. Some were beginning to question the dominant traditional paradigms of experimental research and hypothesis testing. Ethnographers were increasingly making their presence felt in the field of education. Rist (1980) writes of blitzkrieg ethnography: the transformation of a method into a movement. Many researchers equated qualitative and ethnographic.[7] By the middle of the1980s, approaches other than ethnographic began to take hold in the educational community. It was no longer sufficient to say that qualitative research was the same as doing ethnography or a modified ethnography/case study. The idea of doing research in a naturalistic setting began to surface (Custer, 1996; Lincoln & Guba, 1985) although, as Custer acknowledges, it by no means was accepted as a better alternative to traditional work. Voices of feminists began to be heard as well (Harding, 1987; Reinharz, 1992; Roman & Apple, 1990).

This was a time when researchers tried to clarify what research approaches to take and how to legitimize their alternative ways of thinking, and the road was somewhat rocky. I agree with Eisner and Peshkin (1990) when they state that "there were no accepted models to which educational researchers with a qualitative bent could turn for direction" (p. 1). Crabtree and Miller (1992) concur that "no prepackaged designs exist from which to choose" (p. xiv).

Denzin and Lincoln (2000) see this period as a time of blurred genres. It seemed as though almost anything fit. They acknowledge that the "naturalistic, postpositivist, and constructionist" paradigms gained power during this time period. During the mid 1980s they speak about the crisis of representation and suggest that in the 1990s "the ethnographer's authority remains under assault" (p. 17). Yon (2003) maps the transition from modernist formulations of the field in its formative days, when ethnographies laid claim to being sealed and scientific texts, to the more recent formulations shaped by postmodern and poststructural ideas that undermine earlier meanings of culture and call attention to the explanatory limits of ethnography.

According to Campbell (n.d.),

the research paradigm shift has to do with major shifts in the way knowledge is constructed and created. Associated with this is the further question of whose interests are served by the dominant paradigm? Research has been dominated in the last hundred years or more by what is commonly known as the scientific method. Also known as positivist or quantitative research, its emphasis is on objectivity, neutrality, measurement, and validity. To live in the scientific method means to live within an understanding of the beliefs, values, and techniques that guide scientific inquiry (Lather, 1991). Those working within the scientific framework also accept the conventions, language, and methods of carrying out research in this way. Those living within the scientific paradigm judge other ways of carrying out investigations as too open to multiple interpretation, too biased, too subjective, simply not scientific or rigorous enough. (¶ 5)

Denzin and Lincoln (2000) characterize this latter period as a time of crisis. One crisis is what they refer to as the representational crisis. As such, they question the assumption that qualitative researchers can capture lived experience. They argue that such experience is created in the "social text written by the researcher" (p. 17). For them, this is the crisis of representation. The other crisis they pose is the question of legitimating. They suggest that traditional criteria for evaluating and interpreting qualitative research need to be rethought. They also briefly mention new ways of writing and representing information. They suggest that "fictional ethnographies, ethnographic poetry, and multimedia texts are today taken for granted" (p. 17).

At the end of the one hundred years or so during which education training moved from being dominated by the training of women teachers, through the adoption of the scientific method to lend an air of legitimacy to research, to a questioning of traditional approaches, educational researchers and those who describe themselves as qualitative researchers find themselves in somewhat of a dilemma. No longer are the rules clear. No longer can they feel secure in how to conduct research. No longer do they know how to evaluate research. They have opened themselves to new ideas, to new paradigms, to new ways of thinking, and to the creativity of those who follow.

2000 AND BEYOND

As I write this book in the year 2005, I find myself wondering what I should tell you about the state of qualitative research today. I recognize that by the time you read this material, "today" may be quite different from what we know now. This is interesting because for many years educational research was fairly predictable and consistent. We knew what to do and how to do it. And now I am not sure what we know except that we don't agree on what to do and how to do it. I speculate on some ideas here and rely on recent writings of others.

Things have flipped almost 180 degrees in a very short time. It has become almost impossible to keep up with the writing and publishing in the field. No longer is qualitative research dominated by the anthropologists and ethnographers. Many disciplines and subdisciplines inform the field. Creswell (1997) singles out five traditions to discuss, although he acknowledges others as well. More recently, Creswell (2003) has emphasized also looking at a mixed methods approach in which elements of both qualitative and quantitative research are combined to enlarge an investigation. Merriam (2002) and Patton (2002) also acknowledge various approaches and methodologies. *The Handbook of Qualitative Research,* first published in 1994, adds other ideas. The second edition of the *Handbook,* issued in 2000, introduces still more ideas, and the third edition, published in 2005, expands our horizons even further. Now it seems that almost anything can be labeled qualitative research. I will talk later about how this is confusing for you as a student and how you can begin to make judgments about which way works for you.

SPECULATIONS FOR THE FUTURE

I have been in the field for a long time. I have seen many things become popular. Education is a discipline replete with fads. We tend to react and are often driven by forces beyond our immediate range. I suspect this will be true for qualitative research as well, but here are some trends that I see.

Greater Diversity and Creativity. This new millennium will be a time for greater diversity and creativity in answering questions about human interaction and in representing information. The doors have been opened, and I believe we will see creativity unlike anything we can imagine. I know the art and music worlds have gone in directions we could not expect. Why not the world of research and education?

I think we have just begun to scratch the surface in terms of our thinking about how research will be done and who will be doing it. The field has opened up dramatically since the 1980s. Women have taken leadership roles in all aspects of the profession. I remember clearly back in the mid 1970s when I was interviewed for a position at a university in a department of educational research. The chairman of the search committee called me and invited me to come for an interview. He said he was especially pleased that I was a woman; I would be joining a department of almost a dozen men. In 2005 that department is almost exclusively women. People of color have made contributions to the field and heightened awareness of issues. These voices were not heard in the past. Now they are heard.

How research will be done and how it will be transmitted will continue to be examined. Representations will not be strictly textual. I hope we will move more toward the visual because it is well known that so many gain their information through television, the Internet, DVDs, and other visual media. I wonder why we think it is important to convey our information solely through words and traditional text?

Greater Access and Availability. The revolution of the Internet has affected all aspects of our lives. Instantaneous communication around the world is now available to almost everyone. One way this will continue to affect qualitative research is to make information readily available through online journals and discussion groups. No longer do we have to wait until a journal is published in hard copy. This means what you read is current, not a year old or more. Another fact of instant worldwide communication is worldwide influence. No longer will the U.S. or Europe be the dominant force. I suspect we will see new ideas from Asia, Africa, and South America. At the time of this writing, we already see influences from Asia and much greater impact from Europe.

More Voices Heard. Educational research began with voices of men. They were remote, objective, and scientific. You may know that research in the medical field began the same way. In fact, in medicine, much of the research was done on white men (usually doctors) and extrapolated to other groups. Once women became a greater force, they began to design studies and conduct them on women. The qualitative research field has opened up to many voices. But, although we have a greater representation of women and minorities than ever before, we still hear from those with more education and traditional schooling. Since much research emanates from universities—either by professors or by students—this is not surprising. But I wonder if there is not a way to include a broader perspective of education and experience in the planning and design of our research. I predict that this will be so and in ways we can't now imagine.

Creative Flow That Does Not Follow Any One Pattern. If we look at the field of art, we have seen a variety of movements since the center of art moved from Paris to New York. Just as in research, art was initially dominated by men. Now we see women and minorities making enormous contributions. Their creative ideas are astounding. In the year 2004, for example, I visited an exhibit at the Saatchi Gallery in London of Richard Wilson's 20:50, which is an installation of a lake of sump oil that reflects the ceiling and completely disorients the viewer. It was quite fantastic. Some would probably say this is not art, but I do not agree. Installation art is not new, but reusing oil probably is. What else can we expect of qualitative researchers? We have performance art, dance, play reading, and **blogs**. I believe that multimedia is an area that will be used to a much greater extent. Chenail speaks about a research park similar to Disneyland (Lichtman, 2004). Without rules and restrictions, who knows where we will go.

Is It Good Enough? As researchers grapple with what qualitative research is, what it should be, how it should be done, and what it should look like, I suspect we might see conservatives moving to more traditional approaches. Some will ask what the rules are and begin to set rules that will follow a traditional paradigm. Davis (2002), in an editorial in the *Journal of Curriculum and Supervision,* speaks about the future of educational research:

> It seeks new ends, for example, reliable research conclusions, causal relationships, and replicable "best practices." At first blush, its aim appears to represent a political "back to the future" policy in which a "new educational scientism" will flourish. This educational research policy, however, differs profoundly from the multiple approaches, even the "scientific" rationale, used by researchers during most of the 20th century. In the past, educational researchers adopted and shifted their research paradigms and techniques on the bases of scholarly exposition, demonstration, and persuasion. In the current scene, on the other hand, bureaucratic mandates supersede the reasonableness of research options. (¶ 2)

From Davis's viewpoint, bureaucracy and politics take a more prominent role in determining research agendas. I, for one, hope he is in error.

A related issue is a concern by some that research will not be taken seriously because the rules are not hard and fast and therefore it is difficult to judge what is "good" or of high "quality." I think there will still be those who are of this view.

Keeping Up With the Explosion. Information access and retrieval is a challenging pursuit. I suspect that by the time you read this document you will be able to access an enormous amount of material on the Internet. Some of it will be scholarly; some of it will be personal and specific to an individual. I don't hold to the admonition that the only good material needs to be peer-reviewed. I know there are politics that affect much of what we hear and say and what gets printed. It will be your challenge to locate information, judge its merit, and integrate it with what you already know. This will be a greater challenge than ever before because the Internet makes so much material instantly available and retrievable. This is true for you and for the students you might teach and for their parents. Ten years ago Denzin and Lincoln (1994) wrote about the concept of the qualitative researcher as a bricoleur. A French term, this concept suggests someone who has the tools to get the job done. According to McLeod (2000), a bricoleur's image is a tension between creativity and conformity. He sees creativity as one of the core characteristics of a good qualitative researcher. How the new qualitative researcher will be creative is a matter of speculation. I believe we will continue to see creativity and resourcefulness, and those characteristics will overcome the need by some to move into a more traditional and conservative posture.

SUMMARY

In 1934, Cole Porter's *Anything Goes* opened in New York. The screen version appeared in 1936. A revival appeared in 1987. In 2004, the film *De-Lovely* portrayed the life of Cole Porter. I think of this music when I think about the field of qualitative research. It is rich, long lasting, and ever fresh. It is as good today as it was when it was first written. Qualitative research is a field with a long tradition. It is rich, long lasting, and ever fresh. I hope as you continue to read this book you will be open to these new ideas, to new ways of doing things. At the same time you will look for quality, integrity, and value. You should find yourself on a new pathway. It is time to jump in and learn how to do it.

GROUP ACTIVITY

Purpose: To identify the latest trends in the field.

Activity: Join a team of two other students. Identify possible new trends—I suggest many will involve technology and the Internet. Prepare a brief one-page synopsis of what you think you know about the topic. Now you are going to find out what else is out there. Use a search engine (e.g., Google) to search the Internet. Allow at least two hours for your search. Save your information online and be prepared to send it to your other teammates online. You may engage in a discussion online before your next class meeting. Prepare a summary to send to each other and other class members.

Evaluation: Determine whether you have located new information that supports, adds to, or contradicts what you know so far.

INDIVIDUAL ACTIVITY

Purpose: To examine your own views on the appropriateness of qualitative research as a tool for answering questions in education.

Activity: This is a self-reflexive, introspective activity in which you will write in your qualitative research journal. The topic to think about is how you view the field based on what you know so far and how it fits with your own belief system.

Evaluation: Determine to what extent you are able to examine your own motivations and thoughts. Decide what additional information you need to obtain a clearer understanding.

NOTES

1. I had the good fortune to attend The Laboratory School at the University of Chicago while Tyler and others were conducting research on the students. We used to move to the "Experimental Lab—Room 400" during certain periods of each week. We were told they were studying us. I think most of us tried to mug for the cameras as pictures were taken. You can read more about the Eight Year Study at http://fcis.oise.utoronto.ca/~daniel_schugurensky/assignment1/1930eight.html or http://www.coe.uh.edu/courses/cuin6373/idhistory/8year.html.

2. You can read more about Skinner in his 1938 work *The Behavior of Organisms*. Skinner died in 1990 after a long career at the University of Minnesota, Indiana University, and Harvard. Skinner also studied his daughter, whom he raised for a time in a box called the Skinner box.

3. Frederic Lord, who died at age 87 in 2000, is said to be the father of modern testing. G. Stanley Hall (1844–1924) was an American psychologist and founder of the testing movement. He also founded the American Psychological Association and *The American Journal of Psychology*. E. Paul Torrance, who died at age 87 in 2003, is said to be the father of creativity. E. L. Thorndike, who died at age 98 in 1998, was known as the father of educational psychology. But no one was named the father of educational research. Lewis Terman, a professor of education and psychology at Stanford between 1910 and 1946, was instrumental in bringing the scientific approach both to research studies and to the training of researchers. He became president of the American Psychological Association in 1923.

4. How ironic, though, that in 2004, the majority of the more than 20,000 members of the American Educational Research Association are female. The president of the organization is female as well.

5. See Becker's (1976) study of medical students, Liebow's (1967) study of street corner men in Washington, D.C., and Agar's (1973) study of urban heroin addicts.

6. For an excellent account of the history, read Chapter 1 in Bogdan and Biklen's 1992 *Foundations of Qualitative Research in Education*.

7. You can read many ethnographies on such topics as drug dealing, girl gangs, or psychiatric clients. Few ethnographies were actually conducted in schools.

CHAPTER 4

Learning How to Be a Qualitative Researcher

Education is a kind of continuing dialogue, and a dialogue assumes, in the nature of the case, different points of view.

—Robert Hutchins

I have found over the years that sometimes it is best to do something rather than to plan to do something. In 1990, while attending my son's graduation from business school, I heard Tom Peters speak to the newly minted MBAs from UC-Berkeley. We were sitting outside in the Greek Theater. Peters advised them: ready, fire, aim. Some 15 years later, these words stay with me. Get out and do something, he advised the graduates. You can make adjustments and corrections later. (See Cox, 1994 or Schrage, 1999 for their comments on Peters's advice). I couldn't agree with him more. In my experience, many students get turned off when they have to write draft upon draft of plans on how to do a piece of qualitative research. They like to jump in with both feet and begin the process rather than plan and ponder. For the most part, I agree with this idea.

In this chapter, I discuss some of the ways you can get out and do something about learning to be a qualitative researcher. After all, qualitative research is an inductive approach. One of the best ways to learn about such an approach is to practice its principles. (You will recall that inductive means moving from the particular to the general.) So, get your notebook and pen ready, charge the battery in your digital camera, get your laptop out, and embark on this new adventure. I promise you that you will learn something; you will enjoy yourself; and, most importantly, you will gain some insight into being a qualitative researcher.

SO YOU WANT TO BE A QUALITATIVE RESEARCHER

If you have finished skimming or reading the first few chapters, you will have a taste of what qualitative research is. Many of you will be very intrigued. It sounds like something that is interesting to you and something that you can manage to do. If you are working on a degree, you know that any discipline is informed by research efforts and findings. As a practitioner, you can learn about how to do something, but why and what works is what we gain from conducting research.

Use this checklist to see if being a qualitative researcher seems right for you.

1. You are interested in people and empathetic toward them, their situations, and the environment around them.

2. You want to study questions about how people interact, how social networks develop, or how cultures are nurtured.

3. You like to be with people and see how they tick.

4. You are interested in studying schools and classrooms and kids.

5. You see value in going beyond facts and tables.

6. You like new ways to do things and are innovative in your approach to research.

7. You are willing to deal with some ambiguity.

8. You have a tolerance for lack of structure.

9. You like to write and are good at it.

10. You like to look further into things.

11. You have to write a research paper or a thesis.

12. You are willing to see research as more than testing hypotheses.

13. You are open to new ideas.

14. You want to know more in depth about how humans interact.

15. You recognize that all research is complex and challenging and you are not necessarily looking for an easy way out.

I offer these as guidelines so that you can gauge how you fit into this type of research approach. In my own experience, some students like the rules laid out for them in advance, while others are challenged by lack of structure and ambiguity. To begin doing qualitative research, an open mind is critical.

In keeping with the inductive nature of qualitative research, I want to begin with an example. Sandra is just beginning her advanced degree in education. She hopes to obtain an endorsement in special education. She has worked with children in her rural home town where she grew up and in the adjacent city where she attended college. She found the work stimulating and challenging, but she continued to ask questions about what she was doing. She wanted to know about ways to work with these challenging children. She especially wanted to explore ways to socialize them into the larger school community. She began taking notes about how these kids behaved when they were having lunch and passing through the halls. She often thought about what she might do to help them feel more comfortable.

Sandra sounds like a good candidate to begin to learn some of the skills of doing qualitative research. She asks questions about her own practice. She has had several types of experiences and remains open to improve her own teaching. And she is a careful observer and recorder. I see her as someone who would benefit tremendously by jumping into the field. From those experiences she can begin to build her repertoire of qualitative research skills.

Why does she want to do qualitative research? I suspect Sandra doesn't know explicitly that she wants to do qualitative research. She probably has heard the term but doesn't have a clear understanding of what it is. In this chapter I will offer some advice about when you might want to do qualitative research, and I will provide you with some practical suggestions to get started. I conclude the chapter with several ethical considerations.

Why would someone want to do qualitative research? One way to think about qualitative research is that it is a way to answer questions. In fact, most research deals with finding answers to questions. But the kinds of questions qualitative research tends to focus on are those that take place in real settings and not in a laboratory. They are not contrived or manipulated by the researcher. The questions are often about human or social interaction. The questions are often somewhat general and not well thought out. I have listed some advice that I offer you as you embark on your qualitative experience. If you fit into any of the areas, then it is time to begin to identify some kind of qualitative research question.

Advice Number 1. When you have a question that deals with real people in real settings and you want to study some general ideas about the people and how they interact in these settings, you may want to use some type of qualitative research.

Advice Number 2. When you are interested in looking at behaviors, thoughts, or feelings of individuals with certain traits or characteristics, you may want to use some type of qualitative research. You like the opportunity to explore ideas in depth. This is especially critical if you want to study underlying meanings by using thick descriptions.

Advice Number 3. When you are attracted to what people say, how they portray themselves, or how they talk to each other, you may want to use some type of qualitative research.

Advice Number 4. When you look at yourself and see yourself as a good listener and good at asking questions, you may want to use some type of qualitative research.

Advice Number 5. When you find you are a good judge of self and others—you have a kind of introspective viewpoint— you may want to use some type of qualitative research.

Advice Number 6. When you find you are intrigued with the details of how people interact, you may want to use some type of qualitative research.

POTENTIAL RESEARCH QUESTIONS

I know how very difficult it is to come up with a suitable research question. Here are some ways that might be helpful to you. Begin by thinking about different categories: people, concepts, places, and events. I have constructed a table so you can think about this more clearly.

People	Concepts	Places	Events
students	power	classrooms	hurricanes
teachers	leadership	playgrounds	pep rallies
parents	loneliness	malls	parties
adult students	mentoring	coffee houses	athletic events
administrators	gender differences	homes	assemblies
high-achieving girls	violence	lunchrooms	concerts
children at risk	cooperation	schools	parades
gangs	friendships	adult centers	flood
pregnant teens	mentoring relationship	places of worship	holidays
beginning teachers	teacher burnout	online chat rooms	mealtimes
students in same-sex classes	aggression	rural classrooms	elections

Of course, the examples under each category are those I have thought about. You can substitute any you wish. Very often researchers begin by identifying individuals of interest to them. Some find it helpful to select a particular concept to study. I think this helps you to focus your ideas as you begin your study. Once you have selected who and what you plan to study, you need to determine where the study will take place. I have listed some places for you to consider. Lastly, some people find that they are motivated by a particular event and want to study the event itself. The event can be unique, such as a hurricane or disaster, or more common, such as a sporting event or assembly.

Before you embark on the steps I have outlined below, use the table to help you formulate a research question.

GETTING STARTED

Now that you have determined that you might want to do qualitative research, I will talk about some ways that you can get started.

Jump right in. I think too many people spend a lot of time planning, making sure that everything is just so, and perhaps avoiding the actual task of collecting and analyzing data. One way to avoid this is to just get started and jump right in. Here are some things that you can do.

- Select something, some place, and someone to study. Most people like to begin by selecting something to study. And since you are doing this just for practice, I think it is advisable to make your selection from something that is immediate, accessible, and of interest to you. I've made some suggestions below. Since you are going into a public place, you do not have to seek permission, worry about privacy, or otherwise get bogged down in technicalities. Remember, your purpose is just to practice and begin to think and act like a qualitative researcher.
  - Select something or someone to study within your own college setting. You can study people in the library, individuals at a sporting event, students as they interact between classes, students at coffee breaks, or small group work efforts. You can position yourself in the lounge areas of buildings and watch as students leave and return to their classes. I had a student who studied an aspect of personal space (she was getting her degree in architecture) by observing in the campus library for an extended period. She was interested in the physical use of space, how students surrounded themselves with books, whether they sat near others, and so on.
  - You can venture outside of your immediate campus and study social interaction in fast food places (e.g., McDonalds, Burger King, or Starbucks). I often get my best practice watching and listening to people in public places. You will find that if you frequent one of these places at about the same time each day, you will see the same people. You can look from afar, or you can interact with them more directly. Many of them will be happy to talk with you since they may have some time on their hands. I have studied retirees, young mothers, and young professionals. By the way, the crowd is different during the week than on weekends.
  - You can identify other places where groups of people tend to congregate: parks, playgrounds, grocery stores, malls, airports, or train stations. Malls are a great place to study teenagers. If you live in a suburban area or a city, these places offer insight into contemporary society that may be quite different from when you were a teenager. The airport is another place where people congregate. It is especially interesting to see how different cultures greet one another.
- Select a co-researcher. Doing research can often be a very lonely task, and here you are doing something you don't really know how to do and you are on your own. Remember, there is no right way to do something; there are many ways. You will have to identify what works best for you, but in my experience, it is a good idea to work with someone else. So pick someone from your class who wants to study the same thing that you do. My suggestion is that you do not talk about what you are going to do in advance—just that you are going to study the same thing.
- Get yourself ready. Since this might be an impromptu task, there will not be much that you need to do. Decide on what, where, or who you are going to study. Allow at least 30 minutes for your observations. Bring a note pad and pen with you to take notes. You might also do some thinking about what you will be looking for in advance. I do not

recommend that you do a literature review at this point. I find that it tends to close you off and dictate what you will look for rather than let the data emerge from the setting.

- Now go out there. Depending on which place you select, you might have to figure out where to sit or stand, whether you really want to take notes or not, and how you will position yourself so that others will not become wary or suspicious. If you are in a college campus, you might find it easy to observe in the library or at a coffee house. Both locations will provide you access to a variety of people. Since many people stay in these places for a long period of time, you will be able to work on your skills easily. You can take notes about how people are dressed, how frequently they interact with others, whether they use their cell phones, or the extent to which they are aware of others in their surroundings. Your note taking should be inconspicuous because others will be writing as well.

- Debrief with your partner. After you finish your 30 minutes, plan to meet with your partner for at least 30 additional minutes. Have a general discussion about what you did, what you noticed, what seemed important, how you felt, and what you think you learned. This session will be invaluable as you will see what someone else thought and did in the same setting as you. Your purpose is to talk about process, not necessarily about what the findings are. But I know that you will begin your discussion talking about what you saw and what it meant. That is only human nature.

Practice, practice, practice. You can never get enough practice. You know that professional athletes practice every day. But for you this task is new and perhaps somewhat foreign to your own daily behavior. You might be more likely to do something rather than to study how others are acting or doing. If you are a counselor, you might be more likely to want to help someone you see in trouble. If you are a special education teacher, you might want to provide additional assistance to a needy student. If you are working as an administrator, your inclination might be to just get the job done. But you are training to be a researcher, and that is something with which you have little or no experience. So I suggest you continue your practice. You might want to refine what you did in your first practice session. Perhaps as a result of your dialogue with your partner you get the idea that it would be good to focus on one particular aspect of what you observe. Maybe you decide that you want to look at the interaction between teenage boys and girls in the mall. Maybe you want to focus just on how they talk to each other and the informal body language they demonstrate. Do you see what you have done? You have begun to work your ideas around to something that you found interesting, unique, or unusual. That is what qualitative researchers tend to do. So let's look at some ways you can practice and build your own repertoire and your confidence.

- Look at the same or a similar site. Use the same partner. Try to identify at least one thing that you will do differently from your first time out. It might be to focus on a particular aspect of the interaction, as I suggested above, or it might be to decide to take more extensive notes than you did the first time. Or it might be to actually talk to someone you are observing.

- Choose a different kind of site, either one where the people you are observing are of a different age, involved in different kinds of activities, or are in a very different type of setting. Follow what you did initially, but now your site has changed.

- Select a different partner with whom to work. You might get some new insights by talking to someone else.

In any event, your purpose is to continue practicing.

Work with others. We can learn so much by working with others. That is why I stress that you should begin with a partner. There are a number of things that you can do with a partner or with a larger group.

- Plan together what you will look at or how you will look at something. Alternatively, work separately and then compare what you have done afterwards.
- I find it especially helpful to work with others on data analysis. Although there is no one right way of making sense of your data, sometimes it is helpful to see others' response to your ideas.

Read work by others. There are different kinds of things you can read. All are helpful, but I don't think it is critical to read before you set out into the field for your practice work.

- One thing you can read is what others have to say about the topic. How do teenagers interact with each other? What are effective ways of working with students with special needs?
- Another kind of material to read is what others have to say about doing qualitative research. This material would be considered methodology. You can read about how to do qualitative interviewing, how to observe, what kind of data analysis to do, and you can read about theory. What are qualitative research traditions? What is grounded theory? What is phenomenology?
- To make your life easier, I suggest you begin by reading through material that is readily available. Two good sources are *The Qualitative Report* (http://www.nova.edu/ssss/QR/) and *FQS* (http://www.qualitative-research.net/fqs/fqs-eng.htm).

Don't be afraid. At this point you cannot make a mistake. Remember, you are not working on writing a journal article or your thesis. You are developing skills. Since there is no one right way of doing something, you need to experiment with what works best for you. Your creative juices will flow as you begin to go into the field. You might begin one way and then see yourself moving toward something else. It is often the case that new researchers try to write down everything they see and hear, but quickly they will notice how difficult this is to do. What should they write down? What if they miss something? What is important and what is not? I suggest that you also need to rely on what you see, so I like people to write a detailed description of the setting. If you have a digital camera, you might want to take pictures of what you see. This combination of visuals and words often leads to a much richer set of data with which you can work.

Keep a journal. Write early and often. I cannot emphasize this enough. You need to write down your reflections. They can be about the process, they can be about what you are thinking, or they can be about what you found. What is critical is that you write. I suggest you take a laptop with you to any site. If convenient, you can write while you are observing. If this is too cumbersome, you need to allocate some time in the following day or so to write your reflections.

Join an online discussion. There are a number of online discussions that are often very helpful. Many of them are supportive of questions from students. One Listserv that has become very useful emanates from the University of Georgia. You can join it by going to listserv@listserv.uga.edu

Seek out others with similar interests. Learning to become a qualitative researcher sometimes places you out of the mainstream of others doing research. If you are taking a qualitative research class, find others in the class with whom you seem compatible and form a small discussion group. If you are taking the class online, initiate a chat room or other discussion forum. If you are reading the material and not enrolled in a course, use an online discussion.

Be an advocate, not an apologist. In the early days of qualitative research practice, I found that students would say something like, "I am doing qualitative research. I know it is not as good as quantitative but that is what I want to do." Qualitative research has an important and legitimate role in the research community. You can contribute to this growing field by accepting what you are doing and being positive about it.

Believe in what you are doing. I am a firm believer that qualitative research can be used to answer questions that other approaches cannot. This does not mean that other forms of research are wrong or bad, but certain kinds of questions lend themselves to be answered by looking and listening.

THE ETHICS OF CONDUCTING QUALITATIVE RESEARCH

There are many ethical questions that you might consider as you begin working in the field of qualitative research. In this section, I will discuss three areas. First, I deal with appropriate and inappropriate behaviors on the part of the researcher. Second, I discuss actions you need to consider as a consequence of information you gain. Finally, I offer some suggestions and guidance as to how to conduct yourself.

I want to make some general points first. In many different kinds of qualitative research, you develop a close relationship with your participants. You may spend extensive time with them. You may learn intimate details of their personal lives. They may reveal information to you that they have not told anyone else. Now you face a dilemma. As closeness develops, how do you deal with it on a personal level and what are your obligations to keep information confidential if you determine the information is damaging to the participant or to others?

Researcher Behaviors. In the 21st century, it seems that nothing is surprising to us. You have read with shock and sadness of the inappropriate behaviors of many priests with their young parishioners. But you might be surprised to learn about inappropriate behaviors of qualitative researchers. Roth (2004) reviews Wolcott's personal account of his homosexual relationship with his research participant, as described in *The Sneaky Kid and the Aftermath.* I need to provide you with some background. Harry Wolcott is a prominent qualitative researcher. His seminal work, published in 1973, in which he follows a principal for a year, was one of the first ethnographies I remember reading. Much of his writing has influenced the field tremendously. Imagine what courage it must have taken for Wolcott to reveal his inappropriate relationship with Brad, the 19-year-old studied in his work about "the sneaky kid." We learn that two years after the study, Brad returned and beat up Wolcott and burned down his house. Wolcott reveals this information as he discusses ethics and intimacy (Wolcott, 2002).

Roth (2004), in his critical work on qualitative research and ethics, reminds us that Malinowski's[1] field notebooks reveal that such relationships may take place in the field, although they are not usually reported in a write-up. Roth also discusses Wolcott's work. I wonder if perhaps the positions of power and status somehow influenced the behaviors both of the researcher and participants. Feminists are particularly interested in power issues as they approach qualitative research.

More familiar examples of inappropriate conduct by researchers have been written about more widely. Do you know that in some early research studies, the issue of ethics was not really considered? Drug studies were conducted on prisoners with the promise of reduced sentences. Prior to the 1980s, clinical trials for new drugs were conducted in prisons. Studies included the Tuskegee syphilis study with African American men, a study of mentally retarded children exposed to hepatitis at the Willowbrook State School, and the injection of live cancer cells at the Jewish Chronic Disease Hospital in New York. Prisoners were especially highly motivated to participate because often their sentences were reduced. Since that time, the government and universities have developed specific policies to protect human subjects. For the most part, such vulnerable subjects are now protected.

Other illustrations of inappropriate behaviors are shown in these two experimental studies. You can look at a slide show of the Stanford Prison Experiment on the Internet at http://www .prisonexp.org/. It describes a 1990s study in which students were in simulated prison situations. The study had to be discontinued after a few days because the sadistic behavior of the guards led to depression and stress in the students. You can read the comments of one of the participants at http://www.stanford.edu/dept/news/relaged/970108prisonexp.html.

You can also read about the study of obedience and individual responsibility developed by Stanley Milgram, a Yale psychologist, at http://www.cba.uri.edu/Faculty/dellabitta/ mr415s98/EthicEtcLinks/Milgram.htm. It involved teachers punishing learners for incorrect responses.

In a somewhat different vein, you can read about how a controversial topic presented a serious problem for one graduate student. An early work that caused much controversy involved Laud Humphreys. For his dissertation, Humphreys (1970) studied homosexuals in public restrooms ("tearooms," as they were called), a topic very avant garde for the time. While much controversy surrounded his work (including a fist fight among faculty members and a request to rescind his degree), he won a prestigious award for the work. He was an activist most of his adult life and died in 1988. While I am not suggesting that his behavior was inappropriate, at the time it caused great consternation about privacy.

Questionable Information. Now, you might say that qualitative research does not involve drugs or inappropriate experimental manipulation that might cause harm to a participant. After all, how can talking to people or observing them or looking at what they have drawn lead to any danger? Here are some ideas you might want to consider. What if in the course of an interview you discover that a young person is engaging in illicit drug use or promiscuous sexual behavior? Or if you learn that someone is the object of abuse by a teacher or a family member? Or if you observe that a student is carrying a weapon in school? Are you obliged to do something with this information? How do you reconcile that with the fact that you have promised that you will keep all information confidential? That is a dilemma that some qualitative researchers face.

Suggestions and Guidance. What are your roles and responsibilities as you begin your research planning? You might be surprised to learn that there are no specific rules of conduct for an educational researcher; however, there are many guidelines you can use. As a teacher, counselor, or administrator you have guidelines and codes of ethics recommended by your profession. For example, the American Psychological Association's code of ethics and conduct is available for psychologists. (http://www.apa.org/ethics/code.html). As a student, your university most likely has an Institutional Review Board with specific rules you must follow for conducting research with humans. The United States Department of Health and Human Services offers guidelines for the protection of human subjects (http://www.hhs.gov/ohrp/humansubjects/guidance/45cfr46.htm). You can look at the National Institute of Health's courses and tutorials about conducting research with human subjects (http://www.cancer.gov/clinicaltrials/learning/page3). You can even read about conducting human subjects research in cyberspace (http://www.aaas.org/spp/sfrl/projects/intres/main.htm).

One way to think about the problem is to consider different viewpoints or stances you might take. If you choose what is called an absolutist stance, you would consider four central issues: protection from physical or psychological harm, prevention of deception, protection of privacy, and informed consent. Many people take this viewpoint. But others adopt a relativist stance, which provides you freedom to study whatever flows from your own experience and holds that ethics are dictated by your individual conscience. Here you would strive for open relationships with the participant. A less desirable option, in my view, is the deception stance, in which you use any means necessary to understand a particular situation. In such cases, you might find yourself telling lies, misrepresenting yourself or others, or setting people up. This approach would be used if you are studying participants who are uncooperative or unwilling to reveal information about themselves. I caution you against using this approach as a beginning researcher.

Roth (2004) provides a history of the issues and writes about evolving a community of ethical practitioners. He suggests that our research ethics are continuously evolving and would benefit from active reflection on issues associated with practice. He continues, "Because we constitute the community, our collective reflection not only will make ethical concerns more prominent but also move them along to make them more appropriate" (¶ 14). This leads me to my last point regarding learning about being a qualitative researcher. I think it would be helpful for you to begin to assess how you feel and what you know about doing qualitative research. This self-reflection is a very important component of qualitative research.

McGinn and Bosacki (2004) suggest that instructors can model their own thought processes and emotional reasoning strategies as they work through research decisions and related ethical dilemmas in their own research. Although the ideas are thoughtful, I question to what extent instructors should be privileged holders of high ethics. We certainly learn from recent experiences with large businesses that the leaders are not necessarily in possession of high morals or ethics.

Breuer and Roth (2003) remind us that it is necessary for researchers to abandon the conventional textbook approach and to take a decentered and reflexive position. Researchers observe not only participants but also themselves, which allows them to document how their presence affects the research process and its products. As individuals we are the determiner and judge of our own behaviors. All the guidelines and regulations are only that; ultimately, how we behave is our own personal responsibility.

SUMMARY

This chapter introduced you to some general ideas about doing qualitative research. It asked you to take a look at your own skills and temperament for doing qualitative research. I suggested that you need to think about your own desire and ability to approach research of this kind. I then made some specific suggestions that you can follow in order to jump into being a qualitative researcher. I concluded with some ethical issues. I want you to recognize that you haven't really learned any specific skills yet. Now it is time to look in greater detail at qualitative research and how it is characterized and defined in the field.

GROUP ACTIVITY

Purpose: To explore alternative ways of gathering information.

Activity: Identify a television program that focuses on family or friend interaction. Many programs are available to watch in reruns or on an unscheduled basis. Decide on a particular aspect of the interaction that you might find interesting. It might be looking at gender differences, interplay of parents and children, or couple interaction. I like to use the topic of power. Watch the program together in class. Following the viewing each person should prepare a written statement of examples of how power is displayed between individuals.

Evaluation: Look at the variety of responses people offer. This activity should help people to see how one's perspective influences interpretations.

INDIVIDUAL ACTIVITY

Purpose: To continue practicing alternative ways to gather data.

Activity: In your own home, identify pictures, photos, or other symbols that describe who you are. Select several to bring to class. In class, explain what you chose and why you chose it. Then participate in a discussion of how others learn about you.

Evaluation: This will help you move away from the literal into the meaning behind what you see.

Of course, you need to keep up your journal writing. Your question this week might be "What else can I do to get myself ready? How do I feel about where I am so far?"

NOTE

1. Bronislaw Malinowski, a prominent anthropologist who lived from 1884 to 1942, founded the field of social anthropology. During World War I, he studied Trobriand Islanders of New Guinea. Subsequently he came to the U.S. where he held prominent positions at Cornell and Harvard.

CHAPTER 5

Exploring Traditions and Approaches

Those who cannot remember the past are condemned to repeat it.

—George Santayana

The next step was how to approach the qualitative research. The words learning the experiences that are "lived" and "felt" led me to the phenomenological aspect of research. This directed me to intense reading and inner searching as to how to conduct phenomenological research. I needed to divorce myself of my personal thoughts about retirement, my viewpoints, and biases. I had to listen to the story that the professional women in my research would tell me. I could not embellish or put words in their mouths. This would be the study of their stories and experiences.

—Mary Repass

In previous chapters I mentioned various traditions and provided a brief overview of their elements. This chapter includes detailed information about the major traditions, approaches, and methods that are associated with qualitative research. Is ethnography qualitative research? Yes, say some. Is it the only way to do qualitative research? A few might say so. And you could substitute other terms for ethnography: grounded theory, anthropology, case study, phenomenology, feminist, narrative analysis, poststructural. Can you do an ethnographic case study? What about a phenomenological feminist study? I could go on and on.

I guess you see that there is no one tradition or approach, or combination of approaches, that is generally accepted as characterizing the field. In fact, some would say you don't have to adopt any of the traditions.

What is clear is that there is not general agreement about what qualitative research is, even though many seem to write and talk about it. The variety of approaches to qualitative research presents a challenge both to the novice and experienced researcher.

The material that follows is included here to help you set this field in a larger context of research methods and philosophy. In my experience, however, putting a particular piece of research into a neat little box is not always so easy. Often you will encounter a joining or overlap of two or more traditions. So you might come across an ethnographic case study, or you might find a phenomenological ethnography. You will find some overlapping and use of terms in more than one way.

TRADITIONS, APPROACHES, AND BEYOND: THE DETAILS

Before I proceed to details about any of the traditions, I think it is important to place the various traditions in a larger context. Recall that earlier I described qualitative research as a kind of umbrella term. You will remember that some people who choose to conduct qualitative research do not select any one particular tradition but follow general principles that include hearing the voices of those studied, using the researcher as a conduit for the information, studying things in a naturalistic manner, looking at the whole of things, and avoiding testing hypotheses. Results rely heavily on words, and often quotations from those studied are included in the document. In fact, these principles are common to all kinds of qualitative research, whether a general approach or one that follows any of a number of traditions.

Others who conduct qualitative research choose a tradition that serves as a guide and defines how the study is to be conducted. The most common are ethnography, grounded theory, phenomenology, and case study (Creswell, 1997). In the sections that follow, I discuss these traditions in depth as well as provide examples. Although strictly speaking not a research tradition, I also include a brief section on feminist research. Other possible traditions that influence the field include oral history, biography, auto-ethnography, video-ethnography, narrative analysis, content analysis, visual analysis, postmodernism, and poststructuralism.

Anthropology and Ethnography: Studying Cultures

I divide this section into four parts. First, I begin with an introduction. Second, I talk about the history of ethnography and how it came to be adopted into the general field of education and qualitative research. Next, I include some examples from the field. I end with a summary of the main ideas about ethnography.

Introduction

It was not until the second half of the 19th century that the field of anthropology developed. Originally from England and Europe, the field was brought to the United States at the beginning of the 20th century. Course work was offered at Columbia University in the 1920s under the leadership of Franz Boas. Ruth Benedict (Boas's student), and Margaret Mead (Benedict's student), became leading figures.

The field remained fairly traditional and attempts were made to use scientific methodology. However, by the 1960s and the emergence of the civil rights movement, there was an acknowledgment of a power struggle between those who did the studying and those being studied. Shifts in the discipline led to the view that perhaps it was not possible to study culture using the scientific method. By the 1970s, postmodernism and feminist anthropology became popular and the rigid scientific approach was no longer the only way to conduct ethnographic studies. In the 1980s, ethnography made considerable inroads into the study of educational issues (Fetterman, 1998). Postmodern and critical ethnography, in which the observer was no longer privileged but rather became involved with those studied, emerged in the 1990s. Doing ethnography today involves recognition of "contemporary technological, global, and multicultural, racial and linguistic existence" (LeCompte, 2002, p. 283).

Educators adopted some of the basic principles of studying cultures. Instead of traveling to remote locations in the world, they began to study the culture of schools and classrooms. More recently, studies of online cultures have become popular.

When reading about ethnography, you might encounter the term field methods. This is associated with methods of cultural anthropology. Field methods are the procedures used to collect and analyze data.

History of Anthropology and Ethnography

Anthropology and ethnography are two related terms. Anthropology is a general term used to describe the study of cultures. Ethnography refers to a systematic description of a culture that is based on direct observation of a particular group. Such observation usually involves a detailed study of physical characteristics and social customs. The science of anthropology began at the end of the 19th century. E. B. Taylor (1871) from Britain is considered the father of anthropology.[1] He and the American scientist Lewis Henry Morgan (1818–1881) were considered the founders of the study of cultural or social dimensions. Boas[2] and Malinowski, together with Benedict[3] and Mead, came to be identified with anthropology and ethnography. Boas contributed the idea of cultural relativism to the literature. Boas's approach was to utilize documents and informants, while Malinowski believed that the researcher must immerse himself for long periods in the field. He urged ethnographers to live with their informants, learn the language, and participate as allowed. From him we get the idea of interpretive anthropology since it was the viewpoint of the "native" that was important. As part of the immersion process, Malinowski traveled to New Guinea during World War I. Due to the war and limited funds, he stayed there until the war ended in 1918. So this is the origin of fieldwork. Mead and Benedict immersed themselves in primitive cultures as well.

From the latter part of the 19th century until the 1950s, anthropology was aligned with a strong scientific foundation. As the field developed, one concern was the power relationship between anthropologists and the subjects they studied. As colonialism ended, new ways of conceptualizing anthropology emerged. In the 1960s, the climate shifted toward acknowledging that the scientific study of culture might not be possible. There was recognition that change and conflict might be as prevalent as stability and harmony. By the 1970s, postmodernism and feminist anthropology became dominant.[4]

Although anthropology as a discipline has been around for well over one hundred years, the field of educational research did not adopt ethnography to any great extent until the 1980s. Yon (2003) suggests that

> the growth of educational ethnography as a subfield within anthropology reflects a growing focus on prescriptive, applied, and reformist research within urban contexts. It maps the transition from modernist formulations of the field in its formative days, when ethnographies laid claim to being sealed and scientific texts, to the more recent formulations shaped by postmodern and post structural ideas that undermine earlier meanings of culture and call attention to the explanatory limits of ethnography. (Abstract)

He argues that these developments are not distinct phases but overlapping moments in the evolution of the field of study. In particular, he notes a move toward reflexivity in educational ethnography. Actually, this move toward reflexivity permeates many traditions in qualitative research.[5]

Offshoots of ethnography/anthropology include autoethnography (Bochner & Ellis, 2001; Jewett, 2004) and photo-ethnography (Aldridge, 1995), which is said to be the art and science of representing other cultures through visual means. Ellis and Bochner describe autoethnography as a "systematic sociological introspection and emotional recall" as a way to understand personal experiences (Ellis & Bochner, 2000, p. 737). A related area is visual anthropology, which is premised on the belief that other cultures can be understood through the visual symbols that they use, based on an analysis derived from long-term participant observation of that culture. Photographs and films of other cultures have a seemingly objective explanatory power that masks the subjectivity implicit in their making (Nakamura, 2003).

Examples From the Field

Much of the ethnographic writing comes from sociology departments rather than from departments of education. In a recent edited book on ethnography, for example, a distinction is made between qualitative research and ethnography (Van Den Hoonaard & Schouten, 2004). I find this distinction somewhat confusing in that I see ethnography as a subset of qualitative research rather than parallel to it.

Ethnographers often choose as their area of study subgroups within their own culture that operate outside of the mainstream. So you might encounter studies of gangs, of drug dealers, of psychiatric patients, or of people with disabilities. Adler's 1993 *Wheeling and Dealing* is an account of a drug dealing and smuggling community. Campbell (1984) and Schalet, Hunt, and Joe-Laidler (2003) write about girls in gangs; Armstrong (1998) provides a portrait of football (soccer) hooligans; Estroff (1985) describes psychiatric clients in an American community; and Goode (1994) describes the social construction of children who are born deaf and blind.

Some ethnographies are about schools or school children. Aggleton (1987) informs us about middle class youth in transition from school to work in his book *Rebels Without a Cause;* Hey (1997) describes girls' friendships in *The Company She Keeps;* and Thorne (1993) selects the topic *Gender Play: Girls and Boys in School.* Conteh (2003) writes about a group of bilingual learners in the United Kingdom who have achieved success. While not strictly ethnographies, Kearney (2003) conducts life histories of six academically successful people in their 30s who come from a range of cultural heritages. Their stories unsettle the myths surrounding culture and identity. The voices of the six individuals are powerful, clear, and distinctive, providing fascinating insight into what changes when we cross boundaries and borders. They show how we construct our individual identities and how certain aspects of culture and identity persist across time and space. The book highlights the need to afford a central place to autobiography and life history in children's exploration of their world.

Summary

The study of cultures is an approach to research that educators find attractive. Schools and classes are studied extensively. Subgroups of students, especially those who have a particular behavior or characteristic or trait in common, are appealing to researchers. Becoming immersed in a classroom is highly interesting to many researchers who are too often put off by test scores and surveys. So ethnography has become a popular approach adopted by some qualitative researchers. A word of caution, however. De Welde (2003) reminds us that "it is in fact ethnographers themselves who are battling it out over what ethnography should look like, how it should be done, how it should be presented, and what the goals should be" (p. 233).

Grounded Theory: Placing Theory in Its Context

I divide this section into four parts. I begin with an introduction. Second, I discuss the history and meaning of grounded theory and its adoption into the field of education. Next I give some examples from the field. I conclude this section with a summary of the main ideas about ethnography.

Introduction

Ethnography and phenomenology have a long history as research approaches and philosophies. In contrast, grounded theory is a newcomer to the field. You might be surprised to learn that Glaser and Strauss wrote *The Discovery of Grounded Theory* in 1967. As its name implies, this book dealt with theory, but not in the traditional sense. The authors suggested that theory emanated from the data, rather than the more typical view that data are used to test a particular theory. This way of thinking is called inductive reasoning. I believe that some researchers are attracted to grounded theory because the research being conducted could be taken beyond a particular data set and applied to theoretical issues. Others are attracted because its methodology is closer to the scientific rigor of quantitative approaches than some other qualitative methods.

Glaser and Strauss came to see grounded theory in different ways as their thinking developed. Strauss, writing with Corbin in 1990, took a somewhat different approach and Glaser (1992, 1998; Glaser & Holton, 2004) responded to Strauss's views. I will talk about a few of these differences subsequently; however, I don't think it is critical that you understand the nuances of the differences between these two writers. Rather, I would like to stress what I see is the essence of the approach.

Theoretical sampling and saturation and specific approaches to coding are key elements of grounded theory. Unlike phenomenological or ethnographic methods, grounded theory emphasizes a specific approach to coding the data. Three terms you often will encounter are open coding, axial coding, and selective coding. Davidson (2002) explains coding thusly:

There are three distinct yet overlapping processes of analysis involved in grounded theory from which sampling procedures are typically derived. These are: open coding, axial coding, and selective coding. Open coding is based on the concept of data being cracked open as a means of identifying relevant categories. Axial coding is most often used when categories are in an advanced stage of development; and selective coding is used when the "core category," or central category that correlates all other categories in the theory, is identified and related to other categories. (¶ 4)

I believe that a number of people are attracted to grounded theory because the coding process is systematic and described in detail. McCarthy (1999) suggests that it was the rigor involved in grounded theory that led her to that approach for her dissertation. For those who like structure, this works for them.

History and Meaning of Grounded Theory

In the 1960s, positivism dominated the social sciences. Many researchers were drawn to methods that involved hypothesis testing, statistical manipulations, and computer analyses. I think this is because the scientific method was thought to be the *sine qua non* of methods. Those in the social sciences—who were often seen by other disciplines as "soft" and "lesser" and sometimes saw themselves in that vein—either believed they were practicing "true" science or thought they could convince others that they were. By using statistics and experimental designs, they believed that they were exercising rigor and searching for the truth. Like many of my colleagues, I adopted that view.

And although some were attracted to ethnography or phenomenology, by far they were in the minority. They did not have the scientific rigor that was thought to be part of positivism and postpositivism. Words like "touchy-feely" and "soft" were bandied about.

So who should come on the scene but Anselm Strauss? Strauss was involved in studying death and dying and care of the chronically ill. After earning his degree, he went to San Francisco to head up a new sociology department as part of the school of nursing. He did extensive writing prior to his work on grounded theory. I suspect that he found quantitative methods lacking in terms of understanding the needs of the physically ill.[6]

What emerged was his seminal work (with Barney Glaser) on grounded theory (Glaser & Strauss, 1967). Initially it was directed at sociologists and accepted by many because it offered an element of scientific rigor and intellectual rationale. Haig (1995) concurs with this view and suggests that Glaser and Strauss thought the approach met accepted standards for good science. Haig argues that grounded theory "offers an attractive conception of scientific method." Grounded theory appealed to those in higher education, adult education, and nursing education (Askew, 1983; Babchuck, 1997; Conrad, 1982) for these same reasons.

As I said above, after their initial writing Glaser and Strauss took disparate views of what they meant by the concept. Glaser's view is that grounded theory looks at a particular situation and tries to understand what is going on. As with other qualitative approaches, data are gathered typically through observations and interviews. The researcher jots down the key issues as data collection proceeds. What distinguishes Glaser's view is the constant-comparative method. This data analysis technique involves comparing data from one interview (or observation) with data from another interview or observation. He suggests that theory quickly emerges.

Imagine that you are studying teachers from urban school settings. You are interested in investigating how administrative support enhances teaching. As you collect data from teacher 1 and then teacher 2, you write down the issues they present and compare the two interviews. You would then follow with additional interviews and compare what you learned with what you already have. You would write down—or insert in your database—some simple codes that express what you think each is saying. You would then move from these specific codes into more general categories or themes. From these themes, you begin to develop a working theory to help explain the key concepts of administrative support, teaching, and urban settings. Actually, the coding procedures are very specific.

Now, how does this process lead to theory? I think Dick (2002) says it very nicely.

> As you code, certain theoretical propositions will occur to you. These may be about links between categories, or about a core category: a category which appears central to the study. As the categories and properties emerge, they and their links to the core category provide the theory.

Glaser and Holton (2004) despair that grounded theory has eroded with remodeling used in qualitative data analysis. They remind us that grounded theory actually emerged from doing research on dying patients in the 1960s. As such, they suggest it was discovered and not invented.[7]

Examples From the Field

I have selected a variety of examples of grounded theory so that you can see the range of topics that are covered. McCarthy (2001) studied parents from various socioeconomic backgrounds to gain an understanding of the process they go through to make school choices. She reminds us that coding begins after the first interview is completed. Allen (1998) studied parenting classes and practices in her grounded theory dissertation. Petrie (2003) studied ESL teachers' views on the innovation of visual language using grounded theory. Here is a brief excerpt from her results:

> First, graphics, etc. presents students with a different sense of relevance. Graphics, etc., appears next to the words in e-texts, sometimes misleading students from the main message of the text (the linguistic one). One teacher referred to the presence of graphics, etc. as "cluttered": Most websites are so cluttered. So, unless they are just pure text on the screen, they are so cluttered that you really have to get good at scanning. And I don't know. It's not textual scanning. I guess I don't even know what the term would be, because it's not all text. (pp. 153–154)

Starbuck (2003) relies on data from the Internet in her unusual dissertation about art and collage. Here is an example taken from her work. This dramatic and unusual dissertation offers insight into as yet rarely tapped sources.

> You enter an artist's studio outside of Paris to find an animated group of artists. A heated conversation is in full swing. A dramatic French woman looks around the room and passionately exclaims, "Mail art must move, change like the world. Mail art is just at his [sic] starting, we have to re-invent it." . . . Message boards are an art supply in the studio of the

networking artists. Artists use message boards to achieve a continuation of correspondence art networking goals. However, in many cases, artists feel that the real communication still takes place in the mail.

Brown, Stevens, Troino, and Schneider (2002) suggest that by using grounded theory they can increase understanding of the college student experience. They also provide a detailed explanation of the coding process as well as how to enhance credibility.

Summary

The newest of the qualitative approaches, grounded theory has become a popular paradigm for many who value structure and order. I believe it is closest to using a quantitative approach of all the traditions. Some students are attracted to it because they can offer a logical and coherent, if not somewhat cumbersome, method of data analysis. On the other hand, those very characteristics seem to limit its usefulness, in my view. I suspect that much of what is found in the field does not really contribute to theory.

Our Lived Experiences: Phenomenological Inquiry as a Philosophy and Method of Study

In this section, I talk about several ideas. First, I provide an introduction. Next, I discuss a brief history of phenomenology. I then address phenomenology in today's world and provide examples. Third, I distinguish between phenomenology as a philosophy and as a method. I conclude with a summary of the main ideas about phenomenology.

Introduction

I want to begin with a little story. I have been a teacher for many years. I have thought a lot about what it is to teach, what I was trying to get across, how to assist my students to find their own way of raising questions and finding answers. I have also thought about how I should do this in the context of a university. Should I provide detailed lectures? Should I have students engage in small group discussions? Should I ask students to read everything about a topic and then write a paper? Should I ask students to find an expert and pick his or her brain? Should I have students do a project reflective of what they understand? You can see that these questions that I raise are not about content *per se;* rather, they center on the pedagogy of teaching.

Now, not all of you have been teachers. But what you each have in common is that you have been students—prior to formal schooling (from the time you played school with your siblings and friends or from the time your parent tried to teach you the names of colors and parts of your body), during your elementary and high school years (in classes with others of your own age or peer group), during your college years (in classes or increasingly mediated with the Internet and computers), and even at this moment. As you continue to read, I would like you to try to recall what it was like to be a student.

So, back to my story. For the last few years I have been engaged in teaching with the new technology facilitated by the Internet. But how to do it? Were the questions I raised earlier the appropriate ones? Were there other things I needed to consider? I lived through this transition for several years, and I wanted to know more about it. Was I alone in my questioning? What did others think? How could I find out?

I had the perfect topic for a phenomenological study. At least, so I thought. I was very interested in the increased activity of online teaching. I recruited one of my doctoral students to conduct the study. She liked the idea. It seemed so simple and straightforward to her. Her committee accepted her idea. We were ready to go.

And now my challenge came. This student had been in one of my qualitative research classes several years prior to her conducting the study. Based on that information, I assumed she had quite a good grasp of the major traditions in qualitative research as well as some knowledge of phenomenology. I suggested to her that the study of online teaching might appropriately be done using a phenomenological approach. I offered the idea to her and she seemed to be taken with it. I thought she understood phenomenology. After all, she just had to go to a few references (e.g., Husserl or Heidegger or van Manen), figure out how to bracket her thoughts, decide what epoche means, and be on her way.

As I worked with her, I came to see that what seemed so simple—studying the lived experiences of individuals who had experienced the same phenomenon—was indeed quite complex. I found myself extremely challenged in trying to make sense of all these complex ideas and bringing them to a practical understanding. At the same time, I did not want to "dumb down" or "make trivial" the philosophical or existentialist underpinnings. In this next section, I will try to take you on the same journey that I took my student.

A History of Phenomenology

It is generally acknowledged that Edmund Husserl[8] is the father of phenomenology, although Priest (2002) suggests that it was Kant who first used the Greek term in 1764. I found it instructive to read from Husserl's inaugural lecture at Freiburg im Breslau in 1917. "A new fundamental science, pure phenomenology, has developed within philosophy. . . . It is inferior in methodological rigor to none of the modern sciences" (¶ 4). Husserl continues somewhat later in his talk to acknowledge that empirical science is not "the only kind of science possible" (¶ 39). I think this issue is important because it highlights the idea that an approach other than a pure science is acceptable as an alternative to traditional paradigms.

Husserl's writings on phenomenology served as the impetus as this philosophical movement spread throughout Europe. Heidegger (a German, who ironically later joined the Nazi party) and Merleau-Ponty (from France) were leading proponents of the philosophical concept of phenomenology. Sartre's writings on existentialism were closely related.[9] Influences from European writers and philosophers were dominant for phenomenology, unlike other qualitative research traditions.

Phenomenology in Today's World

You might be wondering why you are reading about a movement that had its origins in Germany around World War I and was not practiced much in the United States. What does that have to do with studying one's lived experiences? What kinds of links can be made to the use of phenomenology in the current climate?

Phenomenology is not an easy concept to understand. It is said to be both a philosophy and a method. My intention here is to first tell you about key elements of phenomenology and then to introduce you to some of the newer thinking. Researchers, philosophers, and writers do not agree on what phenomenology is. So how do you, as a new learner, come to understand this field?

Phenomenology as a method looks at the lived experiences of those who have experienced a certain phenomenon. Suppose you have selected some experience that you want to study and you have located individuals who have lived that experience. Let's follow my earlier example with my student. She decides that she is interested in studying the experience or phenomenon of teaching online. She identifies individuals who she knows have taught online. She places her own thoughts on the topic in brackets so as not to influence or color her thinking as she continues her investigation. She interviews a number of people who taught online. After transcribing her data, she moves on with the process of reducing the data so that ultimately she is able to discern the essence of the phenomenon. Think of it as moving from very specific and detailed statements about the phenomenon, or even examples of the phenomenon, ultimately to the essence of the phenomenon. One way to think of it is that we begin to stretch out our understanding of something into an interpretation of it, and the researcher is the interpreter of the data.

The process is completed when you reduce the data you have to its essence. I often see people begin with 25 themes. By the time the reductive process is complete, there might only be three essential components to describe the lived experience. In a later section, I will talk more about phenomenology and its methodological process.

I want you to appreciate that phenomenology as an approach has taken hold worldwide. From its roots in Europe it has now spread broadly into the United States, Canada, and parts of Asia. I want to talk about three trends: first, the use of a phenomenological method in a variety of disciplines including, but not limited to, education, nursing, adult learning, allied health fields, art education, and special education; second, the broadening scope of interest in phenomenology worldwide facilitated, in part, by the Internet and the opening up of travel throughout the world; and third, the expansion, modification, and in some instances reinterpretations of the application of a phenomenological method.[10]

A Variety of Disciplines. The use of a phenomenological approach has taken hold, especially in education and nursing. Beginning in the 1990s, phenomenology in education became fairly widespread (Barnacle, 2001; Vandenberg, 1996; van Manen, 1997).

Examples of phenomenological studies in education and related fields include Nielsen (2000), who writes about using a hermeneutical phenomenological approach in art education; Stanage (1995), who writes on adult education and phenomenological research; McPhail (1995), who writes about phenomenology in remedial and special education and why it is an appropriate approach; and Janetius (2003), who writes on how he used a phenomenological approach to studying indigenous people of the Philippines to understand their world. Robinson (2000) reports on her study of students who are involved in online learning and presents an alternative to traditional linear writing by using what she called a "Web-based spatial dissertation."

With the development of postpositivist approaches, phenomenology has been adopted by different disciplines as an appropriate way to explore research questions, which leads to a different way of knowledge being constructed. Rose (1993), in a book called *Feminism and Geography,* describes how she sees the discipline of geography being influenced by feminist studies and phenomenology. In particular, phenomenology has become a way to research the gaps in the discipline, those areas which previously were not considered important to research because they had little to do with the public and patriarchal world of geography. Nurse education, in recent moves to define itself as a separate and different discipline from the rational, scientific medical model, has adopted phenomenology as a way to research previously uninvestigated areas in order to inform the theoretical base of nursing practice on which nurse education is based.

Growth Worldwide. There has been an enormous resurgence of the study and use of phenomenology worldwide. Embree (2003) speaks about phenomenology in the 21st century. He suggests this is due to the collapse of the Soviet Union, increased international travel, and the Internet. It is interesting to see how this resurgence has developed. A 2002 conference in Prague on the topic of issues confronting the post-European world led to the founding of The Organization of Phenomenological Organizations. In an essay published to celebrate that event, Embree (2003) informs us that there are at least 20 countries with traditions of phenomenology and 22 disciplines outside of philosophy that have conducted phenomenological investigations.

He offers a number of reasons to explain the worldwide growth. Colleagues with no personal affiliation with World War II are coming into leadership positions, and so phenomenology has been restored following fascism in Germany. You will recall that I said earlier that Heidegger was a strong proponent of phenomenology, but his fascist persuasion put him in disfavor with many academics. Embree also suggests that while no tradition in philosophy prior to the 1970s has generally been receptive to women, there are now many women new to the field. Although the center of the phenomenological movement is still in the West (remember that its center had been in Europe for long periods of time), greater international travel and the Internet and the use of English has led to a greater interconnectedness among countries.

There are many recent writings in phenomenology that represent a much larger viewpoint, especially from the Far East. From Malaysia, Scown (2003) studied the process of phenomenological inquiry on the lived experience of being an academic. You can read about reflective analysis in the phenomenology of photography by a Chinese colleague in Korea (in Embree, 2003). In the *Finnish Journal of Education,* Perttula (2000) writes about transforming experience into knowledge using a phenomenological approach. There is also the *Journal of Phenomenology and Education,* published in Italian.[11]

Reinterpretations of Phenomenology. You have read above about the burgeoning of the phenomenological movement worldwide. I imagine that you will not be surprised, then, to discover that there is no one thing that is considered phenomenology. Although most acknowledge Husserl and his influence, what you will find in the research and writing today is that many things, many ways, and many approaches take on the phenomenology label. These approaches range from very strict, conservative, traditional approaches to very broad interpretations and applications to the study of lived experiences, the thread that holds the various applications together. It is unclear how phenomenology evolved from a rigorous science to anti-foundationalist position. Ihde (1995) writes about post-phenomenology in his essays in the postmodern context.

Phenomenology as a Philosophy and as a Method

Here are some ideas about phenomenology as a philosophy. Dermot (2000) suggests that the phenomenological movement reflects European philosophy in the 20th century. Husserl's idea was that phenomenology was a new way of thinking about philosophy; rather than being esoteric and metaphysical, this would enable the philosopher (and phenomenologist) to come into contact with matters, the actual lived experiences. It is quite beyond the scope of this book to get into the philosophical voyage that Dermot takes.[12] The philosophical underpinnings are very complex and are not necessary for you to understand as you begin to learn the elements of phenomenology as a method.

As I said earlier, we can think of phenomenology as a philosophy and we can think of it as a method. I don't think you can begin to understand one without the other, which is why I have tried to give you some key elements of the philosophy. Now we turn to phenomenology as a method. If the philosophy is about the lived experiences, and the essence of these lived experiences, how is it that we should go about "doing" a phenomenology? I have gone into some depth about the method of phenomenology because at times it is somewhat confusing. You know that it is a study of lived experience. But it is more than that because ultimately the researcher's role is to extract the essence of that experience by means of a reductionist process.

1. What do we mean by the lived experience? The lived experience is a term from Husserl.[13] Lived experiences or life experiences are those in which we are all involved. Often a researcher selects a particular experience or event on which to focus. In the adult education field, one might study the lived experience of professional women as they plan for retirement (Repass, 2002). The individuals who are studied have been involved in the experience. In education, one might study the experiences of families living with a child with autism (Glass, 2001) or one might study educational leadership (Van der Mescht, 2004).

Boeree (1998) offers some insight into understanding the lived experience. Think of it this way: Every experience has an objective and a subjective component; thus, you must understand all aspects of a phenomenon.[14]

2. What is meant by the essence of the experience? And on a deeper, more philosophical level, we can ask how does the nature of the experience indicate the nature of the human being's existence? I agree with Bottorff (2003) that when we consider the essence of the experience we are moving to a deeper level of understanding. It is this last part that gets a little difficult to understand and that is related more to the philosophical underpinnings. You can see that a description of an experience, while interesting, is not the full intent of the research.[15] I believe, however, that you will encounter a number of studies that are phenomenological in intent but do not go to a deeper level of understanding. Perhaps that is because some are reluctant to bring too much interpretation to the data they have. Or perhaps it is because we do not trust ourselves to move to an understanding of the inner self.

3. What is the reductionist process? How are bracketing and epoche related to it? Phenomenological reduction is the process that is used to facilitate seeking the essence of a phenomenon. It is here that bracketing, epoche, or eidetic reduction (terms often used interchangeably) describe the change in attitude that is necessary for the philosophical reduction. Bracketing involves placing one's own thoughts about the topic in suspense or out of question. Epoche involves the deliberate suspension of judgment. Giorgi (1989) suggests that the researcher should search for all possible meanings of the phenomenon.

Husserl suggested that a researcher could set aside his or her own views about the phenomenon by using a process of bracketing. As a mathematician, he was interested in objective and logical approaches, so he thought that this act of setting aside would accomplish objectivity. It has been almost 100 years since Husserl gave us this idea of bracketing. I have found in my own experience that it is too simplistic to think that a researcher can set aside his or her own ideas about a phenomenon. I like to think of making explicit one's ideas on the topic. This is accomplished by writing down one's ideas, preferably prior to immersion in the literature on the topic. The mere task of writing puts the researcher in a mind-set that forces him or her to make explicit his or her ideas.

A term related to phenomenology is hermeneutics.[16] Hermeneutics is generally thought to be the science of interpretation and explanation. In the hermeneutical process there is an inter-action or link between the researcher and what is being interpreted. I don't want to get involved in too much detail, but you should know that hermeneutics was originally associated with interpretation of textual material, especially the Bible. Byrne (1998) suggests that herme-neutics and phenomenology are often used interchangeably. She reminds us, however, that phenomenologists focus on lived experiences and hermeneutics refers to interpretation of lan-guage. Two assumptions of hermeneutics are that humans use language to experience the world and that we get understanding and knowledge through our language. Its name derives from the Greek god Hermes, a son of Zeus, and the fastest of the gods.

Summary

You have read about the philosophy and methodology of phenomenology. With an almost 100-year history, this tradition has become widely used in education. Starting in Europe and transported to the United States, it has now become a dominant tradition worldwide. I think you will find yourself very attracted to the elements of the tradition. However, as with many of the other approaches to research, details of how to do a phenomenology are not readily available. Further, current writers do not agree on what phenomenology is and even how to do it. You would be well advised to read some completed phenomenological studies to decide whether this tradition is right for you.

Case Study: A Look at the Particular

This material on case study is divided into five sections. I begin with an introduction. Second, I talk about the history and meaning of case study and its use in education. Following, I include a section on selecting a case. Next, I provide some examples from the field. I conclude with a summary of the key ideas about case study.

Introduction

Case study is often recognized as one approach to qualitative research. Creswell (1997) includes case study as one of the five traditions of qualitative research. Case study seems to be primarily a method without any philosophical underpinnings. In most instances, when a researcher says he is doing case study research he is most likely identifying a single entity to study. The entity could be as small as one individual or as large as an entire school. It is the researcher's task to identify the case and set the boundaries of what is being studied. It is quite common to encounter case study methods combined with some of the other paradigms I described earlier, so you might come across a phenomenological case study or an ethnographic case study.

History and Meaning

No doubt you have heard of case studies in many disciplines. Business schools use case studies from real life. Psychologists use case studies of individual patients or families. Product designers use case studies to examine new products. Case studies were used fairly often in the early days of sociology when an interest developed in studying various groups or programs. But case study research methods were not accepted by many who saw them as less rigorous and not scientific. According to Tellis (1997), the history of case study research is marked by periods of activity and inertia. He attributes early use in the United States to the Chicago School of Sociology. The study of immigrants presented ready-made cases for researchers. However, in a move to make research more scientific, sociologists at Columbia University began to discredit case study methodology. For many years, the Columbia view became predominant. However, a resurgence of interest in case study research emerged as qualitative methods began to be accepted in education.[17]

Case study as an approach to qualitative research involves the specific and detailed study of a case or cases. I recall a student of mine who studied the case of the development of a nursery school in an urban neighborhood of Washington, D.C. For years the community was interested in building a school for the children, many of whom were non-English speaking. But most who lived in the immediate area did not have the experience or means to tackle the assignment. It took an outside group of concerned citizens, working together with the clergy and members of the local community, to secure a location, build a staff, and develop a program. Her research documented this process and the program. Case studies are often of this type.

What is a case? What do we mean when we talk about a case? Here are some ideas that might help you sort through this murky area. A case can be limited to a characteristic, trait, or behavior. You might study a child (or children) with a particular type of learning disability (characteristic). Or you might study an administrator who exhibits particular behaviors such as cooperative or collegial interactions (behaviors). Or you might study a teacher who is outgoing (trait). The key to this kind of case study is that you identify the characteristic, trait, or behavior in advance and then identify individuals who have or are thought to have the characteristic. This is a somewhat narrow view of case study and might result in missing the very information that would be enriching or informative.

More often a case is limited to a particular entity, for example, Mr. Brown's special education classroom, Ms. Hernandez's honors English class, or an athletic team with the highest win/loss record. By extension, more than one case could be studied.

A case can be limited to one type of situation. These situations are often special or even unique. For example, you might come across a case study of the experience of 9/11. Or you might come across a case study of those who lived in Prince Edward, Virginia, when the public schools disbanded rather than integrate. Or you might read about a case study of individuals who attend year-round schools.

So we might have cases that are designed to study behaviors, traits, or characteristics. We might have cases that are designed to study a particular program or classroom. Or we might have cases that are designed to study a particular situation. You can see in all of these examples that what is studied is critical to the design, analysis, and interpretation.

Selecting a Case

How do you select a case? I propose you consider one of three types of cases: the typical, the exemplary or model, or the unusual or unique. Other kinds of cases you might select could be the constructed or the borderline. One of the most common methods is to select a case that is considered typical of others in the same set. For example, if you want to study fourth-grade classrooms, you can ask someone knowledgeable in a school system to nominate a typical class or classes. What is typical? It is up to you, the researcher, to think about the criteria you want to use. You might give some guidelines; for example, you could decide that the class test scores should be average for that school system or the racial composition should be similar to that of the school system, and so on. It is usually a good idea to identify more than one case because it is possible that a particular case does not want to participate, or you find you need additional information. Of course, you might have decided to do a multiple case study so you would need to have several cases. What I want to stress here is that the case you study is considered typical. Since you are not trying to generalize to other fourth grades, it is not important that you cover the range of possible fourth grades. Patton (2002) and Donmoyer (1990) remind us that we are more interested in the richness of the information we generate from the case rather than the ability to generalize.

Another approach is to select a case that might be considered exemplar. For example, you might want to study the best or the most outstanding fourth-grade classroom in a specific area or system. Again, you would have to rely on nominations from knowledgeable individuals to get the appropriate case. For an unusual exemplar case study, you can read an account of football in Bath, England, in the late Victorian era that was designed to illustrate cultural imperialism (Henson, 2001). A third type of case you might select is one that is considered unusual, unique, or special in some way. While this sounds somewhat similar to an exemplar, it does not have to be. For example, you might ask for nominations of a sixth-grade class that is doing something unusual or creative or groundbreaking.

Often students think they have to identify a case that is representative of all cases of a particular type. This kind of thinking occurs because the novice researcher is thinking about making generalizations to other cases. In qualitative research, this is definitely not so because you do not have sufficient breadth to make generalizations. So, it is not important to get a case that represents all other cases. Your goal is to get detailed and rich descriptions of the case you select.

We can look at some examples from education as well. If you wanted to study reading programs serving urban youth, you might come up with the following:

- Typical case: A program that exists in a school division with average test scores.
- Exemplary or model case: A program nominated by a school division with high test scores.
- Unusual or unique case: A program identified by a school division using special materials.

Of course, you could select criteria other than test scores. There are several important ideas to remember. Your case does not have to be one type or another, nor must you be inclusive in terms of having all types of cases.

Still another take on selecting cases is one offered by Jensen and Rodgers (2001). They mention snapshot case studies, longitudinal case studies, pre-post case studies, patchwork case studies, and comparative case studies.

While most suggest selecting cases using the methods I describe above, Garson (n.d.) takes the position that the selection of a case should be theory driven. This is in keeping with his scientific orientation. His views represent a more scientific, traditionalist view of research. I think you would find his views in the minority, however.[18]

Examples From the Field

There are many different kinds of case studies. Typically researchers study a program or project on which they have been working. I find it interesting that case studies of online programs or multimedia are readily available. Kearsley (2002) is a typical example of a case study. In this example, 22 students who had completed an online masters program in engineering were studied. However, the article provides little information on the methodology of case study. Piper (n.d.) conducts a case study of her own interactive and multimedia dissertation.

You can read very comprehensive case studies such as a case study of the educational systems in Germany, Japan, and the United States funded and published by the United States Department of Education (Stevenson & Nerison-Low, 1998). This broad ranging study is described in the Executive Summary.

> The Case Study Project is a component of the Third International Mathematics and Science Study. It was designed to provide in-depth information on education in three nations: Germany, Japan, and the United States. The four research topics which were the focus of the case studies in each of these countries were selected by the U.S. Department of Education in an effort to collect qualitative data which would complement and amplify the quantitative information obtained through the main Third International Mathematics and Science Study. The topics investigated in the Case Study Project were: education standards, dealing with differences in ability, the place of school in adolescents' lives, and the training and working conditions of teachers. (Executive Summary, ¶ 1)

Together with Izumi Taylor, I conducted a case study of the Kawasaki Kindergarten (Lichtman & Taylor, 1993). Izumi Taylor, originally from Japan, had studied the school on several occasions and had close contact with the principal. I traveled to the site and spent several days observing classes, interviewing the principal and teachers, and photographing various situations. We addressed typical case study issues including identifying a single unit, developing boundaries, the larger context of the case, the in-depth and longitudinal nature of the case, and finally the process we followed. We selected a case study approach because we were interested in the particularistic and descriptive nature of the case.

I use this example to illustrate the power of working together and working apart. In our presentation, we emphasized the use of multiple perspectives. Our own backgrounds—one native Japanese and one native American—enabled us to see things through different lenses. Our paper interweaves our different perspectives to describe the school. We began with no particular ideas in mind. Our major findings identified the importance of rituals, especially at mealtimes. We also noted group effort and cooperation as important components of this modern Japanese preschool.

Summary

The use of case studies has had a resurgence of interest along with other approaches to qualitative research. The process is similar to many other approaches. I think you will find it helpful to remember that information from case studies provides rich and detailed insight into the case or cases being studied. As with other approaches to qualitative research, generalization is not expected or viable. You will probably locate case studies that also are referred to as ethnographic, grounded theory, or phenomenology.

Feminist Research Methods and Feminist Theory

Although not always seen as a research method, feminist research is included so that you can see approaches that take a more active stance. This material on feminist research methods is divided into four sections. I begin with an introduction. Second, I talk about the history and meaning of feminist research and its use in education. Next, I provide some examples from the field. I conclude with a summary of the key ideas about feminist research.

Introduction

Feminist research emerged as a reaction to several methods and approaches described earlier. As the field of research began to be open to female scholars, there were increased questions about the appropriateness and adequacy of prevailing approaches. In particular, questions of power disparities were on the minds of many women. This field actually has many principles in common with critical theory, queer theory, and postmodernism. I see it as anti-foundationalist. But like many of the other traditions I have discussed, there is not general agreement on what is meant by feminist research. And more recent writing introduces post-feminist concepts.

History and Meaning

Harding (1998) is one of the key figures in this movement. She combines elements of feminist, postmodern, and postcolonial critiques of modern science. Brayton (1997) suggests that what makes feminist research uniquely feminine are "the motives, concerns and knowledge" brought to the research process (¶ 1). Here are the principal concepts Brayton includes. She suggests it differs from traditional research for three reasons: it removes the imbalance of power (Fine, 1992), it is politically motivated and concerned with social inequality, and it addresses experiences of women. Maguire (1987) defined feminism as "(a) a belief that women universally face some form of oppression or exploitation; (b) a commitment to uncover and understand what causes and sustains oppression, in all its forms; and (c) a commitment to work individually and collectively in everyday life to end all forms of oppression" (p. 79).

Fine (1992) identifies other aspects of feminist research as well. I see many of these as being common to all qualitative research. I wonder if these principles were identified first by qualitative researchers and then feminist researchers, or if the reverse is true. In any event, Fine identifies the unequal power issue and the need to eliminate this. She talks about making research participants true participants by calling them co-researchers. Others speak to eliminating the word "subject" as a masculine term. Related to making participants share in the research is the view that they are experts about their own experiences. Fine also speaks about the researcher taking an active role, not as a detached and objective observer. Related, then, is the need to address the actual and apparent inequalities between those being studied and those who are doing the study. Research as consciousness raising and transformation is another element. I recall hearing a researcher at a conference speak about sharing the proceeds of her book with the participants. Social change is also important to feminist research. Rosenberg (1999) describes how a feminist research circle promotes changing power relationships and contributes to social change.

Scheurich (1997) says there are four parts to feminist research. Feminist research aims to create social change; it strives to represent human diversity; it is a perspective, not a research method; and it frequently includes the researcher as a person.

Examples From the Field

Here are some recent studies you might find interesting. Clinchy (n.d.) writes about women's reflections on their undergraduate experience. Ellingson's (2001) dissertation is a feminist ethnography in collaboration with a geriatric oncology team. LePage-Lees (1997) studies academically successful women from disadvantaged backgrounds. Aparicio (1999) presents a video project about women of color. Deutsch (2004) reflects on the process of becoming a feminist researcher and writer. These examples highlight how feminist research topics address social change and power relationships.

Summary

Feminist research methods and theories acknowledge disparities in power between those who are studied and those who study. They are also interested in issues about women and women's ways of knowing. Like some of the other new approaches, they are critical of the presumed objectivity and remoteness that characterizes traditional methodologies. They align themselves closely with critical theory and postmodernism. New on the horizon are some post-feminist approaches, which suggest that there be a reexamination of the premises of feminist theory.

Generic Approach to Doing Qualitative Research

You have read in depth about a number of approaches or traditions in qualitative research. Many have been used in education and serve as a guiding force for those beginning a research project. Sometimes a researcher selects a single approach; often a researcher combines several qualitative approaches. Sometimes a researcher combines both qualitative and quantitative approaches. I want you to understand, however, that you can do qualitative research and not choose one of the traditions you have just read about. If you decide to take that pathway, you will be following in the footsteps of many others.

While many researchers choose a particular orientation or combination of approaches, others do not make such a choice; rather, they take a generic approach. Chenail discusses this idea in a recent interview (Lichtman, 2004). While many may have operated this way, it is fairly recently that it has been articulated as a generic approach (Caelli, Ray, & Mill, 2003). Further, they see this as a trend that is growing. If the researcher takes a generic viewpoint, it is not necessary to adopt any one approach to doing qualitative research. While Caelli and her colleagues suggest that this presents a challenge in terms of evaluating a study, they acknowledge that people are conducting studies that do not adopt any single type of methodology. The issue of evaluating the worth of a study is certainly not limited to evaluating generic studies. I have devoted an entire chapter to this topic. They express the view that this offers a challenge because there is little in the literature about how to do a "generic" study well. They offer four areas that could be considered in evaluation of generic qualitative research: noting the researchers' position, distinguishing method and methodology, making explicit the approach to rigor, and identifying the researchers' analytic lens.

Merriam (2002) discusses a basic interpretive qualitative study. Such a design is used when the goal of the researcher is to understand how participants make meaning of a situation or a phenomenon. The researcher serves as the filter for the meaning, using inductive strategies with a descriptive outcome (Imel, Kerka, & Wonacott, 2002; Merriam, 2002). Of course, these ideas are prevalent in almost all approaches to qualitative research.

SUMMARY

By now you might find that your head is swimming with many new ideas and thoughts. Some are quite technical. Some are very detailed. Some seem abstract. Some seem to bear little relevance to what you are thinking. I included them in order for you to understand that this field of qualitative research is dynamic, ever-changing, and yet has a long history and tradition that informs it.

Your next step is to read about the role and function of a literature review in the conduct of qualitative research.

GROUP ACTIVITY

Purpose: To organize your ideas. You need to extract the essential elements about the various paradigms.

Activity: Develop a series of questions and answers that would be suitable for a Jeopardy game. Work with three or four other students. Put your questions on cards with answers on the reverse side. Play the game with volunteers from the class.

Evaluation: Determine to what extent your questions get at key elements and how your responses reflect your new knowledge.

INDIVIDUAL ACTIVITY

Purpose: To design your own research study.

Activity: Identify at least three research questions that lend themselves to qualitative research. Write a one-page outline of how you would answer the questions. See if you can determine which paradigm would be most appropriate for each of the questions.

Evaluation: Assess the extent to which you believe you have captured the essence of the paradigm.

NOTES

1. In 1871, Taylor defined culture as "that complex whole which includes knowledge, belief, art, morals, law, customs, and many other capabilities and habits acquired by members of society" (p. 1).

2. Boas worked at Columbia University, which was thought to be the seat of the anthropological movement.

3. After earning her Ph.D. under Boas, Benedict went to Barnard. Mead became one of her students. Benedict's *Patterns of Culture* and Mead's writing were significant contributions.

4. See Barrett (1996).

5. In recent years, the swing has been back to broader theoretical models. Most influential over the past 20 years has been Lévi-Strauss's (1968) structural model, which seeks to look below the surface of culture to identify the mental structures of human thought that underlie all cultures.

6. Strauss died in 1996. Strauss was trained as a sociologist at the University of Chicago but established his career as the founder of the Department of Social and Behavioral Sciences in the School of Nursing at San Francisco State. Glaser was part of his research team. Strauss's initial writings were in medical sociology where he studied chronically ill and dying patients. Glaser continues to work in the field. His book discusses the remodeling of grounded theory methodology by ascendant methods of qualitative analysis. There is also an international journal called the *Grounded Theory Review,* edited by Glaser.

7. You can read Glaser's current thinking on the topic in his comprehensive article entitled *Remodeling Grounded Theory,* available at http://www.qualitative-research.net/fqstexte/2-04/2-04glaser-e.htm.

8. Husserl, born in Czechoslovakia in 1859, studied mathematics and astronomy in Berlin and Vienna. Brentano, an Austrian philosopher, led him toward philosophy and away from mathematics. In 1907 he gave five lectures on phenomenology. Although he planned to come to California in the mid-1930s, he became ill and died in 1938.

9. Other leaders include Levinas, who studied with Husserl and developed a philosophy of ethics, and Derrida, a French philosopher, whose contribution concerns the idea that there is no single meaning to language or text. He suggests that language is constantly shifting.

10. Go to the Center for Advanced Research in Phenomenology to read the latest ideas. They can be found online at http://www.phenomenologycenter.org.

11. If you read Italian, it can be located at http://www2.unibo.it/encyclopaideia/.

12. Dermot (2000) and Dillon (1997) provide additional and clear information on Husserl, Heidegger, Brentano, Sartre, Merleau-Ponty, Gadamer, Arendt, and Derrida. See also Sokolowski (2000) and Hopkins and Crowell (2003).

13. In its original German, Lebenswelt, or the world of lived experience, comes from Husserl's last work.

14. For more information, see Byers (2003) and Moustakis (1994).

15. Heidegger provides an alternative to bracketing. He acknowledged that our own culture, background, and gender influence our experience. He did not think bracketing was possible. Instead, he talked about authentic reflection that would enable us to know our own assumptions about a phenomenon.

16. Byrne (1998) offers a clear explanation of various aspects of hermeneutics. Lye (1996) also identifies some basic principles of phenomenological hermeneutics.

17. You will learn something about the history of this field by reading Yin (2002), Merriam (2002), and Stake (1995).

18. Soy (1997) provides some specific directions on how to do a case study.

PART 2

Gathering, Organizing, and Analyzing

The four chapters in this part focus on the methodology of qualitative research. Chapter 6 addresses embarking on qualitative research. Chapter 7 addresses the role and function of a literature review. In Chapters 8 and 9, I offer you many practical suggestions on how to collect data through interviewing, observing, and other techniques.

I have said several times that qualitative research follows an inductive approach. I follow these principles in this book. I ask you to begin with the particular and move to the general.

Many of the suggestions I make are based on practical experience. I ask you to use the suggestions as you practice gathering data.

When you finish this part, you should have collected a considerable amount of data. You will then need to turn your attention to deciding what to do with the data. That information is contained in Part 3.

CHAPTER 6

Embarking on Qualitative Research

The position of the artist is humble. He is essentially a channel.

—Piet Mondrian

I was initially excited about the idea of doing a qualitative study. Though I had very little background I knew that I was much more interested in qualitative research than quantitative research. Even though I had a strong background in math and statistics, I never quite bought into the quantitative techniques. I guess this is so for me because as an individual, I never quite fit into any of the stereotypes or norms that statistics claimed. I always thought that we could learn so much more in some cases by going out into the environment and investigating for ourselves.

—Donna Joy

In this chapter I provide you with a concrete example of an extensive study that I have conducted with members of several of my classes. This study uses in-depth interviewing as the primary source of information. I use it for illustrative purposes only. Of course, other studies often rely on other methods of gathering information including observation, examining records, or collecting visual data. I begin the chapter with 20 questions that students typically ask. Then I lay out in detail the elements of the study and include much information drawn from student output. I hope you will find this interesting and that it will give you some ideas on how you and your colleagues can proceed.

TWENTY QUESTIONS

Did you know that "Twenty Questions" began in the 1950s as a BBC radio game show? The premise was that the host was thinking of something that could be animal, vegetable, or mineral. The questioners had 20 chances to ask the host "yes" or "no" questions about the object. At the end of the allotted number of questions, or earlier if a questioner wanted, a guess was made. If the guess was correct, prizes were awarded. When it was a game show, the audience was told by a mystery voice what the object was. The questioners could not hear. I want to begin with a variation of this game. I have chosen 20 questions that students typically ask me or get asked by others, and I have provided my responses.

Q.1. How do I convince my adviser that doing a qualitative study will be worthwhile?
A.1. Prepare. If you come to a meeting with knowledge you are always in a one-up position. So, read this book, read other material, and read completed qualitative research studies.

Q.2. How many research questions should I have?
A.2. Usually you have only one or two main questions. The questions you ask your participants are not considered your research questions.

Q.3. Since I only talked to three people, how can I generalize to similar individuals?
*A.3. Generalization is a concept used in scientific research where you draw **random samples** from populations and generalize back to the populations; you are interested in testing hypotheses. In qualitative research, you do not generalize or test hypotheses. Rather, you describe, understand, and interpret.*

Q.4. How do I keep going when I do not seem to be getting anywhere?
A.4. Find a support group. Your fellow students are often the best source of support. If they are not available, rely on your faculty mentors or other supportive faculty. Try to locate a chat room on the topic. Remind yourself why you are in school and the goals you plan to achieve. Take a break and treat yourself to something that does not have anything to do with school.

Q.5. How do I form a good committee who will understand what I am doing and assist me in the process?
A.5. Rely on your advisor to guide you. Fellow students are also very helpful.

Q.6. Why won't they tell me how to do it?
A.6. I know how frustrated you are, but since this field is dynamic and creative, there is no right way to do something. There are several ways and new ways emerge all the time. Use your own creativity and talents here.

Q.7. What should I do with all the data I collect?
A.7. Well, you should have thought about this before you started, but I would strongly suggest you rely on the computer. You need to develop a system to organize and manage your information. At the very least, you should become familiar with a word processing program and a filing system.

Q.8. Do I need to back things up?

A.8. How often have I heard students say their computer died, the hard drive crashed, it rained on their files, and so on? I can't urge you enough to save your work often and in at least two locations. There are many easy storage systems available for use on your computer. Make sure you are familiar with them.

Q.9. I plan to do interviews. Should I develop a detailed interview script?

A.9. I expect you are used to having questions written out in advance and that you want to follow the same format for each participant. I would state an emphatic "no" about doing this. Your interview should be more like a conversation that you guide. You need to provide a chance for participants to tell their story in their own way.

Q.10. Which is easier to do—quantitative or qualitative?

A.10. I would say that ease is not a deciding factor. What questions do you have? Are you trying to study people, their lives, and their interactions? If so, qualitative research might be suitable. That is what you need to think about.

Q.11. I have read some things about triangulation. What is it and should I use it?

*A.11. **Triangulation** is based on the idea that something (e.g., a submarine, a cell phone) can be located by measuring the radial distance or direction from three different points. Some writers hold the view that validity can be established by triangulating data, investigators, and methodologies. I believe, however, that the concept is more appropriate to traditional or positivist paradigms and should not be used in the newer forms of qualitative research.*

Q.12. What style of writing should I use?

A.12. It is strongly recommended that you use a narrative, first person style. In that way, your story has more impact. Some resist this, but I do not. You can read Holliday (2001) or Wolcott (1990), who provide good resources for writing up your work and recommend using first person.

Q.13. I want to do something different. What else can I do?

A.13. There are many new ideas out there. I like the idea of using images to convey messages, and I strongly urge you to explore alternative means of presenting information.

Q.14. Why should I waste my time keeping a **journal**?

A.14. Self-reflection is critical in the new qualitative traditions. By keeping a journal, you will be able to examine your own thinking and motivations and how they influence and are influenced by the work you do.

Q.15. I have read some things about feminist research, yet I am a man. Am I precluded from this methodology?

A.15. As with most questions, it depends on whom you ask. I would say that sensitivity to feminist issues is critical. I suggest you explore with your female colleagues their reaction.

Q.16. This seems overwhelming to me. How can I do all of this and still live my life?

A.16. My two watchwords are priorities and balance. I often tell my students that they need to take time for themselves and build it into each day. I know so many of them have family and work responsibilities and often feel cut into many pieces. Of course, it helps to have supportive and understanding friends and family.

Q.17. How will I know when I am finished?

A.17. This is not an easy question to answer. You need to remember that you are capturing a slice in time and space of thoughts, actions, and beliefs. From a practical standpoint, finishing often relates to deadlines imposed by your institution or yourself.

Q.18. How do I learn about computer software packages, and should I use them?

A.18. You actually have two questions here. In my experience the more sophisticated packages are quite difficult to learn on your own. If possible, you should attend a training workshop. You can also join a Listserv so you can ask questions of others. But the learning curve is steep and you may decide it is not worth the trouble. So you might have to revert to the colored pencils and note cards. I remember one student of mine used tape and poster board and had things pinned up all over her basement. I wonder how her family managed.

Q.19. How do I know if my work is worthwhile?

A.19. This is a question that is relevant to anything you do. From the lowest level of doing laundry to making decisions about war, we strive for the best and put forth our best efforts. Qualitative research is no exception, but judging is quite complicated. Who is the judge? On what basis does he or she judge? You know whether the pillow case is clean. Do you know whether going to war is right? And since one of the vexing questions now about qualitative research is its merit or worth, it is incumbent on you to be prepared to document what you did, how you did it, and what you found.

Q.20. So, I'm ready for my first steps. How do I begin?

A.20. I have included many suggestions throughout this book. Read below for a detailed account of a study conducted in my classes. Its topic—My Life as a Graduate Student—should be near and dear to you.

MY LIFE AS A GRADUATE STUDENT

This project began with my desire to have students practice interviewing. It evolved into a complex, multiyear project with many documents. I have chosen to include some of the material that was developed by my classes over several years.

Let me tell you briefly what we did so you can get an overview. I identified the parameters of the project: We would explore life as a graduate student. I chose this topic because I knew that everyone in the class was going through the experience at that very moment. I could not think of another more pertinent topic than this. We would begin by discussing what interviewing was and then practice interviewing each other in class. In this way, we were able to immediately identify a participant who met the criterion. We did not have to seek permission or go through an institutional review board. Next, we would identify someone else to interview. Our interviews would be recorded and transcribed, and we would bring in copies for all other students or post them as attachments to be accessed online. We would work in teams practicing data analysis, first by hand and later by computer programs (such as NVivo).

Finally, we would each write up our own interpretation based on our own data and data of others. We would also keep a journal of our experiences. I, too, wrote up my interpretation of the process and the findings.

What follows is a detailed account of what we did at each phase of the project, why we did it, and some examples. These are the phases of the project:

Phase 1: Getting Started

Phase 2: Modeling Good Practices

Phase 3: Practicing Interviewing and Debriefing

Phase 4: Conducting Outside Interviews

Phase 5: Doing Preliminary Analyses as a Group

Phase 6: Doing Analyses as an Individual

Phase 7: Preparing Individual Papers

Phase 1: Getting Started

If you want to do qualitative research, it is critical that you get involved in a qualitative research project and actually collect and analyze data and write about what you learned. I decided that it would be valuable for my class to become involved in a group research project. In this way, I could deal with some common questions, some common data, and a topic that would be interesting to students. I don't remember precisely when I came up with the idea that the best topic would be to study the lived experiences of graduate students. I don't recall telling them that they were doing a phenomenological study. I thought that would be too complicated. I didn't ask them to do a literature review. But I knew they had a wealth of experience and their own thoughts on the topic.

Like much of qualitative research, the details were not all worked out before we began the project. But I knew there were certain things I wanted them to do. My three main goals were for the students to practice interviewing, practice coding, and practice writing up results. I was on my way. I developed a set of materials for the interviews, worked out the details of the assignment, and introduced the project.

Phase 2: Modeling Good Practices

The first step in this phase was to record our own views about the topic. I knew that talking about them was not sufficient; we had to write our thoughts down. We took some class time to do this. I did not tell them that we were bracketing. Bracketing, as I discussed in the section on phenomenology in Chapter 5, is a concept that comes from Husserl (1917/1981) and Moustakis (1994). Its purpose is to set aside our views on a topic that we are studying so that they will not have undue influence on what we ask and what we learn. Actually, I don't really believe that you can set your views aside. Rather, I take the position that by making them explicit and overt you will be well on your way to accomplishing the same purpose.

I did not give students specific questions to follow. I wanted them to practice the interview as conversation (Rubin & Rubin, 1995), but I knew that they would feel more comfortable if they had some general topic areas. So I asked them to write down what areas they thought they might find interesting. We discussed these thoughts in class prior to doing our interviews.

I encourage questions that are of a "how" and "why" nature. I also encourage questions that are neutral in nature. I avoid questions that are "who" and "what." These latter kinds of questions lead to very specific answers and then just stop. They do not lead to a conversation.

The first thing I did was to demonstrate how to conduct such an interview. I asked for a student volunteer and I began my interview. Although I knew these students, I still wanted to model appropriate behaviors. I asked permission to record, gathered my paper and pen, and placed myself in the center of the classroom with onlookers on all sides. I began by making the participant feel at ease. We talked about her family and school in general. I asked what her major was and what kind of work she did. She seemed ready to begin. Now I was ready to conduct the interview.

I have two favorite ways to begin an interview. I either begin with a Grand Tour question (Spradley, 1979) or ask the participant to tell a specific and concrete story about the topic—something that happened to her last week or last month. I find these concrete stories very meaningful and reflective of underlying thoughts. They are especially useful for getting material that is not full of jargon. Grand Tour questions usually begin with something like, "Tell me what it is like . . ." In this case, I asked, "Tell me about your being a graduate student." Notice that the question is neutral and non-directive. I don't want to ask, "Tell me about the difficulties you face as a graduate student." I continued my interview for some time. I asked specific story questions, such as "Tell me something that happened to you last week while you were in school." Due to time limitations, I tried to illustrate different aspects of interviewing strategies, so I asked questions that permitted comparisons and contrasts. I asked questions that probed more fully. In Chapter 8, you will see my complete Interview Guide that illustrates various principles.

The next step in my modeling was to debrief with class members. I do this in several ways. I ask questions that try to get at points I was intending to illustrate. For example, what behaviors did they notice that showed my neutral stance? How did I provide wait time for the respondent to answer? How did I let the respondent's story come out in his or her own language?

Phase 3: Practicing Interviewing and Debriefing

We were ready to begin our practice interviews. Tape recorders were assembled, teams of three were chosen, and places selected for the interviews. The students were told they had about 30 minutes for the task. One was to conduct the interview, a second was to take notes and observe, and a third was to be interviewed. If time permitted, they could trade places so each would get an opportunity to do each thing. During the interviews, I moved among teams and made mental notes of practices that illustrated certain points. I try to operate in a positive manner and usually point out things that are done correctly rather than dwell on mistakes made.

As I recall, this task took quite a long time and some of the actual practice time had to be cut short. Different classes operate differently. Some get right to it while others seem to get lost in trivia or just take a much-needed break from their studies. In an ideal world, I think I would allocate two or three class sessions to practicing interviewing techniques. But given the reality of much material to cover and too little time, I suspect that some people did not get as much time as they needed.

We concluded with a debriefing time. I called for volunteers. The observer/recorder commented on what was done. The other two members of the team talked about their experience. If time permitted, we listened to the tape. We discussed the merits of doing an unstructured interview and why I thought it was so important. I remember more than one student expressed a concern that she or he did not really know quite what to ask and what to do without formal questions. We discussed how important it was to think about the topic in advance and to get their thoughts clear in their minds. I recommend using a general outline of potential topics to cover. I reiterated the idea that the interview was a conversation and thus not meant to be planned in advance. While I knew that everyone was not ready, time was passing, and I decided to ask them to commence with their outside interviews.

At this point, it is important to know that individual in-depth interviews are a type of qualitative interview that is described as a conversation between interviewer and participant (Kvale, 1996; McCracken, 1988; Rubin & Rubin, 1995; Spradley, 1979). Our purpose in such a style of interviewing is to hear what the participant has to say in her own words, in her voice, with her language and narrative. In this way, participants can share what they know and have learned and can add a dimension to our understanding of the situation that questionnaire data does not reveal.

Individual in-depth interviewing is a process, not just a predetermined list of questions. The process builds in several stages. It begins with developing rapport and getting the participant to trust you and to open up to you. It is advisable to talk about why you are there, why they have been selected to be interviewed, and how you will use what you learn from them.

Although this class example involved adult students, I want to mention some issues that might develop when interviewing younger students. While procedures are quite well-established for interviewing adults, they need to be modified somewhat when interviewing students, especially those who might be suspicious of adults in formal school situations.

Once rapport has been established, it is desirable to find a way to connect with the student and his or her experiences. One way that works well is to have a student relate stories about his or her school successes. This use of the concrete guarantees rich data. This use of the narrative and concrete stories is well documented in the literature on qualitative research.

Phase 4: Conducting Outside Interviews

Students were asked to identify someone who would be willing to be interviewed. They were left on their own to schedule appointments, conduct the interview, transcribe the interview, and prepare copies for classmates. As students became more technologically savvy, they transmitted material via e-mail attachments. Initially, however, I remember they brought me a diskette and hard copies for classmates.

Before we began any analysis, we debriefed our experience. These are some of the comments I recall: I really liked doing this. I learned so much from talking to someone else. I felt uncomfortable when I asked a question and it was not answered. I did not know where to go next. I found transcribing took so much time. Is there an easier way? Why can't I just summarize what I learned? I could identify with things that others told me. You can see quite a range of reactions.

Now let's take a look at some of these interviews. I have chosen excerpts from a number of interviews, and have modified the interviews to shorten them, to remove personal information, and to provide uniformity of presentation. Although I modified some of the interviews, I did leave much information intact. I want you to see that often the information you gather may not be directly on point or provide insight into what your participant thinks about the topic. My comments should help you to see how you might formulate your questions and how you might follow up based on the responses you receive.

Although each student had the same assignment, they approached things differently. Some clearly had questions that were predetermined; others were more open in their approach. Some elicited responses that were more informative while others were less successful.

This particular activity is one that can be used in any situation. Its main advantages are that it is easy to locate respondents and select questions about which each has some thoughts and knowledge (since they are currently in school). By using this common activity, students begin on a similar footing and can practice technique and skill with less emphasis on the questions.

Interview A. Jon Interviews Paul

I am here with Paul, who is a second year ALHRD Ph.D. candidate. The purpose of this interview is to find out how the graduate student experience has been for Paul and to perhaps gain some insight into how students balance their work, family, and school commitments.

Q1:   PAUL, ARE WE READY TO START THE INTERVIEW?

A1:   Absolutely. Let's go for it.

Q2:   I WANTED TO THANK YOU FOR TAKING THE TIME TO TALK WITH ME. AS YOU KNOW, WE BOTH STARTED THE PROGRAM AT THE SAME TIME, AND I'M CURIOUS AS TO HOW WE BOTH PERCEIVE THE GRADUATE STUDENT PROCESS. PAUL, HOW IS IT THAT WE HAVE GOTTEN SO FAR THAT NOW WE ARE LOOKING AT THE DISSERTATION IN THE NEXT YEAR?

A2:   (Laughs) I have no idea, Jon. It just seems like yesterday that we started this program. It has been a real adventure so far.

Q3:   WELL, PAUL, WHY DON'T YOU TELL ME A LITTLE BIT ABOUT YOUR GENERAL EXPERIENCE HERE AS A GRADUATE STUDENT AT VIRGINIA TECH?

A3:   Well, my experience has been one of . . . change.

Q4:   CHANGE?

A4:   Yes, change. We both started in Fall of 98, and the whole experience has been hard at time, eye-opening at times . . . you know it's hard to juggle family, work, and school, taking quite a load every semester, and it's starting to wear on me now. By May, I will have taken over 60 credit hours of coursework. At times, I can see glimpses of the end, and at others, it's hard to see the end. . . .

Q18:   AS A GRADUATE STUDENT NOW, GOING THROUGH WHAT YOU HAVE GONE THROUGH, HOW WOULD YOU IMPROVE YOUR EXPERIENCE AS A GRADUATE STUDENT FOR OTHERS?

A18:   For myself, I would gear my core Foundational courses toward the Cognate, which would determine what my interests and coursework would be. I would definitely get a good overview during the first foundations courses, and then move towards fleshing out the requirements and targeting the coursework towards the Cognate as soon as possible.

Interview A: My Comments

These two students were friends outside of class. Notice Jon's introduction prior to the interview. He talks about his purpose and sets the stage. His Q3 reflects a general Grand Tour question. His Q4 reflects a probing or "tell me more" question. Q18 is more directive, but it is not leading.

Interview B. Valerie Interviews Annette

Q1:   TELL ME SOMETHING ABOUT YOURSELF.

A1:   I'm Annette, a Special Education teacher in Fairfax County. I'm in my first semester in the doctoral program at Virginia Tech in Adult Learning and Human Resource Development.

Q2:   ANY OTHER INFORMATION YOU WOULD LIKE TO SHARE? ANY FAMILY?

A2:   I'm married and have a 17-year-old and a 20-year-old.

Q3:   HOW DOES IT FEEL TO BE A GRADUATE STUDENT?

A3:   Well, for me being a graduate student means furthering some of the knowledge that I already have to a different level. I'm totally out of my career—I guess my field. I'm a Special Education teacher and this is Adult Learning and so right now learning the history has really made me think a different way about adult education. But, I truly like it and I don't mind going to school. I love the camaraderie of my classmates and the professor. So, it has been, you know, pretty good. It's just my first class and it shows my rustic [sic] spots.

Interview B: My Comments

Q1 and Q2 get at general information about the respondent. This information is often important for a later analysis. While we didn't specifically discuss it, I think students knew to gather information about work and family and school. Q3 illustrates another Grand Tour question.

Interview C. Bob Interviews Student by Phone

Q1:   THINK BACK. WHAT EXPECTATIONS DID YOU HAVE OF GRADUATE SCHOOL?

A1:   I am not so sure I had too many. I expected to be challenged, particularly in a new area for me. I expected a different level of interaction from faculty as it relates to the student. That's it. By the way, that is compared to my undergraduate or master's.

Q2:   CURRENTLY, HOW WOULD YOU DESCRIBE YOUR EXPERIENCE AS A GRADUATE STUDENT?

A2:   Very stressful. It is a lot more stressful than I expected. It is a lot more stressful, certainly, than my bachelor's and master's were. It's a lot more (pause) in some cases, it is a lot more philosophical in how it relates the data. The flip side is a tremendous amount of application in it. May very well be the nature of where we are located, being the Capital, very political, very government, and in the amount of government students we have in the program.

Q2a: LET'S EXAMINE STRESS. WHAT CONTRIBUTES TO THE STRESS?

A2a: In some cases it is the amount of material that has to be read in order to come up, not necessarily with an answer, but sometimes even in deciding how you think or where you stand relative to an issue. Or you're pushed to find a paradigm in which you belong.

Q3:   WHAT STRENGTHS OR LIMITATIONS CHARACTERIZE YOUR STUDENT AFFILIATION WITH YOUR SPECIFIC ACADEMIC DEPARTMENT AT THE NORTHERN VIRGINIA CENTER?

A3:   Okay, definitely feel at a disadvantage academically as compared to the Blacksburg students. Their, first of all, their experience is different than ours. I don't think there are any part-time students that work. They're all not working or graduate assistants. So they're not working a 40- or 50-hour week. They don't have the same commitments that we have. I believe there are not any exceptions to that, but I could be wrong. The diversity in professors—what is an "A" paper with one professor is a "B" paper with another, and it teaches you a lot about looking at all the different perspectives. It is sort of like writing for a different journal.

I also think that there are some limitations, in addition to the library part of academic life and working in that part of academic life and working, is that we don't have—I forget the verbiage that I hear—a sense of community. There is a sense of community within a small group or a few here and there, but it is a little different if you're at a satellite campus versus a main campus. College life—they have places to go and socialize and places to go to sit and study. We don't have that.

Interview C: My Comments

This interview illustrates a somewhat different style. Bob is a more formal student than the others. He knew this person and they were in the same program. Q2 and Q2a illustrate how he picks up on something his respondent says and explores it more fully. He picked up "stressful" and pursued it. This is typical of a good interview. When you are not sure what the respondent is getting at, explore it more fully. Sometimes you think you know what the respondent means, but instead you are looking at what you believe. This is where your own thoughts and those of the respondent need to be disaggregated. I think Bob did an excellent job. Now look at how Q3 released a large flow of information. I think perhaps Bob had hit a sore point with the respondent. In any event, it led to a wealth of information that can be used in subsequent analyses.

Interview D. Leslie Interviews Tammy

Q1:   THUS FAR IN YOUR PROGRAM, WHAT HAS BEEN YOUR MOST MEMORABLE EXPERIENCE?

A1:   I gave a speech on "How to Find a Job" and four of my classmates thanked me for helpful information. Two of them found new jobs within a month. They really did, they actually followed my advice. They didn't have a clue.

Q9:   WE'VE DISCUSSED A LOT OF TOPICS DURING THIS INTERVIEW; IS THERE ANYTHING ELSE YOU'D LIKE TO TELL ME ABOUT YOU AND YOUR GRADUATE EXPERIENCE?

A9:   Being a full-time employee and attending school is very challenging, but the rewards will be well worth it.

Closing Comments: TAMMY, THANK YOU FOR TAKING THE TIME TO HELP ME WITH MY PROJECT. I REALLY APPRECIATE YOU TAKING THE TIME OUT.

Interview D: My Comments

Leslie tended to ask very direct questions that led to very specific answers. She never quite got a conversation going. Part of that, I believe, is her own personal style. I chose this brief section to illustrate a favorite closing question of mine: Is there anything else you would like to add that we haven't talked about? Sometimes this leads to a wealth of information. I find it interesting that Tammy speaks about the rewards of being in graduate school.

Interview E. Karen Interviews Jimmy

Q1:   UM, WELL, AS I HAD SAID TO YOU, WHAT ARE YOUR THOUGHTS ABOUT BEING A GRADUATE STUDENT?

A1:   Um, I like being in graduate school. I don't really associate it with being in graduate school. I associate it more with being in pharmacy school, and I think that's how a lot of people back home address me as being in pharmacy school rather than being in graduate school. . . .

Q5:   UH, HUH. UM, LET'S SEE, YOU ARE CURRENTLY A P-3, THIRD YEAR IN PHARMACY SCHOOL, UH . . . YOU'VE GONE THROUGH THREE YEARS WORTH. WHAT ARE SOME OF THE MAIN BARRIERS THAT YOU HAVE HAD TO OVERCOME TO BE SUCCESSFUL IN GRADUATE SCHOOL?

A5:   Um, well, there's a lot of barriers. Moving was one. I think that was a good thing for me because it got me out of a small town life. It got me away from friends and made me make new friends. It got me out of everyday habits of doing things and made me change my whole lifestyle.

Q6:   THAT'S A CHANGE IN LIFE.

A6:   That's a change in lifestyle. It just didn't work out for both of us. She [his wife] started going to school at JMU. There was a lot of stress for both of us. We both had to be away from each other. So that was one thing I had to give up [laughter]. . . .

Q9:   I SEE. HAS ANYTHING IN, AH, GRADUATE SCHOOL SURPRISED YOU OR WERE YOU UNPREPARED PER SE FOR SOME OF THE EXPERIENCES HERE?

A9:   Um, yes. The level of intensity of teaching has increased a lot from undergrad. That was a big surprise. I wasn't expecting, like, when I was an undergrad I worked full time and went to school full time and had no problem, and here, my first year I didn't work. I took the first year off from working and just went to school. It was all I could do just to keep up with classes. There was no way I could have worked.

From Karen's Journal

Bottom line, the interview went well. I think there was a comfortable atmosphere where the student could speak candidly and fully.

Reviewing the tape, I think I was too leading with two of my questions, actually offering an answer or an explanation. That must be avoided in the future. I heard myself on the tape several times giving an encouraging uh-huh, or yes, which is a natural part of the way I engage in conversation but may not be appropriate for this type of interview.

I found myself almost embarrassed by the willingness of the interviewee to reveal such personal things about his life such as a divorce, but, upon reflection, I am glad he felt comfortable enough to do so. Dr. Lichtman is right, if we just keep our mouths closed, people will talk.

I was able to handle silences and pauses well, not feeling like I had to jump in to fill the silences. This I have learned in teaching for the past 18 years. Silences help draw out thoughts and reflection. I covered all the parts of the interview. In terms of mechanics, I would like to get a smaller, less obtrusive recorder. I learned that it takes a very long time to transcribe a 30-minute interview!

Interview E: My Comments

I believe Karen was on the faculty and interviewed Jimmy who was a student. This may have changed the nature of the interview, but I don't know for sure. Karen illustrated good practices when she picked up on the term "lifestyle" and asked for elaboration. Notice that Karen observed that this was a change in life and Jimmy pointed out that it was a change in lifestyle. Karen's thoughts on the interview illustrate how observations of our own thoughts help.

Phase 5: Doing Preliminary Analyses as a Group

Each student had copies of everyone's interview. I learned as I went along with this project that it was best to print the interviews on about 2/3 of the page with a very large right-hand margin, about 1/3 of the page, for notes and themes. But initially I don't think I asked students to transcribe in this way, so we worked as best as we could. We began without any direction except to write down notes in the margin of ideas or observations based on the actual transcripts. I worked together with the students. We spent about 15 to 20 minutes on the activity. I tend to make many very specific and detailed comments. I noticed that some did that while others tended to write down only a very few things. I thought that they wanted to get to the end before they were ready.

We then reflected on what we wrote, and one student volunteered to put the comments on chart paper for future reference. This is actually the beginning of our data analysis and search for themes. Initially what each person said was recorded. We began to see that some people had used one word to convey a meaning while others used a synonym. We tried to combine these and choose a common word. We worked through this process for another hour or so. We moved back and forth between the transcripts and our group discussions.

We began to move from having all comments on the same level to a hierarchy of comments. Some were major headings while others were subheadings or minor headings. Some appeared more important while others seemed less so. Those that kept popping up in a number of interviews took on greater salience than those that appeared only one time. This process of winnowing down is what our data analysis is all about. We begin with all our data. We move to some preliminary topics. We organize these topics in some logical order. We select major and minor topics. We eliminate those that seem irrelevant. We add those that we might encounter as we read more data. Our ultimate goal is to identify a few themes that convey the essence of the data. In other words, what is the essence of the lived experience of being a graduate student?

I believe that this activity is extremely valuable. You gain new ideas and insight. You think about justifying your thoughts about the meaning of what someone says. And you have an enormous amount of data rather than just an interview of one individual.

Phase 6: Doing Analyses as an Individual

Students were now on their own to pursue their thoughts. Their assignment was to write a paper based on the interviews. They were not to value their own interview over others; they were to treat all data equally. I suspect some gave greater weight to their own data, perhaps being mistrustful of data that they did not collect.

Another cohort of students worked with qualitative software to organize and locate information. These students also worked in teams. One group developed a hierarchical model representing major and minor themes that they anticipated finding in the data. Another group worked together coding the data from transcripts imported into the software program. A third group coded separately and then got together to coordinate their individual work.

Phase 7: Preparing Individual Papers

Each student was asked to prepare a paper based on the data from all interviews. I have selected several to illustrate various points.

Paper 1. James's Paper

In this paper I take a bio-phenomenological look at the life of "Maggie" a third-year doctoral student at a major east-coast university. Her story is compared to those of others collected by graduate students, to include myself, studying qualitative research methods. While the goal of the exercise was to glean data from the interviews and distill them into an understanding of the "typical" graduate experience, Maggie's story is used as the focal point of discussion. A narrative of her life in graduate school is generated from her own answers to an interviewer's questions. Whenever possible Maggie's own words were used to tell her story. Her experience, while presumably not typical, incorporates the themes identified as typical in the lives of all of those participating in the study: Age in life; Full-time or Part-time; More Women than Men; Finding Balance; Support; and The Positive Experience. While Maggie's story reads somewhat like a soap opera, it allows the reader to gain a glimpse of the true-life experience of a graduate student.

The image of an hourglass is projected on the screen of my TV and the narrator speaks those famous words, *"Like sands through the hourglass, these are the days of our lives."* I stop, mesmerized for a moment anticipating the picture on the screen to change and a world of love, hate and intrigue to take its place. Like sands through the hourglass, the seconds slowly fall away as the music fades and the program goes to commercial. Disappointed and awakened from my trance I turned off the TV. *"I don't need this,"* I say to myself as I fill my arms with books and papers and head off for yet another class, yet another meeting, yet another day in MY life. I'm in graduate school. MY life is a soap opera.

Paper 1: My Comments

Jim's work is so poetic and heartfelt. I love his soap opera **metaphor**. This sets the stage for what is to come. I remember that Jim spoke of how hard it was for him to write. I believe he is too critical of himself. I think Jim accomplishes one of his goals in writing: setting the stage and drawing the reader into the story. Aren't you ready to continue reading after this brilliant introduction?

Paper 2. Leanne's Paper

In many respects, this paper is an ethnographic tribute to the graduate student journey. I have sought to share the cultural behaviors, language, and artifacts of the graduate student through a descriptive storytelling format that presents an "everyday" perspective. Of course, this topic also positions me as the researcher in the somewhat precarious position of "going native," as I am actively engaged in doctoral coursework. Certainly I am "immersed in the day-to-day lives of the people" (Creswell, 1997, p. 58). The bracketing cautions loom tremulously. Or perhaps my immersion merely positions me for the **emic perspective** [boldface added] of an insider's view of the graduate student culture (*Ways of approaching research: Qualitative designs,* n.d.). While there are also admitted limitations in the variety of data sources, the nature of the research question, as well as the data itself, suggest the opportunity to provide a holistic portrait of the graduate student experience. Fully realizing that this qualitative effort may not generalize to the larger population, I acted on the opportunity to capture a glimpse of this world.

This paper represents my maiden exploration of qualitative research methods. The significant portion of this paper plunges the reader into the world of graduate school as the journaled account unfolds from application process through the end of the second semester. I follow this with a briefer description of the ethnographic tradition, research methods, analysis and comments, and conclusion. Throughout, I have added subtle—some perhaps not so subtle—touches that reflect the personality of this author. Constant Reader, I trust you will sit back, relax, and enjoy the journey.

Paper 2: My Comments

How beautiful this journey is. Leanne weaves her thoughts, what she learned, and discussion of qualitative research approaches into her opening paragraph.

Paper 3. Talisha's Paper

In preparation for the interview, I thought about the topic "My Life as A Graduate Student." Because I am currently a graduate student and have had the experience of being a graduate student before, I had a lot of thoughts on the topic myself. I know the positive and negative experiences and stresses that I endure and endured as a graduate student. For this project, I had to attempt to "bracket," as introduced to the class in Frank's presentation on Phenomenology, my thoughts and feelings on the topic so that I would not impose my feelings and thoughts on the participant. I attempted to "bracket" my feelings and thoughts by writing them in my journal. My journal excerpt read:

When I think about the topic "My Life as A Graduate Student," the first thought that comes to mind is the hard work that comes along with being a graduate student. As a first-time graduate student, I was a full-time student and worked full-time while working on my master's. It was really difficult because I was coming out of undergrad

(Continued)

(Continued)

where I worked a few hours a week, but my primary focus was on classes and I knew that I had the support of my family. Then as a graduate student I was working full-time to support myself and going to school. I had to learn how to successfully balance work, school, and my personal life. And although I knew I could count on my family, I did not want to depend on them for financial support. There were times when I would work a 16-hour shift (3 p.m.–7 a.m.) and go to an 8:00 a.m. class when I got off work the next morning. In spite of the stresses, the students in my master's program were really supportive. We would work together in groups and consult each other about assignments, which was really helpful for me. Obtaining my master's was a personal goal of mine. Not only did I want to pursue higher education, but I also knew that I did not have too many options with a bachelor's in Psychology. I endure the same stresses right now as a doctoral student. I am working full-time and attending school part-time. An additional stressor is the commute from Richmond to Northern VA. But, like my master's degree, obtaining my doctorate is a personal goal as well as a professional goal so it is worth the drive to me.

Paper 3: My Comments

This excerpt illustrates how Talisha chose to bracket her thoughts on the topic. I liked both her description and her journal entry. You will see that her style is more straightforward and less poetic than the others you have read.

Paper 4. Annette's Paper

I enjoyed conducting the interview. I learned that the process can be challenging and very time consuming. We were asked to conduct a 30-minute interview, but some student's interviews lasted as long as an hour. The amount of questions varied for each student as well as the length of pages. At least two of the interviews were about sixteen pages in length. Therefore, some students are quoted more than others due to the fact more information was provided from their interviews.

This was a good exercise. I would like to continue to practice the interviewing process to sharpen my skills in developing questions and transcribing the responses. It would have been helpful to have practiced in class as a group and gotten feedback before conducting the actual interviews. Another practice strategy would be to compare my hand coding to a computerized coding program to determine if the same themes would emerge.

Paper 4: My Comments

I think Annette makes some interesting observations. She participated in a class that met online part of the time, so she did not have the full experience of practice interviewing as I described above.

Paper 5. Stephanie's Paper

The theme of this project evolved from the "My Life as a Graduate Student" interview project. In coding and reviewing the data from the interviews, a number of themes evolved that were of interest to me. Specifically, themes around support systems for female graduate students. This project is a case study that will review the impact and types of support systems used by married female graduate students. As described by Creswell, a case study is an in-depth analysis of multiple cases using a variety of sources. With this in mind and considering the type of study that this project entails, the case study research method was most applicable.

Paper 5: My Comments

I always encourage students to feel free to do what they want. Stephanie chose to reinterpret the assignment and construct it as a case study on a specific topic. While I was surprised by the turn this took, I thought it quite interesting.

Paper 6. Paul's Paper

The following report presents the case of 'Stuart,' an imaginary individual who is currently dealing with life as a graduate student. Although this particular case is fabricated, it is based on the real life experiences and attitudes of graduate students, as reported through a series of focused interviews that were conducted as part of a qualitative research methods course at a local university. It is the intention of this presentation to model a case that illustrates the real life experiences and challenges that many graduate students face on the path to learning. They are a population that has been relatively unexplored by educational researchers and as such, behoove our investigation.

Graduate students are challenged by life, both within and outside their respective programs. They assign value to certain areas of their life and are often times motivated and required to prioritize its components, based on the perceived value they are assigned. While faced with these multiple challenges, graduate students search for the 'light at the end of the tunnel,' but still stop to smell the roses, once in a while, as they tread down the path of education toward self-enhancement. It is on this journey that graduate students acquire substance that they believe will transport them to a more personally fulfilling place, while gaining a more introspective view of themselves.

Although Stuart sees graduate school as a gateway to bettering himself, perhaps in his career or in a financial sense, it is the learning that he insists is the most important among the various sources of motivation that keep him in the program. Stuart recalls that on several occasions his classmates have claimed that they are "not necessarily driven by money or furthering their professional careers." Stuart respects this view and

(Continued)

(Continued)

feels as if there are a number of valid reasons and motivations for graduate students to continue their education, with a genuine love of learning being one. Becoming a life-long learner is a reality that Stuart has begun to embrace. He "likes to learn," calls learning new things "wonderful" and actively seeks out new opportunities in this vein. Stuart sees "a tremendous opportunity out there in education" and even believes that he will continue his learning beyond graduation, either by "getting another degree or taking seminars that will help specialize [him]."

Paper 6: My Comments

Paul lays out his purpose clearly. He articulates his thoughts well and demonstrates he has done some thinking about the topic. In a later section, Paul explains his interpretation and the interpretation that others should make. Paul made a decision to create a fictional student to illustrate his thoughts. I believe this is an excellent idea.

Paper 7. Heather's Paper

In an effort to better understand these differences, we have interviewed eleven individuals with the open instruction of discussing their lives as graduate students. As a researcher, I have reviewed these interviews in an effort to find consistent themes and patterns throughout the discussions. As a graduate student myself, my personal experience has likely been woven into the evaluation. These biases and expectations [of graduate student responses] were evident to me as a researcher early on in the semester. My September 18, 2002, journal entry states:

"I think I need to check my own biases going into this interview. I definitely chose these subjects for selfish reasons (i.e., looking for other people like myself who have had to balance school with home/work issues). I haven't felt a lot of stress yet, but I am aware that it is early in the semester. My original impression of the school, the program, the faculty and other students is that many people (not all) are very stressed here. I haven't seen that so much in Terry or Susan, but I sympathize with a lot of people here who appear to have to do so much with so little. I can appreciate that since I also work for a state institution. But I think that I am waiting to find that student who says 'it's really not that bad.'"

Paper 7: My Comments

Heather begins her paper with these comments. You can see how many different styles individuals used and how important it is not to limit what is acceptable.

MY PERSPECTIVE ON THE GRADUATE SCHOOL EXPERIENCE

The insight that is provided in the presentation of this case is based on my interpretation of the experiences and perceptions that have been shared by graduate students. The fact that this is a personal interpretation is evidenced by the use of the first person throughout much of this report. I ask that this be considered as the reader develops his or her own interpretation of the case that I have decided to illustrate. Although data were gathered and evidence has been provided to support the themes that are identified as being associated with a particular graduate school experience, the reader must understand that this is one of many interpretations that may be gleaned. Other interpretations may be accessed through additional research or alternative means of investigation.

SUMMARY

Becoming involved in qualitative research is a challenging and frustrating experience. Often there are many questions that you need to consider. Some remain unanswered; others are answered in different ways by different people. Ultimately, it is up to you to find your own place and way in this maze.

I encourage you to get involved in the My Life as a Graduate Student exercise. I have numerous work products from students that offer insight into the topic, into writing about qualitative research, and into learning about the self. Take the next steps. You will be greatly rewarded as you learn about others and, ultimately, about yourself. From an existentialist point of view, we are forced to define our own meanings, knowing they might be temporary. In this existence the individual defines everything.

GROUP ACTIVITY

Purpose: To practice interviewing other class members.

Activity: Review steps of interviewing by using my protocol. Become part of a team of three. Have one person interview, one take notes, and the third act as the participant. Review the process after 30 minutes. Tape record your work.

Evaluation: Look at how individuals begin to hone their interviewing skills.

INDIVIDUAL ACTIVITY

Purpose: To do a study that follows on My Life as a Graduate Student.

Activity: Examine your own ideas about the concept. Bracket your thoughts by making them explicit: write them down, then share your ideas with the group.

Evaluation: Look at how students are able to delineate thoughts about their own process.

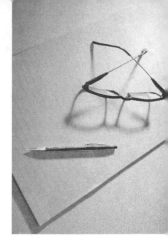

CHAPTER 7

The Role and Function of a Literature Review

Learn as much by writing as by reading.

—Lord Acton

The organization and analysis of the data became the biggest challenge for me. As I gathered information I developed a literature review matrix and letter system to catalog my references (R for research, G for general, N for national trends, S for state trends). I found the variables which were significant in mentoring and the holes in the current research. My professor helped me translate all of this into three research questions and develop a theoretical framework for inquiry. The framework included a graphic model of three intertwining circles for the three variable domains affecting beginning teacher mentor/mentee relationships: (a) participant profile/personality, (b) mentor program, and (c) school environment. This was most valuable and something I could not have developed on my own.

—Judy Smith

Many of you have written reviews of related research or **literature reviews**. They usually involve your going to a library or accessing materials online. Most universities provide access to journals and books either by traditional means or on the Internet. You have learned that one of the best ways to identify a new problem or research question is to find out what others have done on a particular topic, to summarize that information, and to try to find additional areas that need further exploration or investigation. Armed with what others have said, you are able to identify a question to answer.

Now imagine that you are interested in a particular question but not necessarily in what others have found. You have a concern that by knowing what others have found you will close your mind to new ideas. You want thoughts to emerge from what you study rather than having what you study pigeon-holed into particular areas. That is the very nature of an inductive approach: You work from the specific and concrete and move into the more abstract.

In this chapter, I discuss and provide examples of a literature review written from a traditional point of view. I also introduce alternatives to conducting a literature review when doing qualitative research. I provide specific examples that will help you see when to do a review, where to place it in your writing, and how to incorporate new ideas and yet maintain a distance. I hope when you are finished reading this chapter you will be able to make decisions about your own literature review and how your thinking about doing qualitative research and the topic in which you are interested will be strengthened by such a review.

I address several questions: What is a literature review? What is the importance of such a review? How is theory related? What are sources of information? What are the steps in conducting a review? What are some examples? How can you keep track of things?

WHAT IS A LITERATURE REVIEW?

A literature review is an accounting of what is out there on a particular topic. I have written and read many literature reviews over the years. Sometimes I find that students see a literature review as an exercise that needs to be done, but they are not really sure why they are doing it. When they finish, they often say, "Well, now that is done." They do not seem to connect it to the rest of what they are writing. I believe that unless you make your review an integral part of what you are doing it is just an activity that you know you have to do but are not sure why. So it is your responsibility to make this happen.

You need to think of a review as more than just a compilation of individual research studies. It represents a synthesis and critical assessment related to a particular topic. In traditional research paradigms, it occurs prior to the conduct of the research. It is the writer's responsibility to organize the material so that the reader can determine what has come before, what gaps there are in the literature, and how the new research can fill a hole.

I think it would be of value to begin with some traditional ideas about reviews of literature. What is a literature review? This seems like such a straightforward question. A literature review is an account of what has been published on a topic. In writing a literature review, your job is threefold: organize and synthesize what is currently available, identify strengths and weaknesses in the literature, and raise new questions or address areas not yet covered. It is your role to try to organize the material and comment on it in such a way that you convey how well it was done. Some describe it as a critical look or a summary and critical evaluation.

In qualitative research paradigms, the review often takes on a somewhat different function. While some researchers would suggest not conducting a review at all, I think you should consider these alternatives:

- Conduct only a brief review prior to beginning your study and then update and modify it as you collect data. This iterative process helps you maintain an openness that is precluded by an a priori review and avoids leading you down a path already known.
- Select information to review that goes beyond traditional journals and books. Locate information on the Internet that might not be published in other locations. Remember to go into theoretical and philosophical fields as well as some of the newer arenas or those that, at first glance, might not be completely on target.
- In addition to a review of the content of your research, make sure that you review methodological topics that might include how to collect or analyze data; new trends in research paradigms; and postmodern, feminist, or structural arenas.
- Clarify and bracket your thoughts on the topic by writing them down and making them explicit. This process works well for any kind of qualitative research approach but is especially appropriate when you are doing a phenomenological study.
- Integrate your literature review throughout your writing rather than using a traditional approach of placing it in a separate chapter.

The literature review in qualitative research reports may differ from that in the typical quantitative research article, in which all the pertinent literature is reviewed in the introduction to provide a context for the study. When available, it is often useful to cite the important studies published to date that are related to the current study. Alternatively, you may explore the literature sparingly at first to not unduly direct or limit your own research questions or ideas.

IMPORTANCE OF A LITERATURE REVIEW

It has long been a tradition in educational research that a literature review should be conducted prior to actually planning a new piece of research. Most agree that such a review helps the researcher and the reader clarify the current state of research, what has gone before, and what pieces are missing. It then provides a framework for the current research.

In addition to helping readers understand what has come before, a complete literature review might help us understand the theory on which a particular research is based. However, some would argue that theory in relation to qualitative research plays a less critical role because the purpose of most qualitative research is to describe, understand, and interpret and not to test hypotheses.

The limitations of such a review are that it may direct a researcher toward a particular idea or theory and thus not leave open the opportunity to find unexpected things. Another possible drawback to conducting a review prior to embarking on a qualitative research project is that the researcher might not find any relevant research because the topic has not been explored or clearly articulated.

But most would agree that a literature review should be interwoven into the framework of a qualitative research project and be included in the written results. A fully integrated literature review plays a critical role in the researcher's understanding of the relationship between what is presented and what has preceded it. My recommendation when conducting qualitative research is to become familiar with some of the related literature as you proceed with your study, but not be limited by a complete literature review prior to embarking on your own research.

THEORY IN QUALITATIVE RESEARCH

I have been thinking about the role of theory in research. In traditional forms of research we develop hypotheses to test a theory. We gather data and test our hypotheses, often using statistics. Our conclusions assist us in adding to or modifying our theory. You can think about different theories in education. For example, you might be familiar with various theories of learning. Dewey explored how experience influenced learning. Skinner explored the effects of reinforcement on learning. Or you might have studied theories of development. Piaget helped us understand stages of development in young children while Knowles provided us with insight into learning by experience for adults. Over the years, much research has been designed to help test these theories. You could conduct a literature review on either learning theory or human development and identify a large body of literature. Researchers who follow a traditional model have done just that.

But I want to ask whether research can exist without theory. Mitchell and Cody (1993) help us understand several perspectives. While some philosophers and scientists suggest that all knowledge is theory laden and that methods are theory driven, others question the role of theory in qualitative research. These writers contend that since qualitative inquiry is purely inductive, it is not based on any preconceived theory. Mitchell and Cody conclude that inquiry, discovery, and theoretical interpretations coexist simultaneously. Thus, theory does not precede inquiry and discovery but exists as part of the entire process. There are some areas of qualitative research in which you will come across theory, although not in the sense I describe above. For example, grounded theory is an approach that potentially leads to the development of theory as it emerges from the data. Critical theory takes a more active approach and seeks to rid society of oppression and injustices by using knowledge uncovered in the research.[1] Phenomenology is also theory driven. You have read in greater detail about grounded theory and phenomenology in Chapter 5.

SOURCES OF THE LITERATURE FOR A REVIEW

Tradition holds that research that appears in refereed journals should be valued more highly than other research. Reviews are conducted by a jury of peers who presumably review the material objectively. In the ideal world, this might be so. But consider some negative aspects of looking exclusively in journals. Time between writing and publication is often well over a year; thus, information may be outdated by the time it reaches its intended audience. Writers tend to be from the United States, so views from other countries are limited. Some editors may be biased to certain types of qualitative research and may not publish articles that do not fit certain molds. I would suggest that you think beyond print journals for your review.

Limited access to print journals makes their use difficult for those without library access. Some disciplines are looking for alternative ways to present scholarly information. In an effort to serve the scientific community, for example, the American Institute of Physics has decided to provide free access via the Internet to journal abstracts (Marc Brodsky, Executive Director and CEO, American Institute of Physics, personal communication, 2004). Of course, many other sources of scholarly information exist. These include theses and dissertations, conference proceedings, and reports. I have also found quite a bit of valuable information on the Internet. This latter source presents some problems, however, including lack of permanency of Web-based information and lack of peer review.

STEPS IN CONDUCTING A LITERATURE REVIEW

Although Neuman (2003) speaks about four components to a review—surveying what is out there, synthesizing the information, providing a critical analysis of it, and presenting the information—I have elaborated on these ideas and provide you with detailed steps that you will need to follow to conduct a literature review. The steps are identifying and limiting the topic, locating what is out there, reading and evaluating the material to decide what is relevant and critical, sorting and organizing the information you have located into a number of topic areas, and writing what you have in a readable format.

Identifying and Limiting the Research Topic. Let's suppose you are interested in studying teaching mathematics to girls in middle schools. Here are several questions you might ask yourself. Do I want to concentrate on any specific kind of mathematics or should I include all kinds? Would it be important to look at teaching math to boys even if I am not going to study them? How far back should I go in looking up my topic? What do I mean by middle schools? Would it be important to look at elementary and high schools as well? Should I include studies that are related, such as learning mathematics and psychological issues? How do I locate research studies as distinguished from teaching activities or classroom experiences? If I am planning to conduct a qualitative study, do I need to include quantitative studies as well? You can probably generate some other questions, but these are good as you begin to refine your topic. I think with this kind of topic you might find that you have too many studies and you need to narrow down your search.

As the reviewer, it is your responsibility to determine the topic. But I believe that you will find that your topic might change or become altered as you delve into what is available. You might decide that it is in the elementary school literature that most questions are left unanswered, or you might find that you want to expand your topic to include science as well as mathematics. These are all decisions that you make as you begin this task.

Locating What Is Out There. This idea seems so simple yet it is quite challenging. Most of you have access to library facilities (either through traditional means or online or both) at your university. But with the widespread availability of information on the Internet, you might decide to use it as a source as well. I would recommend that you concentrate your search on articles from journals, either hard copy or online, rather than material in textbooks that tends to be older and not necessarily research based. But I believe you also need to be open to examining material from conferences because it tends to be the most recent. One caution: Some material that is on the Internet is just out there and not subject to review by any other group. Some believe that this information is less reliable and should be used with care.

Deciding What Is Critical. Now you have a challenge. You have collected an enormous amount of information from various sources. Can you use all of it? Should you? You need to be the one to evaluate what you read. Does the author provide enough information so that you can determine how the research was done? Whatever the type of study, does the author use appropriate methods? Are the conclusions the author reaches justified by the data presented? How relevant is the particular study to your specific problem? Is one study conducted and described more completely than another? Are some from sources that you can trust more than other sources? You decide.

Deciding What Is Worthy. Ultimately, I believe you need to begin to see yourself as the judge of what is relevant and worthy to inform your own study. While often we tend to rely on research published in established journals, increasingly information from other sources may be of value. Since criteria for judging much of qualitative research are still evolving, you will need to clarify on your own what makes a piece of research useful and suitable for your purposes.

Sorting, Selecting, and Organizing the Information. Now that you have the information, how should you organize it? Suppose you have located 35 studies that seem to be on your topic and that you consider well done. You need to sort these studies into several themes or topics. Although I haven't looked at the literature on this topic, I can imagine that the research could be sorted into topics such as history of teaching math to girls, different methods that have been successful, psychological factors affecting math learning for girls, and comparison of girls and boys in terms of math teaching and learning. If you were to do the sorting, you might choose some other topics. The point here is that you need to decide on some central issues or ideas and organize your studies within these issues. You might find that some studies that you find could fit into more than one issue, but usually that is not the case.

You also need to decide what to include and what to omit. How much detail should you go into? Is it important to include the sample size? Does it matter where the study was done? Should statistical data be included? Should you only include the conclusions that the author stated, or should you draw your own conclusions? How critical can you be of how the study was done? Should you comment on methods used or writing style? Again, these are all questions you need to answer.

As you begin to sift through the information you have collected, I suggest that you find a focus—something that links together the information you have found. You can then use this focus to develop a topic or central idea and sub-ideas. So using the example of math and middle school, your topic or problem statement might be

Educators are beginning to explore teaching methods that focus on attitudes of teachers and female students as they engage in advanced math concepts.

Writing the Review. You are now ready to begin. If you are writing a traditional literature review, your paper should probably have an introduction, the central ideas, and a conclusion. This is a start. Although there are several ways in which you can organize the studies (e.g., chronological, alphabetical, or by trend), in my experience the reviews that tell the best story are organized by themes. Identify the most important theme and place that first.

As you write, consider such things as the use of evidence to support the themes or statements you are making; select only the most important points of a piece of research, use quotes sparingly, avoid the long lists that authors tend to write at the end of their research, summarize and synthesize within each of your themes, take care in paraphrasing so as not to suggest that what you write represents your view, and finally, distinguish between what you think and what others have said.

However, if you are writing a literature review to accompany a qualitative paper, you will often find that you weave your literature into your entire paper. I recall reading a paper by Carolyn Ellis who had three columns in her presentation. One column represented the point of view of the respondent, another column represented the point of view of the research literature, and a third column represented the point of view of the writer. Rather than read in a linear fashion, you could read back and forth between the columns.

EXAMPLES FROM THE FIELD

Although I argue that qualitative researchers have the option of conducting their research throughout the life of the project, when I tried to locate examples for you to review, I found that many still write with a summary and synthesis of related research appearing near the beginning of the work. I have chosen several real and fictitious examples for you to review and use as a guide in writing your own research.

The first one is based on hypothetical literature on the topic of teaching math to middle school girls. It illustrates the use of a central thesis and critical interpretation of what is being offered.

Fictitious Literature Review Example

While math is a subject that has always been taught at the middle school level, it is only since 19XX that an interest has developed in the topic. Achievement test scores reveal that beginning in about the eighth grade, girls do not perform as well as boys (cite references here). This finding is consistent among minority groups (cite reference), across different countries (cite reference), and for different kinds of math (e.g., algebra or general math).

It is surprising that different teaching methods do not seem to make a difference. Some have explored teaching math to classes of girls only (cite references), while others have explored using manipulatives and concrete examples (cite references). In a recent large-scale study in the XXX school system, math was taught to girls attending classes with girls only. Girls did engage in activities and reported doing their homework. They also liked what they did. Yet when given math achievement tests, their scores were significantly lower than those of boys (cite reference).

I found several shortcomings in the literature. Much of the research was conducted some years ago, and it appears that it is time to explore this topic more fully now. Many of the references I located were not based on research; rather, they were accounts by a single teacher of what had been done in a classroom.

Of course, this example is fictitious. I use it to illustrate the point that what you include should be directly on the topic, that you need to include different sections, and you need to include only information that is directly relevant. You can include your own comments about the relevance and recency of the research if you choose to do so.

Another effective way of presenting your research is to build a table that summarizes what you found. Here is a rubric for such a table.

Authors	Title	Date	Source	Sample Size	Type of Study	Findings	Critical Comment

I don't mean to give the impression that such a table is sufficient for writing your review; it leaves out the critical component of integrating the studies. But it is a good way for you to see what you have and for others to judge what you will present.

Neuman (as reported in O'Loughlin-Brooks, n.d.) offers two illustrations of how the topic of sexual harassment might be presented

Example of a Bad Review: Sexual harassment has many consequences. Adams, Kottke, and Padgitt (1983) found that some women students said they avoided taking a class or working with certain professors because of the risk of harassment. They also found that men and women students reacted differently. Their research was a survey of 1,000 men and women graduate and undergraduate students. Benson and Thomson's study in *Social Problems* (1982) lists many problems created by sexual harassment. In their excellent book, *The Lecherous Professor,* Dziech and Weiner (1990) give a long list of difficulties that victims have suffered.

Example of a Better Review: The victims of sexual harassment suffer a range of consequences, from lowered self-esteem and loss of self-confidence to withdrawal from social interaction, changed career goals, and depression (Adams, Kottke, and Padgitt, 1983; Benson and Thomson, 1982; Dziech and Weiner, 1990). For example, Adams, Kottke, and Padgitt (1983) noted that 13 percent of women students said they avoided taking a class or working with certain professors because of the risk of harassment.

At first reading, these two examples seem quite similar. But notice in the second example the writer introduces the subject by speaking of some of the consequences of sexual harassment rather than just stating that there are consequences. The information is summarized and attribution is provided. It takes considerable organizational ability and time to integrate the information you find.

Another example I have chosen for you is a simple paragraph on the topic of sexism and language.

However, other studies have shown that even gender-neutral antecedents are more likely to produce masculine images than feminine ones (Gastil, 1990). Hamilton (1988) asked students to complete sentences that required them to fill in pronouns that agreed with gender-neutral antecedents such as "writer," "pedestrian," and "persons." The students were asked to describe any image they had when writing the sentence. Hamilton found that people imagined 3.3 men to each woman in the masculine "generic" condition and 1.5 men per woman in the unbiased condition. Thus, while ambient sexism accounted for some of the masculine bias, sexist language amplified the effect. (Falk & Mills, 1996)

Adolescent Depression 2

Adolescent Depression and Attachment

Depression affects over 20% of adolescents. It is a disorder taht disturbs their mood, causes a loss of interest or pleasure in activities they should enjoy, and makes them irritable. Several things are thought to be correlated with depression in adolescents. Some examples include, a failure to individuate, insecure attachments, negative parental representations, etc (Milne & Lancaster, 2001; Olsson, Nordstrom, Arinell, & Knorring, 1999). In the present paper, the role attachment plays in adolescent depression is investigated. It is hypothesized that insecurely attached adolescents, (ambivalent or avoidant), will display higher levels of depression related symptoms and behaviors than securely attached adolescents. The following five literature reviews attempt to demonstrate and support the hypothesis.

Explains why topic is important.

Studies are listed in alphabetical order.

Gives reader an idea of what the paper will cover.

This is considered jargon and needs to be explained.

Focuses only on reviewing literature that supports hypothesis.

SOURCE: Online Writing Lab (2004).

Notice that these writers do not use any quotes but restate their findings in their own words.

Above is a literature review written by a student with comments on the way different sections enhance or detract from the review. The topic of the review is adolescent depression and attachment. You should find the specific comments very helpful as you develop your own writing.

The next illustration is taken from an interpretative biographical interview. An extensive reference list is included, but the authors choose to place most of the related literature toward the end of the paper.

As researchers in a qualitative-interpretive tradition, we are open to the findings our analysis generates; we are not out to prove a point, or a set of hypotheses. Inspired by the theoretical foundation and procedures of grounded theory, we are prepared to suspend general assumptions concerning the materials of our analysis, towards attaining "descriptive and sensitizing" (Glaser & Strauss, 1967) concepts. We are aware, however, that our analysis cannot take place "outside of" the contested arenas of Turkish immigration to Germany. If we want to be able to understand what our interview partners are talking about or referring to, we have to take into account how they position themselves within these arenas. We cannot reconstruct their biographical accounts without also reflecting our perceptions and possible positions concerning the issues at stake. Obviously, interpretive analyses can also meaningfully proceed from other perspectives, as documented by other contributions to this issue. Otherwise, doing biographical analysis would be restricted to cases of one's own country and knowledge of the intricacies of debated issues, or to a prolonged study of such debates in the places where interviews have taken place. Our analytical perspective is not prescriptive and certainly not exclusive. But given our situated knowledge as researchers, in Donna Haraway's sense (1991), we cannot abstract from social contexts or from critically examining undisputed beliefs in general public, political, academic terms, which all coincide in that migration is basically and essentially a problematic phenomenon. (Gültekin, Inowlocki, & Lutz, 2003, ¶ 53)

Wright's (2004) case study of teacher burnout in a prison does not include a formal review of research. He incorporates relevant studies throughout his paper, however, and includes a very extensive bibliography. Here are several examples. "In this penal discourse women were positioned (Davies & Harre, 1990) as subjects rather, than objects" (p. 631). "They are the outcomes of a quest for meaning and order (Geertz, 1973). For critical theorists, ideologies articulate the interests of dominant classes through state apparatuses such as prisons (Edgar & Sedwick, 1999)" (p. 632). "I read the transcripts numerous times until I discerned topics which I further examined, chunked and codified into categories and themes (Merriam, 1988)" (p. 634). He very effectively includes literature that relates both to the content of his study and the methodological issues.

I would have liked to see Efinger, Maldonado, and McArdle (2004) provide a better synthesis of their very interesting research. Here is a sample from their recent article on a phenomenological study of Ph.D. students' perceptions of the relationship between philosophy and research.

Each of these theories has had its champions throughout the centuries; likewise, each theory has its own inherent problems. Nevertheless, those who propose research studies may want to consider determining which of these theories is likely to provide a sufficient basis for knowledge and a solid foundation for yielding the truth (Moser & Vander Nat, 1995).

Clark (1998) discusses the positivist view, noting that truth "in positivist inquiry is achieved through the verification and replication of observable findings concerning directly perceivable entities or processes" (¶ 15). Denzin and Lincoln (2000) explain that positivist social science relies on four criteria: internal validity, external validity, reliability, and objectivity. Secretan (1997) points out Sir Isaac Newton's contributions, noting that since the time of Newton, "controlled observation, experimentation, and mechanics" have governed not only "a causal, logical approach to science" but the lives of those in the western world as well (p. 32).

Zucker (1996) maintains that "the positivist claim [is] that scientific explanation is best seen as deduction" (p. 67). Hempel's (1965) covering law model, discussed by Clayton (1997) stipulated "the ideal for science is to formulate 'lawlike' or 'deductive-nomological' explanations." Clayton continued, noting that these explanations "specify the antecedent conditions and the 'covering laws' that pertain to a given situation. . . . [therefore] the thing to be explained (the explanandum) must follow deductively from the conditions and laws" (¶ 7).

Freeman's (2000) ethnography involves what she refers to as a layered text format. Although it includes a dozen or so references, it does not have a section called "Review of Research." Rather, it begins,

It is a cold but bright March afternoon. I am walking through a subsidized housing complex knocking on doors of people who have been identified as having school-age children. There are 110 newly remodeled apartments standing in rows. (p. 359)

The author goes on to quote some relevant references defining ethnography and dealing with culture. She explains a layered account and how she came to use it in her work.

PRACTICAL SUGGESTIONS FOR KEEPING TRACK OF THINGS

The explosion of information is overwhelming. How should you keep track of it? How can you organize it so that you can locate specifics? Where should you keep it? Should you have a hard copy of everything? If so, how do you manage it? Here are some tips that work well for me.

Use your computer. I can't imagine how I finished my own dissertation without the aid of a computer or typist. At that time, students spent many hours in a library, reading and taking notes on 3" × 5" or 5" × 8" cards in different colors. Usually you could obtain a half dozen or so colors. You would find an article, copy the citation, summarize what you read, and perhaps make a comment or two about its quality. All too often, however, you neglected to copy all the relevant information (especially page numbers) and you would have to locate the citation again when compiling your reference list. If you could figure it out, you would choose a different color card for each topic. But often this went astray, and some articles had more than one important idea in them. I don't know whether I have my old note cards, but I suspect that I have them stored where my data cards are for my own dissertation.

Well, you don't need to do that anymore. Most universities will let you download what you need to your own computer. If you are working at the library or not at your own computer, some systems will let you send an e-mail to yourself with references. Here is where your organizational skills come in handy. I strongly advocate starting out with a system, so create a file on your hard drive where you want to keep all your references. Download abstracts and citations. Make sure you save this file in more than one location—usually on your hard drive and on a removable flash drive.

Use technology. Consider talking about the literature rather than writing about it. You can watch videos of two scholars discussing writing the literature review at the following Web site: http://www.library.cqu.edu.au/tutorials/litreviewpages/writing.htm. I enjoyed the interplay between these researchers as they talked about the literature.

Invest in computer software for citations. I cannot tell you how many hours my students spend trying to get their citations formatted correctly and making sure that what they write in their paper also appears in their reference list and vice versa. I know many of you are on tight budgets, but it is a tremendous advantage if you can find the extra money for citation software. I have been very pleased with **EndNote,** which you can find at http://www.endnote .com/. A word of caution: These programs still require careful checking and sometimes lack compatibility with other programs on your computer.

Use qualitative software to access your database. Di Gregorio (2000) provides clear directions on how to use NVivo to organize and access your related literature. This will save you an enormous amount of time later as you progress through your writing. Another advantage to using qualitative software is that you can integrate the research literature with your own research and thus write it up in a more comprehensive manner.

SUMMARY

In this chapter I argue that alternatives to a traditional review of the literature are possible and sometimes desirable when doing qualitative research. I suggest that conducting a comprehensive literature review prior to doing research and treating it as a separate task leads to narrowness and irrelevancy for such a review. Instead, I offer the notion that you might want to do a brief review as a starting point that becomes modified and enhanced as you begin your own research. I also suggest that you consider incorporating your information throughout your writing rather than limiting it to a separate section. I continue to reflect on the idea that your writing should be personal and that your own ideas need to be expressed.

GROUP ACTIVITY

Purpose: To develop a framework for a literature review on the topic of My Life as a Graduate Student.

   Activity: Working with a partner, brainstorm a list of possible topics that might be covered in a review. Refine your list so that you have no more than five topics. Present your list to other group members and eventually develop a master list from the entire class.

   Evaluation: Look at novel ideas that students develop and how they organize their thoughts.

INDIVIDUAL ACTIVITY

Purpose: To gather information from various sources.

   Activity: Use at least one search engine, one online journal, and one paper journal to explore possible topics on the theme of My Life as a Graduate Student.

   Evaluation: Look at the creativity and openness of the students.

CHAPTER 8

Learning About Others Through Interviewing

Know how to listen, and you will profit even from those who talk badly.

—Plutarch

Asking people to share their experiences seems like a simple task but formulating a methodology-based study design can be filled with challenges; who is to be surveyed, how many interviews is enough, how do you formulate questions that encourage study participants to respond openly and honestly, how do you gain a rapport with the study participants and get them involved with your study, writing field notes and observations, transcribing the data, coding the data, sorting the data by categories of response, analyzing and interpreting the data? These were but a few of the challenges that I faced.

—Warren Snyder

Y ou have read a great deal about qualitative research. You know some theory and you have practiced gathering data. You have read what others have done and their thoughts about the process. You know something about how the field began, where it has been, and where it is going. Now I want you to learn what is available to you as you embark on your research. I want you to think about how you might go about gathering your own data.

There are a variety of methods used by qualitative researchers to gather data. In this chapter I describe qualitative interviewing (on a continuum from high structure to low or no structure), focus group interviewing (again on a continuum), and online interviewing. In Chapter 9, I discuss observing in natural settings, using images (created by informants, created by the researcher), accessing chat rooms and online discussion groups (created by informants, created by the researcher), and using diaries and written material from informants (created by informants or stimulated by the researcher).

Before you begin to read about details of each technique, I provide you with a brief overview of different types of interviewing. Each is designed to let you get "the story" from the point of view of the participant. As the researcher, you become the instrument or tool through which participants tell their stories.

- *Qualitative interviewing.* Qualitative interviewing is a general term used to describe a group of methods that permit you to engage in a dialogue or conversation with the participant. While it is a conversation, it is usually orchestrated and directed by you. This can be considered a conversation with a purpose. Usually these interviews are unstructured, but they may be guided by a general set of questions. Some type of interviewing is used in almost all types of qualitative research. There are several types of interviews that are described below, including in-depth interviews, semi-structured interviews, and informal or casual interviews.
- *Focus group interviewing.* A focus group is a special type of interview, usually called a group interview. Its purpose is to provide opportunities for members of a group to interact with each other and stimulate each other's thinking. It is not desirable or necessary for the group to reach consensus in their discussion.
- *Online interviewing.* Online interviewing can run the gamut from informal chat rooms or Listservs to organized and planned e-mail interviews with a single individual. Its purpose is similar to other forms of interviewing.

QUALITATIVE INTERVIEWING

There is so much to tell you about interviewing. It seems so easy. "Just a little conversation between two people. I can do that," you will say to yourself. In this section, I will talk about the purpose of interviewing, provide you with a specific interview protocol that I have developed, and offer some examples of interviews. By the time you finish reading this section, you will be well on your way to conducting a successful interview.

Interviewing is the most common form of data collection in qualitative research. We have all had experience being interviewed or with interviewing. In some instances, interviews are very informal and have little planning at all. You have been interviewed when you visit your doctor and she asks how you are feeling and follows up with additional questions. You have been interviewed when you entered graduate school. Sometimes these interviews are quite formal and follow a strict protocol. In other instances, the interviews may be much more casual. You have been interviewed when you apply for a job, participate in therapy, or talk on the telephone to a marketer. I have no doubt that each of you has had one of these kinds of experiences or ones similar to them.

Many of you have also had experience conducting interviews. You might have interviewed your client, if you are a counselor. You might have interviewed a parent in a special education planning meeting. You might have interviewed a fellow teacher to learn about new techniques.

Many of these interview situations were not planned; they may seem more like discussions than interviews. In some ways, qualitative interviewing might seem like a discussion or a conversation. I want to emphasize, however, whether you adopt a very structured approach or whether you take an unstructured view, there is still planning and thought in advance of the interview.

The Purpose of Interviewing

The purpose of conducting an interview is the same no matter whether you use a structured and formal style or select an unstructured, conversational style. You are gathering information from your participant about the topic you are studying. What does she think about the experience of a new reading program? What does he feel about the new grading policy in your county? What is the culture of your organization and how does it relate to your individual needs? These are all topics you might be studying.

Your goal might be to learn what your interviewee thinks or feels about certain things, or your goal might be to explore the shared meanings that people have who live or work together (Rubin & Rubin, 1995). In either case, you need to think about an interview in this way. You, as the interviewer and researcher, are trying to set up a situation in which the individual being interviewed will reveal to you his or her feelings, intentions, meanings, subcontexts, or thoughts on a topic, situation, or group. It is critical to remember that you are not trying to determine these things as if you did not exist or were some kind of fly on the wall that could transmit the ideas directly. In qualitative research, each idea, interpretation, and plan is filtered through your eyes, through your mind, and through your point of view. You are not trying to do away with your role as you would if you were conducting traditional experimental research. You are not trying to be objective. You will take the role of constructing and subsequently interpreting the reality of the person being interviewed, but your own lens is critical. I think the most difficult task a novice researcher faces is what to do about his or her own role. Should she strive to approximate objectivity? Should she gather multiple sources and use triangulation to make sure that what she says is right? Should she get others—especially those with higher status or authority—to verify that what she writes is the way it is? I would answer all these questions with a resounding NO. I want you to reexamine the assumptions I mention earlier in the book. Accept that there is no single objective reality that you strive for. Accept that you, as the researcher, serve as the filter through which information is gathered, processed, and organized.

A few words about who is being interviewed. You may have heard a number of different terms used to describe the individual you interview. In traditional experimental research, the person being studied is usually called the subject. In anthropological terms, the person being studied is usually called the informant. Feminists tend to use the term co-researcher, acknowledging the shared role between interviewer and person being interviewed. I have also heard the terms interviewee, discussant, partner, and conversational partner. Rubin and Rubin (1995) use "interviewees," "informants," and "conversational partners" depending on the situation. Now you might ask why it matters what the individuals are named. I think it matters a great deal. In traditional research, the term "subject" is meant to be informative and neutral. Yet some have interpreted this term in a negative manner, suggesting that the relationship between the interviewer and the person being interviewed is hierarchical—I am the king, you are my subject. Feminist research describes a dilemma regarding power and the position of the researcher. While there are many terms used to refer to the person being interviewed, it is interesting to me that I have not read about alternative names for the interviewer.

The Structured Interview. You can conduct a standardized or structured interview where the questions and format are the same for each individual. This type of interviewing is an example more often associated with survey research rather than qualitative research. I think most qualitative researchers would *not* recommend that you use this approach. This kind of interview is designed to eliminate the role of the researcher and to introduce objectivity into the situation. You will remember that I do not believe that qualitative research is about objectivity and the omission of bias. I want you to be aware of this type of interviewing technique, but I do not recommend you use it.

The Guided Interview. Another type of interview is the semi-structured or guided interview. This type of interview involves your developing a general set of questions and format that you follow and use on all participants. While the general structure is the same for all individuals being interviewed, the interviewer can vary the questions as the situation demands. I find that some individuals like this format because they feel uncomfortable with not having a clear set of guidelines to follow. Most new interviewers seem to like to have something to use for guidance.

The In-depth Interview. My preference, however, is to use in-depth, unstructured interviewing techniques. I first encountered this kind of interviewing when I read McCracken's (1988) *The Long Interview.* I was so drawn to his writing. For once someone laid out a style of interviewing that did not recommend a specific set of questions. You might think of this as an informal conversation. Although McCracken suggests that a formal set of biographical questions should be used, he recognizes that "the first objective of the qualitative interview is to allow respondents to tell their own story in their own terms" (p. 34). He reminds us that the investigator should remain unobtrusive and ask questions in a general and nondirective manner. Rubin and Rubin (1995) spoke to me when they said that qualitative interviewing "is a great adventure . . . [it] brings new information and opens windows into the experiences of the people you meet" (p. 1). One year later, Kvale (1996) reminds us that qualitative interviewing is a "professional conversation" (p. 5). In keeping with the intent of letting the respondent talk, Boeree (1998) suggests that you should not force the person in any one direction.

Casual or Unplanned Interviews. Often when you are in the field conducting either a case study or an ethnography, opportunities arise for you to talk to some of your participants.

General Issues in Interviewing

Identification of Participants. Who should be interviewed, how should they be identified, and how should they be contacted? Typically, the researcher has identified specific characteristics of individuals to study. She might want to study young pregnant middle school girls, or boys in gangs, or students from homes of divorce, or students who are highly successful in school, or first year teachers, or women principals. After identifying the type of person to be interviewed, the researcher needs to contact individuals who meet the criteria. One way researchers have used to identify additional participants is to ask those already contacted to name others with similar characteristics. This technique, called snowball sampling, is quite useful when studying hidden or hard to reach participants. Atkinson and Flint (2001) provide many examples of the use of the technique. Another issue regarding participants is determining how many should be interviewed. You may know that in quantitative research, determining a suitable sample size depends on how much variation there is in the population and how much sampling error you are willing to accept. Because your goal in qualitative research is to describe and interpret rather than to generalize, there are no hard rules about how many you should study. Sandelowski (1995) suggests that determining sample size is a matter of judgment. For her, there are times when a sample of 10 might be seen as adequate (p. 179). Most qualitative research studies use a small number of individuals and cover material in depth. It is quite common to see studies with fewer than 10 respondents; sometimes only a single person is studied.

Developing Rapport. It is important that you learn to develop rapport in order to have an interview that generates meaningful and useful data. Ultimately you seek cooperation and participation of the person you are interviewing. I don't think I can stress too much that you should include time at the beginning of each interview to establish rapport. We all talk about this and assume that we know how to do it. You could probably develop your own list of what you should do: be relaxed, make the interviewee feel comfortable, be accepting.

Selecting a Setting. Most interviews you conduct will be in a mutually agreed upon location. It is obvious that the location should be quiet and private, to the extent possible. If you go to the home or office of your participant, you can gain a considerable amount of information. I like to look around and take notes. If in an office, does the participant display photographs? What other personal items are around? How does the individual office relate to the larger setting in which it is located? If you are in a school, you may have to "settle" for less than ideal circumstances because there is not usually a private room available for your use.

Observing Surroundings. It is a good idea for you to pay attention to physical surroundings and to the person you are interviewing. Keep notes about your observations. Does the person appear comfortable or fidgety? Does he look at you? Of course, if you are conducting your interviews in cyberspace you would need to begin to develop a sense of what to look for online. Does the person use shorthand in writing? What time constraints exist between your questions and responses?

Details About In-depth Interviewing

Individual **in-depth interviews** are a type of qualitative interviewing that is described by some as a conversation between interviewer and participant (McCracken, 1988; Rubin & Rubin, 1995). Our purpose in such a style of interviewing is to hear what the participant has to say in her own words, in her voice, with her language and narrative. In this way, participants can share what they know and have learned and can add a dimension to our understanding of the situation that questionnaire data does not reveal.

Individual in-depth interviewing is more a process, not just a predetermined list of questions. I want to talk, here, about the interviewing process. The process builds in several stages.

It begins with developing rapport and getting the participant to trust you and to open up to you. While procedures are quite well established for interviewing adults, they need to be modified somewhat when interviewing students, especially those who might be suspicious of adults in formal school situations. Whether you are interviewing adults or children, it is advisable to talk about why you are there, why they have been selected to be interviewed, and how you will use what you learn from them.

Once rapport has been established, it is desirable to find a way to connect with the participant and his or her experiences. This is especially true if you are following a phenomenological tradition of qualitative research. If you are interviewing students, one way that works well is to have students relate stories about their school successes. If you are interviewing adults, you might try to ask them about a recent experience that had a meaningful effect. This use of the concrete guarantees a rich source of data.

Following the introduction of the use of the concrete lived experiences, I suggest you ask a Grand Tour question (McCracken, 1988; Spradley, 1979). This type of question will take the form "Tell me what being in school is like for you" or "What can you say about going to the X school?" The interview proceeds according to the information I have provided below.

It is important to remember that you want to capture the words and ideas of the person you are interviewing. This will be a rich source of data as you begin your qualitative analysis. To the extent possible, the interview should be recorded.

I think it will be helpful to you if you think in advance about five main components of interviews: advanced planning, the opening, getting started, the body of the interview, and the end of the interview.

1. *Advanced Planning.* Since you will not be using a standardized set of questions, you need to think about what you will be doing.
   - Identify 5 to 10 topic areas that you want to make sure you will cover in your interview. Remember, these are to be used as guidelines and you are not necessarily going to use all of them. I like to put these on a single piece of paper with space between each one. Sometimes you need only one question and the interview rolls right along.
   - You can look in the literature about the topic, but I believe that it tends to put blinders on you and that it is better to conduct your literature review at a later time. Use your knowledge of the topic and your common sense to generate your topic areas.
   - Identify some demographic areas that you think you will want to cover with each participant (e.g., marital status, children, or work history). Often these come up in the course of the interview, but you should make them explicit. I also put these on a single piece of paper with space between each one. Of course, the areas to cover are directed by the purpose of your survey.
   - There are three questions that you can use to start with. (1) Tell me a little about yourself. (2) Tell me something that happened to you last week about X. (X is the topic you are studying. Suppose X is "being a sixth-grade student." Then the question is "Tell me something that happened to you last week in your class.") (3) Let's talk about being or doing X (X is the topic. The question is "What is it like to be a student at this school?") Notice that all three questions are personal, immediate, and directed at the topic. They are not "yes" or "no" questions. They usually get the respondent to open up somewhat.

2. *The Opening.* Before you actually begin the interview, you usually have to provide some preliminary information. This would usually include (1) why you are there, (2) your purpose, (3) what you will do with the information, (4) how you will keep the information confidential, and (5) how long the interview will take.

   - You will need to obtain permission to conduct the interview. You might have to obtain a signed formal permission or agreement. Different institutions have different requirements. You should locate the requirements of an institutional review board at your institution. You will need to treat permission from children different than permission from adults.
   - In addition to having your respondent give you permission to conduct an interview, you should ask for permission to use a tape recorder.

3. *Getting Started.* Now that you are finished with preliminaries, it is time to set the stage to conduct your interview. Actually, I think if you get started on a positive note, the interview will proceed smoothly.

   - Develop rapport by introducing chitchat. While it may seem to you that you are wasting time that you would more profitably use to get at the crux of information, this time is invaluable in getting your respondent to be willing to cooperate with you.
   - Make the person feel comfortable. You can do this by using laughter, smiles, and nods. You can offer some personal story about yourself, for example, how long it took you to drive to the site, what fun you had at a recent sporting event, getting your own children ready for school. I stress that you try to remain connected to your respondent rather than staying aloof.
   - One way to get people to feel comfortable is to ask them to say a little bit about themselves (if they say, "What?" say, "Anything you want to share"). Since you have already shared some personal information, they may be more inclined to do so. All of these preliminaries are used so that your respondent feels comfortable with you.

4. *The Body of the Interview.* You are now ready to continue with your interview.

   - Use your semi- or unstructured guidelines to make the interview progress more smoothly.
   - Don't try to take complete notes; it is almost impossible to do so. But do take notes of questions or comments that you want to follow up. Sometimes you will want to probe more fully, but do not interrupt as the interview progresses.
   - Concentrate on listening to what is said and planning your next questions. Perhaps it is like a game of chess; you have some moves and plans, but your opponent may fool you.

5. *The End of the Interview.* Stay aware of the time.

   - My favorite final question is "Do you have anything you want to add that we have not talked about?" You will be so surprised at what you learn.
   - Thank them for their participation.
   - Upon completion of interview, take some time to get your materials in order. Mark tapes, put notes away.
   - Write down your own thoughts and reactions in your journal after the interview is over.

Interviewing Techniques

Conducting in-depth unstructured interviews takes a considerable amount of planning and experience. It may look easy, but it really takes quite a bit of forethought. Now that you have considered the five main components of an in-depth qualitative interview, I want you to begin to think about the questions themselves. I have found that many people focus on the content of the questions. They are inclined to develop a list of questions that they think they want to ask. In my experience, this is a very rigid format and closes the interview rather than expanding it. I would like you to think about questioning in two ways. One way involves the type of questions you might ask; I offer you several types below with some specific examples. The second way is to consider questioning strategies. I provide specific examples of such strategies below. This section concludes with some special areas of concern.

Types of Questions

While you can choose which order to follow, I almost always begin either with a Grand Tour Question or a Specific Example Question.

1. Grand Tour Question. This question gives the participant an opportunity to be open and it should be nondirective. It is a good way to begin because the participant can get started talking to you. Your stance should be open and nonjudgmental.

   #### Examples

   - Very general—What is it like being a graduate student?
   - More specific—How do you see stress related to being a graduate student?

   - Very general—What is it like to work in this organization?
   - More specific—How is it working in this organization with regard to X?

   - Very general—As a new teacher, tell me some of the things you feel.
   - More specific—What are concerns you have as a new teacher in terms of working with parents (with other staff members, with troubled students)?

   - Very general—How would you describe a day in the life of a principal (student, retired person)?
   - More specific—Your challenge as a principal is to modify the discipline at your school. What are some things you have been thinking about along these lines?

2. Specific Examples Questions. This type of question gives the participant an opportunity to be concrete and specific and provide relevant information. A concrete example works well because it is personal and immediate. It is important that it is a specific story rather than some general statement. It helps avoid using jargon and giving responses that the participant thinks you, the researcher, want to hear.

   #### Examples

   - Tell me something that happened at this school that you think is a direct result of the new Site-Based Management plan.
   - What was something that happened last week that you think relates to your stress?

Interviewing Techniques

Conducting in-depth unstructured interviews takes a considerable amount of planning and experience. It may look easy, but it really takes quite a bit of forethought. Now that you have considered the five main components of an in-depth qualitative interview, I want you to begin to think about the questions themselves. I have found that many people focus on the content of the questions. They are inclined to develop a list of questions that they think they want to ask. In my experience, this is a very rigid format and closes the interview rather than expanding it. I would like you to think about questioning in two ways. One way involves the type of questions you might ask; I offer you several types below with some specific examples. The second way is to consider questioning strategies. I provide specific examples of such strategies below. This section concludes with some special areas of concern.

Types of Questions

While you can choose which order to follow, I almost always begin either with a Grand Tour Question or a Specific Example Question.

1. Grand Tour Question. This question gives the participant an opportunity to be open and it should be nondirective. It is a good way to begin because the participant can get started talking to you. Your stance should be open and nonjudgmental.

Examples

- Very general—What is it like being a graduate student?
- More specific—How do you see stress related to being a graduate student?

- Very general—What is it like to work in this organization?
- More specific—How is it working in this organization with regard to X?

- Very general—As a new teacher, tell me some of the things you feel.
- More specific—What are concerns you have as a new teacher in terms of working with parents (with other staff members, with troubled students)?

- Very general—How would you describe a day in the life of a principal (student, retired person)?
- More specific—Your challenge as a principal is to modify the discipline at your school. What are some things you have been thinking about along these lines?

2. Specific Examples Questions. This type of question gives the participant an opportunity to be concrete and specific and provide relevant information. A concrete example works well because it is personal and immediate. It is important that it is a specific story rather than some general statement. It helps avoid using jargon and giving responses that the participant thinks you, the researcher, want to hear.

Examples

- Tell me something that happened at this school that you think is a direct result of the new Site-Based Management plan.
- What was something that happened last week that you think relates to your stress?

studying hidden or hard to reach participants. Atkinson and Flint (2001) provide many examples of the use of the technique. Another issue regarding participants is determining how many should be interviewed. You may know that in quantitative research, determining a suitable sample size depends on how much variation there is in the population and how much sampling error you are willing to accept. Because your goal in qualitative research is to describe and interpret rather than to generalize, there are no hard rules about how many you should study. Sandelowski (1995) suggests that determining sample size is a matter of judgment. For her, there are times when a sample of 10 might be seen as adequate (p. 179). Most qualitative research studies use a small number of individuals and cover material in depth. It is quite common to see studies with fewer than 10 respondents; sometimes only a single person is studied.

Developing Rapport. It is important that you learn to develop rapport in order to have an interview that generates meaningful and useful data. Ultimately you seek cooperation and participation of the person you are interviewing. I don't think I can stress too much that you should include time at the beginning of each interview to establish rapport. We all talk about this and assume that we know how to do it. You could probably develop your own list of what you should do: be relaxed, make the interviewee feel comfortable, be accepting.

Selecting a Setting. Most interviews you conduct will be in a mutually agreed upon location. It is obvious that the location should be quiet and private, to the extent possible. If you go to the home or office of your participant, you can gain a considerable amount of information. I like to look around and take notes. If in an office, does the participant display photographs? What other personal items are around? How does the individual office relate to the larger setting in which it is located? If you are in a school, you may have to "settle" for less than ideal circumstances because there is not usually a private room available for your use.

Observing Surroundings. It is a good idea for you to pay attention to physical surroundings and to the person you are interviewing. Keep notes about your observations. Does the person appear comfortable or fidgety? Does he look at you? Of course, if you are conducting your interviews in cyberspace you would need to begin to develop a sense of what to look for online. Does the person use shorthand in writing? What time constraints exist between your questions and responses?

Details About In-depth Interviewing

Individual **in-depth interviews** are a type of qualitative interviewing that is described by some as a conversation between interviewer and participant (McCracken, 1988; Rubin & Rubin, 1995). Our purpose in such a style of interviewing is to hear what the participant has to say in her own words, in her voice, with her language and narrative. In this way, participants can share what they know and have learned and can add a dimension to our understanding of the situation that questionnaire data does not reveal.

Individual in-depth interviewing is more a process, not just a predetermined list of questions. I want to talk, here, about the interviewing process. The process builds in several stages.

It begins with developing rapport and getting the participant to trust you and to open up to you. While procedures are quite well established for interviewing adults, they need to be modified somewhat when interviewing students, especially those who might be suspicious of adults in formal school situations. Whether you are interviewing adults or children, it is advisable to talk about why you are there, why they have been selected to be interviewed, and how you will use what you learn from them.

Once rapport has been established, it is desirable to find a way to connect with the participant and his or her experiences. This is especially true if you are following a phenomenological tradition of qualitative research. If you are interviewing students, one way that works well is to have students relate stories about their school successes. If you are interviewing adults, you might try to ask them about a recent experience that had a meaningful effect. This use of the concrete guarantees a rich source of data.

Following the introduction of the use of the concrete lived experiences, I suggest you ask a Grand Tour question (McCracken, 1988; Spradley, 1979). This type of question will take the form "Tell me what being in school is like for you" or "What can you say about going to the X school?" The interview proceeds according to the information I have provided below.

It is important to remember that you want to capture the words and ideas of the person you are interviewing. This will be a rich source of data as you begin your qualitative analysis. To the extent possible, the interview should be recorded.

I think it will be helpful to you if you think in advance about five main components of interviews: advanced planning, the opening, getting started, the body of the interview, and the end of the interview.

1. *Advanced Planning.* Since you will not be using a standardized set of questions, you need to think about what you will be doing.
   - Identify 5 to 10 topic areas that you want to make sure you will cover in your interview. Remember, these are to be used as guidelines and you are not necessarily going to use all of them. I like to put these on a single piece of paper with space between each one. Sometimes you need only one question and the interview rolls right along.
   - You can look in the literature about the topic, but I believe that it tends to put blinders on you and that it is better to conduct your literature review at a later time. Use your knowledge of the topic and your common sense to generate your topic areas.
   - Identify some demographic areas that you think you will want to cover with each participant (e.g., marital status, children, or work history). Often these come up in the course of the interview, but you should make them explicit. I also put these on a single piece of paper with space between each one. Of course, the areas to cover are directed by the purpose of your survey.
   - There are three questions that you can use to start with. (1) Tell me a little about yourself. (2) Tell me something that happened to you last week about X. (X is the topic you are studying. Suppose X is "being a sixth-grade student." Then the question is "Tell me something that happened to you last week in your class.") (3) Let's talk about being or doing X (X is the topic. The question is "What is it like to be a student at this school?") Notice that all three questions are personal, immediate, and directed at the topic. They are not "yes" or "no" questions. They usually get the respondent to open up somewhat.

2. *The Opening.* Before you actually begin the interview, you usually have to provide some preliminary information. This would usually include (1) why you are there, (2) your purpose, (3) what you will do with the information, (4) how you will keep the information confidential, and (5) how long the interview will take.
   - You will need to obtain permission to conduct the interview. You might have to obtain a signed formal permission or agreement. Different institutions have different requirements. You should locate the requirements of an institutional review board at your institution. You will need to treat permission from children different than permission from adults.
   - In addition to having your respondent give you permission to conduct an interview, you should ask for permission to use a tape recorder.

3. *Getting Started.* Now that you are finished with preliminaries, it is time to set the stage to conduct your interview. Actually, I think if you get started on a positive note, the interview will proceed smoothly.
   - Develop rapport by introducing chitchat. While it may seem to you that you are wasting time that you would more profitably use to get at the crux of information, this time is invaluable in getting your respondent to be willing to cooperate with you.
   - Make the person feel comfortable. You can do this by using laughter, smiles, and nods. You can offer some personal story about yourself, for example, how long it took you to drive to the site, what fun you had at a recent sporting event, getting your own children ready for school. I stress that you try to remain connected to your respondent rather than staying aloof.
   - One way to get people to feel comfortable is to ask them to say a little bit about themselves (if they say, "What?" say, "Anything you want to share"). Since you have already shared some personal information, they may be more inclined to do so. All of these preliminaries are used so that your respondent feels comfortable with you.

4. *The Body of the Interview.* You are now ready to continue with your interview.
   - Use your semi- or unstructured guidelines to make the interview progress more smoothly.
   - Don't try to take complete notes; it is almost impossible to do so. But do take notes of questions or comments that you want to follow up. Sometimes you will want to probe more fully, but do not interrupt as the interview progresses.
   - Concentrate on listening to what is said and planning your next questions. Perhaps it is like a game of chess; you have some moves and plans, but your opponent may fool you.

5. *The End of the Interview.* Stay aware of the time.
   - My favorite final question is "Do you have anything you want to add that we have not talked about?" You will be so surprised at what you learn.
   - Thank them for their participation.
   - Upon completion of interview, take some time to get your materials in order. Mark tapes, put notes away.
   - Write down your own thoughts and reactions in your journal after the interview is over.

- What did you see (or hear) in your office that indicates that there is sexual harassment?
- Tell me something that happened to you last week that made you annoyed with your boss.

3. Comparison/Contrast Questions. This type of question challenges the participant to think about other times, situations, places, events, or people and draw comparisons with them. Choose comparisons that are meaningful to the respondent. It helps them put their current situation into a meaningful framework. Contrasts and comparisons provide additional insight and serve to highlight what you are studying.

Examples

- How are things at this school now compared to when Mr. X was principal?
- Remember when you were a child. How do you feel now compared to then in terms of your ability to accomplish and meet your own standards?
- Imagine you could choose to have a work setting any way you want. What would it be like compared to the way it is now?
- How does this situation compare with what you had where you worked previously?
- In what ways does what you describe differ from your previous experience?
- How could you compare what you are doing now to what you did in the past?
- Does the situation with Mr. _____ differ from the situation with Mr. _____? In what ways?
- This year you say you are doing (or feeling) in this way. How is that like the way you felt last year? How is it different from the way you did it last year?
- How do you think things would be in the future regarding _____ ?

4. New Elements/Topics Questions. Shifting to a new topic must be done in a very subtle manner. You might feel during an interview that the participant is "stuck" on a particular thing and keeps repeating information about the same thing. Here is a chance for you, as interviewer, to introduce a new topic. You are interested in covering areas that may not have been considered in previous questions. (Note: Some qualitative researchers are opposed to this approach and feel that the areas of interest should emerge from the data.) You might draw from the research literature and your own background areas of importance to the problems at hand. You can introduce areas not previously mentioned by the respondent. Keep your own agenda to a minimum. Avoid leading the respondent to say what you want him to say. Use transition statements to move from one area to another. Use "why" and "how" questions for completeness.

Examples

- We've talked for a while about discipline in the schools. Are there other aspects of working in a school you would like to discuss?
- You've talked about many challenges you face as a new teacher. What can you say about having a mentor?
- Can you think of some other things about the nature of your work life that you think are important?

- We've talked quite a bit about _____. Are there other issues you would like to discuss?
- Let's look at some other areas we haven't yet covered. What do you think about _____?
- Since our time is somewhat limited and I want to be sure we've covered everything of interest to you, let's move on to some other areas. I'd like to talk about _____.
- What else is important to you about _____? Can we talk about some other areas (issues, factors, topics)?
- You mentioned _____ as being an important area for you. What about _____? Do you see _____ as something that you consider important? In what ways?
- Why do you think _____ has an influence in this organization?
- How does _____ work in this school?
- Can you clarify what you mean by _____? How are you thinking of it in this context?

5. Closing Questions. This type of question provides a chance for the participant to add anything else that has not been mentioned.

Examples

- Can you think of anything else you would like to say about working in a school?
- Is there anything else you would like to add to what you have already said?

Strategies for Questioning

"Strategies for questioning" refers to techniques you can use to get the respondent to talk and reveal what he or she thinks or believes about something. I discuss six different techniques or strategies that you can use to get your respondent to respond more completely.

1. Elaboration. This strategy provides an opportunity for the participant to say more, to clarify and elucidate his or her responses, and allows for additional input. It may provide other ideas that the informant has thought about.

Examples

- You've talked about your frustration working with your new principal. What else can you say about why you feel so frustrated?
- You said that you feel so happy working with a new group of classmates. What kinds of things have made you happy?
- What else can you tell me about being in the X school?

2. Probing. This strategy provides the interviewer a chance to try to get the underlying meaning of what is said. Sometimes you think you know what is meant, but it is always better to follow up because words take on many different meanings. Repeat the words that are said or raise an eyebrow. This idea is closely related to elaboration, but

here, the emphasis is on digging down deeper into the feelings. Use the person's own words when restating, use nonverbal cues, and provide encouragement.

Examples

- Can you tell me some more about that?
- What do you mean when you say it is challenging as a teacher?
- I see. What do you mean by_____?
- Yes. Go on.
- Hmm. What else can you say about _____?
- That's good. I'm not sure I understand when you say _____. Can you explain more fully?
- Let's talk about that in more detail.
- I'm trying to find out what you think about _____. Tell me more.
- I'm not clear. Can you give an example of what you mean when you say _____?
- Look at the person, nod your head yes, or use your eyes or eyebrows to indicate that you want the person to continue.
- That's interesting. Give me some additional information.
- I have heard you say during this interview that you feel frustrated. Why do you think you feel so frustrated?
- Happiness means different things to different people. I want to get at what it means to you. Tell me some more about it.

3. Nondirectional. This strategy puts the interviewer in a neutral position, neither for or against something. Very tricky. Your nonverbal and verbal cues can directly or indirectly lead the participant to go in a certain direction.

Examples

- Good: We have talked about being a graduate student. What is the experience like for you?
- Avoid: We have talked about being a graduate student. Don't you agree with me that it is so frustrating because you have so little time to do everything?

4. One Question at a Time. Ask one question at a time. Stop and give the participant a chance to respond. Not giving the respondent time to respond is the biggest mistake I see people make, even experienced interviewers.

Examples

- Good: Let's talk about being in graduate school. Tell me about the experience.
- Avoid: Let's talk some more about being in graduate school. What courses are you taking? What is your major? Why do you think you decided to return to graduate school?

5. Wait Time. After you ask a question, be quiet and let the participant think and then talk. If you add something right away, he or she may lose his or her train of thought. Trust me; your participant will talk if you don't.

Examples

- Good: Look down at your notes. Do not tap your pen on the table or look at your watch. Try to remain neutral.
- Avoid: Jumping in too soon and repeating the question or asking a different question.

6. Use Nonverbal Cues. A number of these are good. In an individual interview, you might look down at your paper or fiddle with your tape recorder to give the participant a chance to formulate his or her thoughts.

Special Areas of Concern

Encourage the respondent to tell her story in her own words.

- Tell me what you think about _____.
- Take some time to tell me in your own words what you think about or how you feel about _____.

Don't assume you know what she means when she says something.

- What do you mean when you say successful? I'm not sure I understand. Can you tell me some more?
- You've said that when your boss does _____ that creates problems for you. Can you give me an example?

Avoid covering your own agenda.

- Do you think _____ is important in this school? If so, in what ways?
- Avoid: Don't you think _____ is important in this school?

Be aware of when to cut the respondent off (he's talking too much) and when not to cut the respondent off (she is saying something you want to hear).

- Well, you've given me a lot of examples of _____. Let's talk about some other areas. What do you think about _____ ?
- That sounds interesting. Keep telling me about it.

Some Do's and Don'ts of In-depth Interviewing

Now that you have thought about different types of questions and strategies for questioning, I have a few other reminders for you. You can also look in the Appendix for a Checklist for Individual and Focus Group Interviews.

Do

- Develop rapport
- Use a tape recorder and have a note pad to jot down notes
- Make eye contact
- Ask open ended questions
- Provide an atmosphere for respondents to tell their own story in their own terms

- Remain low and unobtrusive. Do not put your own thoughts into your questions
- Phrase questions in a general and nondirective manner
- Avoid leading questions
- Use some questioning strategies such as repeating the last word of the response or lifting an eyebrow
- Make sure you get specific and detailed information
- Avoid jargon or situations that are too technical
- Make sure you have enough discussion about the key issues that you will be able to use later for data analysis

Don't

- Depend on your memory. Write it down
- Answer questions for respondents
- Ask a question and then provide the answer (I agree that such and such is a good thing)
- Stop the respondent in the middle of a conversation
- Allow the respondent to spend too much time on one topic
- Act nervous or uninterested

Summary

Qualitative interviewing is challenging. It opens up new doors to learn what others think and feel. It does not rely on a single set of questions; rather, it addresses ways to listen to respondents speak in their own words. I recommend two ways of thinking about asking questions: question types and question strategies. Question types are Grand Tour questions, comparison/contrast questions, and so on. Question strategies are techniques you can use to get your respondents to talk more, answer in greater depth, and ultimately lead you to their underlying meanings. I continue to believe that the best way to learn about how to interview is to practice. Practice with your friends and family. Practice with your classmates. Practice with your co-workers. Listen to yourself on tape and try to determine what strategies you use and what you want to avoid. You should now be well on your way to mastering one of the most important techniques for gathering data in any kind of qualitative research you choose to do.

FOCUS GROUP INTERVIEWING

I was in a large comfortable room, having been invited to participate in a focus group discussion. I wasn't quite sure what was going to happen, but I had agreed to come. I arrived at the scheduled time, got a cup of coffee, and found my name tag. I was not precisely sure what I would be doing, but I agreed to participate because someone called me, asked if I would, and offered me $100 for my time. I took a place at the table and chatted with others around me. I did not see anyone I knew. Soon an individual entered the room, took a seat, and got the group's attention. She thanked everyone for coming and said that they would begin shortly and that they would spend about an hour in a discussion. After getting our permission to record the session, they began. I should tell you that when I was called I was told that someone had recommended me because I had had breast cancer. I confirmed the fact with the telephone interviewer, so I knew that we would be talking about that topic. Anticipating the actual meeting, I had been reflecting back on my own experience. How could I not begin thinking about the topic, especially one so painful and personal?

This is how we began. The moderator said, "I am Mary Jones and I work for the Cancer Foundation. We are here tonight to listen to your views on a topic you know only too well. I am married, have two children, and have been working with the Cancer Foundation for about five years. We're going to begin this evening by learning a little bit about each of us and then share our own journeys. I was diagnosed with breast cancer eight years ago. I didn't know how I would survive or what my life was going to be like, but here I am to tell the story." Mary paused and looked around the room. "Now it is your turn to share your stories. Who wants to begin?" Mary turned her attention to some papers in front of her. She did not look at anyone. The assembled body was silent. I wondered who would lead us off. Soon one of the women sitting across from me began to speak. "I am Ann Spencer. I am not working now, but I used to teach elementary school. My boyfriend and I live together and are trying to decide whether to marry or not." She continued, sharing with us how she discovered that she had a tumor and the treatment she received. When Ann finished, Dianne spoke up. Mary was listening but not talking. She seemed intent on what we were saying, occasionally taking notes. As Dianne spoke, one of the other women—Kelly—asked Dianne a question. She responded. And then I chimed in as well. All the women in the room shared their stories. Mary listened intently but rarely spoke. Toward the end of the hour, Mary said, "We've talked from our hearts about this experience. Let's finish up by talking about how our lives have changed." There was no holding the group back. After we were well into the second hour, Mary indicated that we had to stop and thanked us all for coming. Some of us left the room. Others lingered, talking about our experiences.

I have told you this story because it illustrates one type of focus group interview. It illustrates what Morgan (1988) calls a self-managed group. The moderator introduces the topic, often sharing personal information herself. The group essentially runs itself. When the moderator senses that the group has run out of ideas, she either introduces a new topic or reminds the group to reflect on why they are there. The group interaction is critical. It emerges because individuals who share a common experience stimulate each other to talk. The moderator's role is minimal. She knows that the group will talk and react to each other. For me, this is the best kind of focus group interview to conduct; the data are rich and varied.

A special type of interviewing technique, **focus group interviewing** had its origins in the late 1930s. One view is that this technique shifted the emphasis from the interviewer to those being interviewed, and it became more of a nondirective approach. Merton, a social scientist who studied response to wartime propaganda during World War II, is also credited with its development (Merton & Kendall, 1946). It has been widely used as a technique in market research by Lazarsfeld and in gauging political viewpoints (Lewis, 1995).[1]

Just as qualitative interviewing takes many forms, so too does focus group interviewing. Some see it as a highly structured activity in which participants and leader follow a predetermined set of questions. Others see the technique as much less structured. In the latter type, the leader plays a role of facilitator and lets the group process evolve into questions and responses.

Whatever level of structure, however, there are common elements to focus group interviewing. All agree that a focus group consists of a set of people (anywhere from 6 to 12) who come together for approximately one hour. The purpose is to discuss a specific topic. The leader/facilitator may play a very directive role, leading the group toward specific ends, or she may be very indirect and let the group take the leadership role. It is believed that by participating in a group discussion, members of the group may stimulate others to comment or react in ways that do not occur in individual interviews.

The Purpose of Focus Group Interviewing

The purpose of using focus groups is to gather information from participants about the topic of interest. A focus group is basically a group interview. Kitzinger (1994) refers to an organized discussion. What is critical about the group involvement is that there is group interaction. What distinguishes focus group interviewing from qualitative interviewing with a single individual is that the group interaction may trigger thoughts and ideas among participants that do not emerge during an individual interview. Lewis (1995) talks about putting individuals in a nurturing environment so that they will disclose their own views while at the same time be influenced by their interactions with others.

Another advantage of focus group interviews is saving time. You can interview 6 to 10 people in one hour in a focus group. If you were conducting individual interviews, you might need to spend up to 10 hours to hear the voices of 10 people.

Your goal might be to learn how individuals think or feel about a particular topic that is common to each of them. I vividly recall interviewing parents in military schools in Panama who had experienced site-based school management. I asked them what changes they noticed in their school after site-based management had been introduced. They were able to provide specific and concrete examples of changes that they had tried for years to achieve but had not been able to until management was turned over to the local school. By participating in such a group, individuals were stimulated and thought of examples and ideas that might not have emerged during individual interviews.

Sometimes your goal might be to talk to individuals who have a common experience. Morgan (1988) suggests that while everyone may not want to state an opinion about something, most are willing to share their experiences.

The Structured Focus Group. Focus groups can be highly structured, be self-directed, or fall somewhere between the two extremes. Lewis (1995) and Stewart and Shamdasani (1990) take the position that a formal interview guide should be developed with questions moving from the general to the specific, with those of greater importance at the beginning. Krueger (1988) even addresses the number of questions to be included—no more than 10 and usually about 5 or 6. Other details about the moderator and his specific role in the group are all part of a structured approach. My preference, however, is not to practice such an approach. I believe it limits the nature of the discussion and is used in an attempt to lend a patina of objectivity to the task.

Semi-structured or Guided Focus Group. As with individual qualitative interviews, focus groups can rely on a semi-structured approach. In such an approach, the moderator/interviewer has developed a list of questions and has a preconceived plan for proceeding. Many researchers use such a plan as a guide and are willing to modify it as needed. In my experience, many new researchers find it much more helpful to have a list of questions or question areas that they wish to follow. They seem to need this almost as a crutch. I think it is important, however, that the group lead the way, to the extent possible. With practice, moderators can move into a less structured, less directive approach to conducting focus groups.

Issues Regarding Focus Groups

Deciding on the Size of the Group. Most who write about focus group interviewing recommend a size between 6 to 10 people. I agree with this. More than 10 often results in a session that takes too long, and group interaction becomes more difficult to achieve. Fewer than six may also result in insufficient interaction. On a related note, I often schedule more than 10 people because, in my experience, several participants will fail to appear on a given day, even though they have agreed to participate. This is particularly true if you are not compensating the participants. When I conducted focus groups on a military base, some were called away on temporary assignment and had to miss. When I conducted focus groups with students, some were not available to due to scheduling conflicts or illness.

Deciding on the Number of Groups. I think you need to remember that goals specific to quantitative research, such as generalization, are not applicable to qualitative research, so it is not important to interview a large number of groups. At the same time, however, researchers often seem to be more comfortable having several groups that address the same topic. If you are conducting your own research, you might be limited by time and budget constraints as well as availability of participants. I have heard it said that if, as the moderator, you can anticipate responses and you find yourself being accurate, then you have listened to a sufficient number of groups.

Deciding on the Composition of Groups. How should you choose who will participate? You will not be choosing on a random basis. In most cases, you will select participants who meet the criteria that you have predetermined. If you are discussing those who have survived heart attacks, then of necessity you will need people who are survivors. If you are considering those who like a particular brand of soup, then you need to choose people who have used that soup, unless you plan to have a taste test at the time of the focus group. In most cases, researchers recruit participants by advertising, word of mouth, or nomination. The key consideration is that the participants have experience or expertise with regard to the topic. Again, because you are not trying to generalize in a traditional sense, it is not necessary to make sure that the group represents the population in terms of gender, race, ethnicity, or educational level. Some believe it is best to have homogeneous groups, while others want a greater mix. Some believe that it is better to have participants who do not know each other; others find that a discussion might go more smoothly if participants do know each other. There is no scientific research that speaks to group size, group number, or group composition.

Deciding on the Role of the Moderator. The moderator plays a key role prior to the actual focus group interview. He or she will be instrumental in deciding what questions will be included; whether there will be high, moderate, or low structure; and how the group will be conducted. I have found it very helpful to have co-moderators because they can help keep the flow going and make sure all group members participate. My husband and I worked as co-moderators when he had groups of both men and women.

Locating Facilities and Recording. Ideally, it is best to use a space that is designated as a focus group facility. This type of space usually has oval tables, comfortable furniture, video cameras and recorders, and one-way windows. But most new researchers have to use whatever space they can find. If you plan to conduct focus groups in school settings, you can request quiet and private space, but there is no guarantee that you will get it. I remember conducting focus groups with middle school students in a library. My colleague and I were studying a federally funded program. One of the tasks was to listen to what students thought about the program, the materials, and the staff. We identified what type of student we needed to participate, and at the assigned time they were sent to the library. We had no video equipment; our audio equipment worked reasonably well; we were constantly interrupted with announcements over the loudspeaker system; and others were using the library. But we had a lively discussion and the children shared their views about the program.

Transcribing. You are used to transcribing when conducting individual interviews. While time consuming, it is a fairly straightforward task. You might even use voice recognition software that will facilitate your transcription. But imagine that you have an audio- or videotape with about 10 voices. Some speak at the same time; others interrupt. Others are so quiet that you cannot really hear them. And you do not know the voices well enough to be able to distinguish one from another. I have personally transcribed some of these discussions, and it is daunting. I suspect that most researchers do not make transcriptions of focus groups; rather, they listen and then extract themes.

Example of a Focus Group Interview

The purpose of this focus group is to collect opinions from various constituents about how their school has changed as it adopted a new form of management and control. The schools in this district had long operated from a centralized position. Decisions were made at the central office level, and needs and desires of local schools were largely ignored. A new superintendent decided to implement a plan to move the governance, budget, and decision making to the local level. The building principal, while initially somewhat skeptical about the decision, decided it would be best to implement it. Two years after the plan was implemented, an outside team of evaluators was called in to assess the effect on the staff, teachers, and students. This focus group discussion is illustrative of various discussions that were held. I use it to illustrate how focus groups can yield a large volume of data in a relatively short time period.

Prior to the appointed day, I asked the principal to identify a dozen or so parents who might have knowledge of how the new plan had affected the school. She nominated parents and 12 of them agreed to come. We were to meet in the library of the building at approximately 3:30 p.m., after students had been dismissed. I moved some tables together, arranged my equipment, and waited for the parents to arrive.

As parents began to trickle in after 3:00 p.m., I asked them to wait until all had assembled. I was not surprised that at 3:30 only eight people were there. I had been through this many times before and knew that other activities or emergencies tended to interfere with schedules. We sat down around the table and I wrote my name in large letters on a tent card and put it in front of me so that all could see. The others followed without my saying anything.

I reminded them that they had been nominated by the principal and that we were gathered together to talk about the effects they were aware of since the new plan had been implemented. I reviewed details such as the amount of time we would spend together, that no names would be used, and that all reports would be written and distributed to the principal and to them without identifying which individual gave which response. I asked permission to tape record and all agreed. I tested the tape and made sure it was working. We were ready to go.

I have found it extremely effective to begin with specific and concrete items. In this way, you get comments that are authentic. People do not try to impress you with what they know. Jargon is avoided. So I began, "I understand that this school has had two years to move from a centralized administrative structure and to implement the plan to turn budget and management over to it. Can you think of anything that is different about the school since this plan has been adopted?" I finished my comment and looked down at my notes. No one said anything. I waited what seemed like an interminable time. Still no one said anything. Finally, I heard a voice from across the table. "Well, I know that Timmy's teacher says that she finds it much easier to get materials now than before." The woman seemed to pause. I encouraged her to continue. "What do you mean? Can you give me an example?" She thought for a moment. "The teacher was planning a special art project and she needed a certain kind of paper and paint. It was approved almost immediately and the following week the students began the project." "A good example," I commented. "Can you think of other things that have happened?" I said to the group in general. Two people began to speak at once. One mentioned new equipment for the playground. Another mentioned sending teachers to a special training. One parent asked another, "Do you remember when Mr. Miller tried to get approval for his class to travel to an athletic event? Not until last year was he ever able to get the funds in time." The conversation proceeded in this way for about 20 minutes. I really did not introduce new questions at this point. I indirectly led the group, looking at one person or another. I did not specifically call on anyone. I evaluated the comments mentally as they were made. I determined that it was time to change the direction of the comments and so offered the following question. "We've talked a lot about funds and equipment. Can we shift gears a little and talk about other things that might have been affected by the program?" I waited for people to comment and they did.

After interjecting several other comments that changed the direction of the conversation, I determined that our time was up. I then went around the table and asked if anyone had anything else to add to the conversation. I was quite surprised when one very quiet man chimed in. He had said virtually nothing throughout the past hour, but here was his chance. He expressed some concern about the time that it took and the many meetings that were held when he thought someone should just decide. I suspect participatory management was not his preference. Finally, I thanked everyone for participating, gathered my materials, and took a much-needed break before my next group came in.

With this somewhat long account, I hope to illustrate that a lively conversation can occur when people have some experience and thoughts about a particular topic. You do not have to have a predetermined set of questions to get people to talk. I used a general question to begin the conversation, added a comparison question to change the nature of the discussion, and offered opportunities for all to speak.

ONLINE INTERVIEWING

I first read about the possibilities of doing research online in the very late 1990s. Markham (1998) describes her experiences in cyberspace—she calls them ethnographic adventures. When Markham decided to pursue this idea, she had virtually no experience with going online. Only a few years later, this seems difficult to believe, yet Markham's work, which she calls researching real experience in virtual space, will take you on a wonderful journey.

The Purpose of Online Interviewing

The purpose of any type of interview is to gather information from a participant on a particular topic. I have stressed the idea that the interviewer is the vehicle or conduit through which information is passed. Mann and Stewart (2000) remind us what we know so well. A good interviewer begins by building rapport and making a participant feel comfortable. She is a careful, nonjudgmental, and perceptive listener. Many interviewers know the importance of nonverbal cues: the wink of an eye or a small smile. Pauses and silent time also appear in face-to-face interviews. But without the face-to-face experience, and perhaps without even being online at the same time, an online interviewer might need to develop a new set of techniques or skills.

Online sampling provides some interesting challenges. If e-mail is used as a means of interviewing, there are no issues regarding traveling, recording, or transcribing. Online sampling also makes possible interviewing people who are geographically dispersed. Mann and Stewart (2000) speak of "the challenges of presenting self online" (p. 59). The general idea has to do with getting a sense of the other. In theory, this leads participants to trust the interviewer and hopefully share their private and social worlds. Online interviewing may present special problems because none of the usual cues are available. However, there is not general agreement about how and whether online rapport can be established.

Issues and Challenges With Online Interviewing

There are both technological and substantive issues connected with online interviewing. Technological issues involve such concerns as deciding how the two people should communicate with each other. At the current time, e-mail would seem to be the most logical avenue for communication, but other issues might emerge. They include such things as connection speed (do the interviewer and participant have access to a high speed connection?); computer glitches (unexpected disconnects or files being lost); participants' lack of skill in typing or spelling (which sometimes leads to reluctance on the part of a participant); wait time (how do you know if the person is thinking of what to write or did not really get the question?); lack of nonverbal cues (no look of puzzlement, no smiles); sufficient time for an interview (do you and the participant really have 30 minutes or more of uninterrupted time on the computer?); and difficulties in providing follow-up or probing questions (the interviewer may be unfamiliar with the process and need much more experience). Substantive issues might also raise a problem. Shepherd (2003) speaks about difficulty in gaining rapport and in interpreting meaning. She suggests that it is difficult to interpret the emotional tone in which messages are written, for example, when common online abbreviations are used (e.g., "LOL").

Synchronous, Preplanned Interview. This type of interview involves the selection of a participant who agrees to be interviewed at a particular time and in a particular format. Both interviewer and participant agree to be online at the same time and interview questions may be posed by the interviewer and responded to by the participant. I know that sometimes interviewers provide questions in advance for the participant, but I believe that this format is quite limiting.

E-mail, Instant Messenger (IM) and Online Chat. This type of interviewing is new. Since it is not planned you will need to think about how you can capture ideas that are available. Flowers and Moore (2003) provide a detailed account of how to conduct interviews using AOL Instant Messaging.

Focus Groups on the Internet

As the Internet becomes more available and as high speed connections link many people to the Web and potentially to each other, conducting focus groups online offers a new alternative to the traditional type of focus group setting. Rezabek (2000) used online asynchronous discussions that lasted for more than two months. Sweet (1999) distinguishes between virtual focus group rooms and asynchronous online bulletin board rooms. She reports on studies to evaluate online and offline advertising, evaluate mock Web sites, critique existing Web sites, test and evaluate new products (product mailed in advance of the groups), uncover competitive Web site information, evaluate training programs, explore decision making, uncover imagery, evaluate concepts, evaluate package images, generate ideas, and to ascertain customer and employee satisfaction. Sweet identifies issues specific to the technical aspect of focus groups. My impression is that little research has been done on the topic, but suggestions come from practical experience. Much of what is written about this topic is related to market research. Some distinct advantages are lower cost, immediate transcription, and global participation. Disadvantages might include difficulties with technology, inexperience of participants with format, inability of participants to key in entries and to communicate in this manner, and lack of support for the researcher who is working on her or his own.

I believe there is great potential for online focus groups. It is too early to say what methodological issues may arise. For example, what role should the moderator play? Should the moderator submit a list of questions in advance of the online discussion? Must all participants be present at the same time? Can asynchronous focus groups accomplish the same goals as those that meet at the same time? How does the nature of the group interaction change when the group is not present physically or even at the same time? Do we need eye contact, nonverbal cues, and other aspects of face-to-face meetings? Can we begin to think about alternative ways to elicit information? Does online participation limit the type of person who will participate? Are older people less likely to participate? Are those with limited language skills less likely to participate?

I hope by the time you read this book you will have had the opportunity to participate in one or more online discussions. I believe that the technology will be there. It is up to you to avail yourself of it.

SUMMARY

In this chapter, I have addressed many practical issues regarding in-depth interviewing. While some of the issues are different depending on whether you interview a single individual or a group organized as a focus group, I stressed unstructured interviewing techniques and especially emphasized that you need to think about the types of questions you ask and strategies for asking questions. I provided you with many specific questioning strategies and techniques. I also introduced the relatively new idea of interviewing in cyberspace. You can look in the Appendix for a checklist for interviewing.

GROUP ACTIVITY

Purpose: To develop skill in online interviewing.

Activity: Select a topic of interest to you. Identify an individual who is willing to be interviewed online who has some knowledge about this topic. Set aside at least 30 minutes at a mutually agreed-upon time. Practice the mechanics of interviewing online. Identify at least three types of questions and three questioning strategies and adapt them to the online format.

Evaluation: Complete online comments reflecting on the process of interviewing and share with your classmates.

INDIVIDUAL ACTIVITY

Purpose: To become comfortable with interviewing.

Activity: Identify a topic of interest to you. Select an individual you do not know by using a snowball sampling approach. Assess your own skill level by identifying an area in which you feel some discomfort. Practice those skills.

Evaluation: Comment in your journal about your comfort level with the new skills.

NOTE

1. Paul F. Lazarsfeld was honored for his 30-year contribution to the Bureau of Applied Social Research established at Columbia University in 1941. For details see http://www.columbia.edu/cu/news/01/09/lazarsfeld.html. You can also read about his contributions at http://www.b2binternational.com/whitepapers8.htm

CHAPTER 9

Learning About Others Through Observing

There is an art to living life fully and paying attention to the details.

—Anne Copland

I hear and I forget. I see and I remember. I do and I understand.

—Confucius

In addition to interviewing and focus groups, other means are used by qualitative researchers to gather data. Often interviews or focus groups are used in conjunction with one of the techniques discussed in this chapter. These techniques can be used with any of the various traditions. However, it is most common to find that observations are used with ethnography and case studies.

Observing in Natural Settings. Observations usually occur in settings that already exist, rather than in contrived settings. You can observe naturally occurring groups either at work or in informal settings. You can also observe individuals in their home or work settings. Observations have typically been associated with ethnographic studies.

Writing: What Exists, What You Get Others to Create, What You Create. There are various types of written documents that you can use in qualitative research. Qualitative researchers often use existing documents to gather information. These can include official documents such as minutes of meetings or curriculum guides. They can also include newspaper accounts, letters, diaries or journals, and online course descriptions. You can get others to create written material in the form of e-mail messages, responses to questions, or student journals. Finally, you may create written material in the form of field notes, memos, or a researcher journal. In some cases, you will make notes of your observations; in other cases, you will make notes that are self-reflective or introspective.

Images. You can use images for data collection, such as photographs, films, or videotapes. They can be either existing images or ones made specifically for your research. With the availability of digital and disposable cameras, images can be much more readily accessible. You can also use drawings or sketches. Images can be created by you, by the participants, or by both together, or you can use images that exist already.

Chat Rooms, Online Discussion Groups, and Online Teaching. A new source of data. There is a growing body of literature about the use of data from these sources.

OBSERVING IN NATURAL SETTINGS

As you know, I like to begin with a story. Here is a true story you might find amusing. Several years ago, I was teaching a class in qualitative research and I wanted my students to have some practice observing. I knew how difficult it would be for them to gain access to schools and the length of time it might take for us to receive permission. So I decided we would observe human interaction in a public space. In that way, we would not really need to receive permission. My class of about a dozen or so students discussed what they might want to focus their observation on. They also considered how they could observe and take notes without being seen. We decided that we would select a parent-child pair who were shopping and we would try to follow them unobtrusively. Some decided that they would get a shopping cart and pretend to shop. Others decided that it would be foolish to take notes since they would be spotted too easily. We agreed to spend about half an hour on the task.

Would you like to know what happened? We traveled to a very large supermarket in the college town where our university was located. I positioned myself near the front of the store looking at the video rental selections. Others moved around the store. Within less than 10 minutes the store manager spotted me and asked what I was doing. In fact, he thought I was sent by headquarters to spy on him. I assured him that I was just conducting a class. Shortly thereafter someone else from my class came to me and the manager. He had spotted a shoplifter. Well, the rest of us tried to resume our tasks, but it became clear that we were too diverted. Oh well, it seemed like a good idea at the time.

Traditional observation involved anthropologists going to remote locations, immersing themselves in the settings, and learning about the people they encountered. They often spent months listening to and looking at those around them. They took notes. They often remained in the background and basically acted as a "fly on the wall." What was critical to their work was that they studied individuals and groups in their own environment. Their goal was to try to gain a deep understanding of the social interaction and cultures of these groups. Early in the 1900s it was fashionable to study individuals in cultures that were completely remote and different from our own, so anthropologists traveled to New Guinea, Samoa, Mexico, or other remote locations. Of course, you need to remember that access to these cultures was very limited. There was no television and few Americans had actually traveled to such faraway places.

It was not until the late 1980s that ethnography began to be seen to any extent in education (LeCompte, 2002). Borrowing from the ethnographer, qualitative researchers worked to adapt this tradition to the study of schools and education. Researchers immersed themselves in classrooms and conducted extensive observations and took field notes. As interest in the technique became greater, modifications were made to the length of observations and shorter observation times became more widely used. Beginning in the 21st century, researchers became interested in online cultures and adapted techniques to the study of online chat rooms.

The Purpose of Observations

Gathering data through observation has long been associated with anthropologists. Observing humans in natural settings assists in understanding the complexity of human behavior and interrelationships among groups. When they visited groups of people in remote lands, anthropologists' goal was to study the culture of these groups. One definition of culture is that it is a system of shared beliefs, values, customs, and behaviors that individuals use to cope with their world and with each other. In the early years, non-Western people were studied and their values were often compared to our own values.[1] Although not necessarily made explicit, it was assumed that the values of Western culture were somehow better than those of others. When educators decided to use anthropological methods to study classrooms, I believe many of the ideas about culture were largely ignored. Some of the observational studies in classrooms were done to get a sense of what it was like in a classroom. I recall Kidder's 1989 study of a fifth-grade classroom in Massachusetts. He spent nine months with these 20 children and their teacher. His moving account includes sections on homework, discipline, and the science fair. I do not believe he knew which topics he would write about prior to his immersion in the class. Although not written as qualitative research per se, this is one of the earliest detailed accounts of a classroom that provides a rich context and fabric of life for the children and their teacher. Geertz (1973) reminds us that a thick description is to be valued in ethnography. I think he would agree that Kidder does just so.

But even as educators began to spend extended time periods in classrooms, there seemed to be a desire to study groups of children who were quite different from those who were the observers. Since most researchers who do these kinds of studies are highly educated, they usually are members of the middle class. Yet they tended to study children who were not of the middle class. The greater the difference between those observing and those being observed, the more likely it was that ethnocentric ideas came into play. So, for example, when middle class white observers studied working class black students, they saw many differences and I suspect found themselves making comparisons that were quite judgmental. Other anthropologists studied groups who were outside the mainstream culture. If you read the anthropological literature, you will see many references to studies of groups that could be seen as outsiders: motorcycle gangs, the homeless, homosexuals, pregnant teenagers, drug addicts, and the like.

Many researchers do not have the luxury of studying for such a long time period or in such depth. And many schools and teachers are reluctant to give permission for outsiders to come into their schools and classrooms for such an extended time period. Using observation to gather qualitative data has moved away from the kind of immersion practiced by anthropologists to a shorter and less intense activity. So now you have to rethink what is meant by observing. In my experience, it is an activity that is much narrower in scope. I recall a student who studied kindergarten classrooms to determine how rules were formed. McIntyre (2002) studied violence in the lives of Northern Irish women. I remember reading about a study of teenagers in malls and how groups interacted. I used clips from films to study how families from different cultural backgrounds interacted at mealtimes. In all these examples, the researchers limited themselves to a particular aspect of human interaction. They targeted that information and limited the scope of their observations to a predetermined area.

Issues Regarding Observations

Deciding Who Is to Be Studied and in What Situations. Do you want to study children in bilingual classrooms? Do you want to study high school athletes on the playing field? Do you want to study first year teachers in their classrooms? Do you want to study girls in advanced math classes? Do you want to study nurses in emergency rooms? Often qualitative researchers select one or several key demographic characteristics of a group of people and decide to study them by observing them in their natural settings. Usually the type of individual is first decided. Observations then can occur in a number of places. If school children are selected, then the observations might occur inside a classroom, on the playing field, on the bus, in the cafeteria, or in the hallways. Fordham (1988) studied successful inner city poor minority children and observed them at church, at home, and in social situations. Glass (2001) studied families of autistic children and studied them in their homes. Berger (2004) studied wheelchair athletes.

Formal Groups, Informal Groups, or Occasional Groups. You might not have thought about this before, but there are different kinds of groups you can study. A formal group is one that exists on a regular basis with the same people serving as a nucleus, such as a class, a family, a team, a gang, or a work unit. These same people come together regularly for either work or play. There are usually rules and boundaries that are either formal or informal but that are known by all members of the group. Informal groups, on the other hand, are in contact with each other, but members may move in and out and they do not meet regularly. Examples of informal groups are a card playing group, members of an online chat room, a play group with mothers and children, a community action team, or members of a club or a support group. An occasional group consists of people who might come together once or a number of times but whose membership is constantly shifting. All types of groups can be observed, but you might look for different things in each.

Gaining Access. If studies are conducted in schools, gaining access is often critical. In the current climate, many school officials are reluctant to let outsiders enter the schools. Often researchers have to submit detailed plans for what they want to do and how much time they will take doing it. They may be asked to speak of how the research will benefit those studied. Large school systems are very difficult to penetrate and often receive many more requests than they can handle. If studies are to be conducted with specific subgroups, it is often difficult to get access to these groups. Almost 40 years ago, Liebow (1967) studied black men on street corners in Washington, D.C., and had to overcome reluctance on the part of these participants to let him in to their subculture. Gaining access when you are an outsider continues to be challenging, as Berger (2004) remarks about his surprise as he faced difficulties gaining access to observe people with disabilities. As you think about conducting your own observations, sensitivity and awareness of these issues are important considerations.

What to Study. In my experience, what is most difficult about conducting observations is knowing which of the many things to look at. There is so much going on when humans are together. Should you concentrate on a single person? If so, who? If you try to take in the whole setting, it becomes overwhelming. I find that beginning students are more comfortable with some guidelines. In the next section, I offer you some concrete suggestions. Boeree (1998) distinguishes between the physical nature of human interaction and the meaning of interactions. As the observer, it is up to you to decide when an interaction is meaningful. In my experience, the distinction begins to emerge as you process the data you have collected. It is not evident during an observation which interactions are meaningful and which are—to use Boeree's term—physical.

Frequency and Length of Time. Obviously, this varies depending on what you are studying, who you are studying, and how much time you have available. I suggest that you select at least several times when you plan to observe and allocate at least an hour for each observation. Some settings are routine and predictable while others are extremely varied.

Your Role. Observers take on different roles. Traditional ethnographers describe different observer roles. If you are part of the group you observe, or if you become part of the group, you are called a **participant observer**. Or, you might take the role of unobtrusive or surreptitious observer. In postmodern ethnography, the observer's role is one of an interaction in which his or her own voice is made explicit. This contemporary position reflects the new thinking about power and privilege and the relationship between those being studied and those doing the studying. If you observe in cyberspace, you might be a completely unknown or unnoticed observer.

How to Conduct an Observation

Main Components of Short-term Qualitative Observations. Qualitative observations differ tremendously. They vary depending on the concepts and issues to be studied, location of observation, length of time and number of each observation, and type of group studied.

ADVANCED PLANNING

- Most people prefer to begin observations by deciding on a particular aspect to study. It is difficult to just "go in and look" without knowing what you will look at or what is important. I suggest you identify a specific aspect of human interaction to study. Many educators find it difficult to study culture in general and are better able to identify a particular dimension of human interaction to study. I have looked at interactions of aides with children, families interacting at different occasions (e.g., meals, parties, and leisure time), teachers in faculty meetings, and teacher-parent meetings. I have had students study staking out space in the library, motorcycle gangs in bars, and female athletes in the locker room.

- Identify three to five areas to look at, such as who initiates a conversation, reactions of participants to a particular issue, or nonverbal signals shown by participants. These should be seen as freeing, not limiting. Sometimes observers go into a situation with no agenda and this works well, but other times students report being overwhelmed and not able to focus on a particular thing since so much is going on.
- Decide whether you will take notes, use videos or digital technology, or rely on your memory. If the latter, then make sure that you allow sufficient time immediately after the observation to record your impressions.
- Decide how much time you will allow for your observation. I suggest at least 30 minutes initially. I would then follow up with a one-hour observation.
- For your initial observations, I suggest that you choose public spaces where individuals interact with each other. This way you do not need to obtain permission and you can blend in with those you are studying. I use such places as cafes, fast food restaurants, playgrounds, shopping malls, airports, religious institutions, or any other place where people congregate.

Conducting the Observations

- Once you arrive at your destination, you need to settle down in a place where you will be able to look and listen. I frequently observe at a fast food restaurant. I get some coffee and choose a table where I can be comfortable and can see and hear plenty of people. I find it helpful to drink my coffee and survey the space. I need to take notes and so I use a notebook; however, in some situations you might find this gets in the way and you have to rely on your memory.
- I find it very helpful to begin my observations with a look at the surroundings. I often draw a sketch or take a picture as a memory aid. If I am in a school or classroom, I look at how the chairs are arranged, what kind of art is displayed, the lighting, and the air quality. If I go to the same classroom regularly, I make note of any changes in the physical space.
- Because your study is about individuals, you may decide you want to describe the main characters in the setting. What are they wearing? Is their speech formal or casual? How well do the players know each other?
- Because your goal is to observe human interaction, you need to decide what to focus on. In some settings there may be several different things happening at the same time, and you will need to set some priorities. There is no right thing to look at. You just need to decide what is challenging or interesting to study.

Other Issues

- What is your role? Do you want to participate in the interactions or do you want to remain aloof? Is there a right or best way to behave? Can you behave one way one time and another way another time? I suspect you know that it is up you to choose what you want to do. I have observed in many classrooms where I was silent and sat in the back of the room. I have also found myself helping children who needed help. Should you disclose your role to members of the group or keep it hidden? It depends on the situation.
- Things are not always as they seem. If people know you are observing them they might want to look good, so you might not be seeing underlying human experience. Or people

might decide to behave as they think you want them to behave. If you are in a public setting, this is less likely to occur.

- Should you reveal to people what you are doing and why, should you keep it quiet, or should you tell a fictitious story? These are decisions you will need to make once you begin an actual research study. For now, since you are practicing and honing your skills, this is less critical.

- Should you have a very narrow focus or should you look at everything? Here you need to strike a balance. It should be obvious that you can't look at everything, but you may not know what is important until you have spent some time looking and listening and thinking about the underlying meaning of what you see and hear.

- How much is enough? Since you can only get a slice of life, how large a slice should you get? You can answer this question by beginning your data analysis while you are observing. That means you will either have to take notes while you are observing or when you complete an observation. Sometimes circumstances dictate how long you can observe. I recall being at a preschool in Japan for about a week. I studied several class-rooms, met with the principal, and observed children on the playground. While I would have preferred to be there a longer time, it was not possible.

- Can I really get at the essence of the culture of the group? This is a difficult question to answer. I believe you can come to understand how individuals interact with each other and develop new insights through observation. A word of caution, however. As individuals become more sophisticated and worldly, they may learn to mask underlying meanings. Your task is to uncover deep meaning rather than surface structure.

- I am not sure that practice makes perfect, but I believe you can train yourself to be more observant. Exercises that involve observing the same phenomenon—for example, by looking at films or videos, discussing what you observed with others, and then looking again at the same videos—will heighten your powers of observation. You can train yourself to focus on details or look at the whole and ignore the details. You can train yourself to look for the emotional content and meaning expressed in everyday language.

Examples of Observations

I have found it very effective to have some ideas in advance before I actually conduct an observation. I think of these as scenarios. Consider one of the following scenarios before you actually begin an observation.

Scenario 1

Topic: Using television family settings to study power.
Your role: **Observer**
Setting the stage: Select a current television program that runs as a series and concerns a family. I suggest you pick several different kinds of programs and that you choose traditional and nontraditional situations. Choose at least three different examples of the program.

Providing focus for your observation: You are interested in studying power as it manifests in families. Prior to observations, you need to develop a working definition of power from your own framework. As a start, you might ask yourself these kinds of questions. What are the signs of power? How is it manifested? Who exhibits power in a specific family? What are ways in which it is accomplished? Are there power issues that are appropriate (from your own framework) or inappropriate in the families you observe?

Conducting the observation: The first time you watch the program you may just want to get used to looking at different interactions and taking notes. After you feel comfortable, return to your question and try to jot down an example and evidence related to your focus. Continue this process through several episodes of the program.

Making sense of what you found: Since you are only practicing, you cannot conduct more than a tentative analysis. Begin to write down your general thoughts about the topic.

Advantages: By using a television program you can review it many times. You can also do this observation in conjunction with others to compare your comments with others.

Limitations: Television programs do not really reflect real life; most things are exaggerated. You may not find any evidence related to your topic.

Scenario 2

Topic: Examining the effects of parental cultural expectations on children's behavior.
Your role: **Unobtrusive observer**
Setting the stage: Identify a fast food restaurant near your home where you might encounter families from many cultural backgrounds. Choose a weekend mealtime for your observation. Go to the restaurant several times to determine whether you can sit and observe. You might want to talk to the manager, who may become suspicious and ask why you are there.

Providing focus for your observation: You are aware that family expectations differ dramatically based on cultural backgrounds. You might look at such things as whether there are certain expectations for family members based on gender. Are the adult men and women behaving in ways that might influence their daughters to be more traditional, to act out, or to be subservient? What kinds of rules do you think girls would learn in different cultural settings?

Conducting the observation: This is a much greater challenge than observing a television program. People might wonder why you are looking at them. You might not really be able to take notes while you look. In my experience, however, you should find some interesting things in public places.

Making sense of what you found: You can try your hand at writing some general thoughts about the different styles of cultural groups as they interact over a family meal. You may also want to restate your question because you might not be clear yourself where you want to focus.

Advantages: Understanding different styles among cultural groups is a critical topic, especially as our culture becomes increasingly diverse.

Limitations: Conducting an observation in a public place without drawing suspicion may be a problem in light of increased concerns about security.

Scenario 3

Topic: Examine the discrepancies between verbal behaviors and nonverbal cues.
Your role: **Participant observer**
Setting the stage: Identify locations where you are able to observe adults interacting with each other. If you choose an office, the people might be more careful of their behavior. If you choose a social situation, you might see different kinds of behaviors.

Providing focus for your observation: You have long had an interest in the relationship between verbal behaviors and nonverbal cues. You've suspected that what one says and what one does may often be at odds. You've noticed that when talking to people (in your office, for example) you are struck by the abundance of comments that are socially acceptable. Yet when you observe the way people behave, they often act in ways contrary to their words. You decide to observe people interacting in natural settings and look specifically for nonverbal cues, especially those that contradict verbal statements. You might begin by asking, "Do I see discrepancies? What kinds of discrepancies do I observe? Do people misunderstand the meaning of what others say and do?"

Conducting the observation: This observation can be conducted in any social or work setting. It can be a party, a social gathering, a work environment, or an informal get together. Your role as an observer takes on the status of participant observer here; you are actually part of the setting itself. Practice before you actually observe by paying special attention to certain words and behaviors, then identify several settings where you can see evidence of these behaviors. When you leave the setting, write down your thoughts in your journal because it would be awkward to do so while attending an event.

Making sense of what you found: Again, you have insufficient data to make any meaningful statements. However, you can begin to try to organize your notes into themes.

Advantages: You have immediate access to a natural setting because you are part of the group.

Limitations: You might not see what you are looking for, or you might forget what you see because you are not able to take notes while you are interacting.

Scenario 4

Topic: Study gender differences in a math classroom.
Your role: **Postmodern observer**
Setting the stage: Identify a classroom that meets the criteria. Of course, you probably have some idea in mind before you select this topic.

Providing focus for your observation: You are aware of many issues regarding different behaviors and expectations between males and females. Rather than identify a particular scenario or area of focus, in this observation you will gather data to target your observations. You will enter the situation with predetermined ideas about different expectations of performance by teachers. Since you have already adopted a stance, you might find it difficult to keep an open mind as you observe.

Conducting the observation: I usually find with a general idea such as this that several observations are in order. Once you select a classroom, you might find yourself moving from unobtrusive observer to one who takes an active role. I have seen observers in such classes help students with homework or explain different ideas. In fact, sometimes they forget to do their observations. It takes a good deal of skill to focus your attention and not get caught up in a particular situation.

Making sense of what you found: As with the other examples, you might find yourself having difficulty determining what it is you really have gathered.

Advantages: You are not limited to looking at a particular situation and may discover that new insights emerge.

Limitations: By not having a focus, you might find yourself struggling to determine what it is you should look for, or you might discover that you see what you want to see.

These illustrations should give you some ideas of places to observe and ways in which you can engage in observations. Many students who are just beginning their experiences with qualitative research find that practice that is targeted helps them begin to refine their observation skills.

Summary

Astute observing is an excellent way to gather information in your qualitative study. While it is fairly unstructured, it offers endless possibilities for learning how humans interact. You can increase your observational skills through practice, feedback, and discussion with others. Using television and film enables you to look and look again.

Today, with sophisticated technology readily available, we find observation taking on entirely new dimensions. For example, we have video ethnography, a technique suggested by Genzuk (2003), who recommends that you begin by watching people at school, work, or leisure. I agree with him.

EXISTING WRITING, YOUR WRITING, AND WRITING YOU GENERATE

In addition to interviews, focus groups, and observations, other excellent sources of information appear in various forms. What they have in common is that they are in the form of words. Some of this information exists, and you have to identify it and gain access to it. Other types can be generated by you with responses from participants. A third type is written by you. All types are legitimate and useful as you gather data for your qualitative study.

We have only just begun to tap what is available out there. The Internet is an incredible source of written information; I believe it will revolutionize the type of data we collect and use in our qualitative studies. Whether it is a blog written by one individual, or group blog with contributions from many, the discussion in a chat room, online class discussions, dialogue in Listservs, or some other ideas not yet imagined, the power of this source is yet to be used in a systematic way. I can only mention again its immediacy, its availability for use in your study, its universality, and its ease of use.

I do not want you to think that the only source of written information is the Internet, however. I discuss some fairly common sources in the section titled "Issues Regarding Written Material."

The Purpose of Written Material

Use of documents is one of the watchwords of historical research. Whether it is a primary source, such as the Declaration of Independence, or a secondary source, such as a newspaper account of the times during its writing, documents serve as written records by which we learn and study history. They are evidence of what people did and said and what they thought.

Written material created by participants—either in direct response to your requests or as documents they have created for other purposes—captures the thoughts, ideas, and meanings of participants. As such, they provide a window into the human mind.

Written material you create—whether a journal, a diary, field notes, or a poem—provides insight into your own thinking and reactions to what you are studying and its effect on you and others.

I cannot stress how important such written material is to a study. Of course, one enormous advantage is that its form permits easy storage in a computer and easy use in data analysis.

Issues Regarding Written Material

What material should you use? How do you know what material you should use? How do you find it? What might be valuable and what might be trivial? How do you learn about it? The first type of material I want you to think about is written material already in existence. I suspect that there is no written material that you should reject without looking at it, but it is likely that some sources more than others might prove relevant to your topic. If you were studying teenage pregnant girls, you might find their diaries of interest. If you were interested in teachers serving as mentors, you might find documents prepared by a school system to train teachers valuable. If you were interested in how parents and children interact with each other around homework, you might find the homework itself of interest. Obviously, your question is critical, but here are some other examples of written information that you might find useful: documents provided by schools including school newsletters, school board meeting minutes, curriculum guides, teacher lesson plans, or notes of observations by principals; documents in the public domain including newspaper accounts or editorials; documents provided in a work setting including interoffice memos, reports, or performance evaluations; documents provided by individuals including letters, diaries, or stories.

Written material you ask participants to create might include e-mail responses to your questions. In a study of beginning teachers, I have used a weekly e-mail format with three simple questions: How was your week? What problem did you face? How did you solve it? By keeping the format consistent, participants found minimal burden in responding, and I was able to capture many responses over time. Information was already on my computer so I had little to do before data analysis. You might ask students to keep a journal of their thoughts about being in Mr. Smith's class or about learning a challenging subject. You might ask superintendents to dictate their ideas about school violence into software like Dragonspeak that transfers the material to the computer.

Written material you create might include your online journal, memos regarding your thoughts about the qualitative data you collect, field notes that you develop after an extensive observation, or a poem you might write to express your thoughts on a particularly challenging aspect of learning to become a qualitative researcher. You should not ignore class work or papers you create for a class in qualitative research.

Extracting the Essence. Just like any other data you collect, written material challenges you to find underlying meaning in the words of others and in your own words. Reacting to metaphors is especially exciting because they reveal what is beneath the surface meaning of the words you read. I recall asking students to write a short paper describing one of their parents by using metaphors. One student referred to her father as Santa Claus. She wrote, "In my family we had a wonderful Christmas tradition. Sometime during the month of December, Santa would come in the night and decorate our Christmas tree and fill our stockings. One such night was to be very different, for one of those nights, Santa kissed me good-night."

Another woman wrote about her father in a poem titled "The Perfect Southern Gent—My Daddy." She continued in part, "His color of rich mocha chocolate with a hint of cream." Another student described his father as "a horse that wears blinders." And another student wrote, "Boy, write about your parents using metaphors she says. This sounds simple enough, but for the last 24 hours I've agonized over doing it. Seems this assignment has forced me to think about my Mom and Dad in ways that I haven't (or have avoided) during the last 10 years or so. Forgive me as my submission will probably resemble some postmodern stream of consciousness, but that's how things are bubbling up." And finally, from one of my Middle Eastern students, "My father is the ocean who gives a life to the sand and the rocks that surround him and then retreats to let them nourish with what he gave." We used these submissions as we began our exploration of the meaning given by metaphors. Things are not always as they seem, we began to learn.

IMAGES

I have emphasized throughout that qualitative research relies on the written word; it is the written word that forms the basis of all of your data. But I also suggest to you that visual information is very powerful. Just as with written information, visual information can come in three forms: that which exists already (found images), that which you ask participants to create, and the images that you create.

I would be remiss if I did not mention again the power of the Internet. Images are widely available for your access and easy for you or others to create and display online. Tools are available for you to use or to access images at little or no cost. A digital camera or video camera can be used to transfer information across space in fractions of seconds. You can display visual information in your written reports and use hyperlinks to take your reader to photos, videos, or art. It is only limited by your imagination.

Images that exist or are found can serve several purposes. They document aspects of social interaction, they can be used as stimuli for interviews, and they can be used in presentations.

If you become interested in this topic, you may want to read about the hermeneutics of seeing. Davey (1999) suggests that hermeneutics can embrace visual phenomena as well as the written word.

The Purpose of Images

"A picture is worth a thousand words." I assume you've heard this many times. Did you know that the quotation is actually phony? The "Chinese" quotation on the next page was fabricated by an advertising executive representing a baking soda company. The executive assumed that consumers would be compelled to buy a product that had the weight of Chinese philosophy behind it. A young boy's smile is equal to many words explaining the benefits of the product; the product was baking soda to be used to whiten teeth. The ad was most often seen on streetcars on which customers did not have much time to read advertising copy.

Lester (n.d.) reminds us:

With digital hegemony, visual messages have reasserted their position as an important communication medium, but at the cost of not recognizing the combination of words and

pictures as vital in communication. With the correct interpretation of the proverb, words and pictures live in harmony as they are both used equally in order to understand the meaning of any work that uses them both.

I see images enhancing and embellishing and making alive the words we use to write our thoughts. Whether the images are created by us, our participants, or others, they send powerful messages.

Visual images are central to our culture and our communication. They provide another avenue of meaning. They represent a kind of reality captured by the researcher. However, I think you need to remember that images, while an apparent representation of reality, are actually designed and created by the researcher to reflect a particular stance or point of view. Nevertheless, the power and seductive nature of images cannot be ignored.

Examples of Images

Some research asks participants to recreate scenes from their earlier life. Kelly and Kerner (2004) describe how they used the photographic exhibition Positive Lives and personal snapshots to document the death of a loved one from HIV/AIDS. In a study of childhood sexual abuse, the researcher asked the participant to provide illustrations of the abuse. Kearney and Hyle (2004) discuss how they used drawings by participants to examine the emotional impact of change. I use an exercise where students are asked to represent themselves on a large piece of paper with markers and crayons using only images. Some choose to be literal and often draw a timeline of significant events in their lives; others choose more abstract and metaphorical representations. A number of research projects involve giving participants disposable cameras and asking them to photograph a day in their lives. I have asked participants to bring in photographs of their families and use these as a jumping off point to initiate interviews. Online images can be created and expanded and disseminated to serve as discussion points for online chats. You only need your imagination to think of how images can be used.

Issues Regarding Images

Quality of the Image. One important issue to consider is the quality of the visual representation. If you are going to use an image as part of your document, then how it looks becomes important. Of course, software to enhance or modify images is readily available and fairly easy for even the novice to use.

Manipulation of the Image. It used to be that most people believed an image was a literal representation of an event or a person. But whether you choose to manipulate an image through a computer program or to present an image to highlight a particular aspect of it, the critical point is that as a researcher what you see and subsequently represent visually is your interpretation of what you study.

Its Relationship to Your Words. I think it is important that your choice of images and words enhance each other and are enhanced by each other. Including a photograph must have a purpose in the same way as choosing a quotation from a participant.

USING THE INTERNET IN QUALITATIVE RESEARCH

There are a variety of ways to use the Internet in qualitative research. One way is to use existing chat rooms or discussion groups to study online cultures. Another idea is to convene focus groups through online technology. Online teaching is now possible, and courses in qualitative research are becoming increasingly available. Researchers have begun to examine visual diaries, blogs, and vlogs as sources of information. Another way the Internet is being used is to make available data that other researchers can use for secondary analyses (Lichtman, 2005). Finally, discussions and exchanges among researchers can be facilitated by the Internet.

Chat Rooms and Discussion Groups

Researchers see new arenas for studying culture. Instead of traveling to remote physical locations, they can now travel to cyber locations and study online cultures. Some do this by studying existing chat rooms and discussion groups. I recall first reading about studying life online when Markham's (1998) book reached my desk. In this book, she explores how "users create, negotiate, and make sense of their social experience in computer-mediated contexts" (p. 9). Markham studies the experience of chat rooms, support groups, and virtual communities by spending time online herself. Her goal is to experience the meanings of life online. More recently, Markham (2004) raises several issues about doing research of this kind. Although there are no clear guidelines, she suggests that the research should be both epistemologically and methodologically sound. She defines the Internet as a communication medium, a global network of connections, and a scene of social construction. "As social life becomes more saturated with Internet-based media for communication, researchers will be able to creatively design projects that utilize these media to observe culture, interact with participants, or collect artifacts." Online ethnographies, or "netnographies" (Kozinets, 2002) observe the textual discourse that is available on the Internet.

Using the new technology requires researchers to be creative and diligent as they chart new ground. Identifying individuals to study online is something of a challenge. Flowers and Moore (2003) discuss how they identified participants for online qualitative research studies. Robbins (2001), a graduate student of mine, in her work about adolescent girls' use of the Internet, combined online interviews, reviews of Web sites, and postings from online message boards to gather her data.

Dholakia and Zhang (2004) speak about using data from such e-commerce data sites as bulletin board systems, newsgroups, chat rooms, server log files, and Web sites. They suggest that we no longer are looking at an oral culture or a written culture, but rather computer-mediated communications.

Focus Groups

Another idea for using the Internet is to convene online focus groups. Some organize focus groups where participants are available in real time (synchronous). Rezabek (2000) describes using online asynchronous focus groups in a Listserv to generate topics for future in-depth discussions. Issues to be addressed are the different hardware and software capabilities of participants, role of the researcher, ability of participants to type rapidly, and reluctance to put their words in a permanent form online.

One challenge is to identify participants and get them to participate. Some research suggests that computer users tend to be predominantly male and younger. While this may have been true in the past, I do not think it will be so in the future. Researchers continue to develop new ideas about how to locate people and get them to participate. But I believe opportunities will present themselves as use of technology becomes easier, information travels faster, and more people have access to computers.

You can imagine a number of advantages to using online chat rooms or conducting online focus groups. First, you can capture a wide and varied audience. Data from discussions are easy to download and readily available. The anonymous nature of the online environment may result in participants being more open. New technologies provide readymade written transcripts that can be imported into your personal computer with little cost and fuss.

Online Teaching

The data from courses taught online can be used to study student cultures and interactions. I also find it especially helpful to understand how students process information, especially when it relates to the topic of qualitative research. I began putting my own courses online in the late 1990s. I knew very little about the technology but learned how to make Web pages and how to put together the rudiments of a discussion forum. By putting these courses online, I enabled others to locate them and the information reached a larger audience than my own students. Several qualitative researchers began to search the Web and collect information about such courses. You can easily see what is out there by using a search engine and asking for "qualitative research courses." I hesitate to send you to a particular location since one drawback of using the Internet is that there is little permanence and sites that were operational yesterday may have disappeared today.

One unfortunate consequence of newer technologies, such as the teaching tool Blackboard, is that courses are restricted to registered students and the larger community of scholars cannot gain access. I found that while my later courses worked better technologically, they were not available to anyone other than students at my university.

The traditional ways we think about teaching have been turned on their heads with the ready availability of computers for many students and software programs that facilitate discussions and comments. Most of us are used to providing education on a face-to-face basis. In this section, I illustrate some of the things you can do with computer technology that facilitate comments and thought. This first group of comments addresses the way students have taken the material they read and tried to apply it to their own thinking and practice. Online comments and discussions offer a variety of types of information. Here, for example, is a concern and a response about interviewing offered by someone belonging to a Listserv on qualitative research:

Everyone, I just finished an interview for my qualitative research class, and it went horribly wrong. My participant, who is usually very talkative, locked up completely when the tape recorder went on. I asked him to not even think about it and just focus on our conversation, but his answers were very short and vague. He responded poorly to many of the open-ended questions I was asking him. When I asked him to elaborate, he didn't. I even strayed from the topics and talked with him about video games to loosen him up, and when I went back to the interview he did the same things again. Any thoughts and/or suggestions on what I should do for next time? Mike M.

One response followed:

I have found that interviewing someone you know well—friend or grandparent for example—is difficult. Often students pick someone they know as their first interview as they think the person will be more supportive. But it is really much easier to interview someone you don't know, particularly if you have a couple of open questions to ask. Lesley M.

Here are further examples of students' online comments. Students were asked to describe how they planned to analyze a set of interview data. While they were given some guidelines to follow and had read information in their text, this was their initial attempt to analyze real data. They were asked to analyze several interviews. Each student conducted one of the interviews. After transcription, they were to transmit the interviews to all other classmates via the computer. I asked them to consider the process of data analysis and plan what they would do as they began to think about the data they had received.

I also asked them to respond to my online questions: What are some steps you will follow in beginning your data analysis of the grad student interviews? Why did you select these steps?

I began by reading each interview in its entirety. As I read, I thought about the questions that were being asked and how the subject responded, in order to gain *overall, initial perspective* [italics added] for the interview. Before I began taking any type of notes, I wanted to get a general idea of the direction/intent of the questions that were being asked and how/why the subject responded the way that he/she did. My next step was to read the interview transcriptions again to try and get some general direction and think about how the subjects actually responded/what they actually said. During my second reading, I made some general notes that I hope will aid in the identification of themes that will be amenable to additional analysis. Paul

My first few steps in the data analysis process have been *to bracket my own thoughts* [italics added] and feelings regarding the graduate school experience; to organize each of the interviews provided by the class, and then to read through each interview a couple of times highlighting or circling key words or phrases that "speak to me"—at times even memoing in the margin of the interview transcripts.

I decided on each of these steps based on my readings of Creswell's text and numerous websites, as well as our class discussion. I believe these steps will provide me some initial reflection to prepare me to begin the coding process that comes next.

As I review the above statements, I realize that I'm portraying this as a linear process. Yet, I expect much of this experience of data analysis to be iterative and simultaneous based on my readings and our discussions. Leanne

My approach to this analysis is similar to that of my classmates. However, in reading the interviews, it seems to me that as I read each one sequentially, my thoughts tend to be more of a *forward-leaning spiral* [italics added]. In other words, with each interview read, I learn more for my "database," but also start drawing (perhaps jumping to) conclusions. This is the bane of a "scientific method" based education . . . we always want to get to the (a?) conclusion. Thus, I agree with Leanne when she says that she tries to bracket as she reads. What I am attempting to do as I follow the sequential, linear approach to reading is to practice spiral thinking that characterizes some aspects of South Asian (i.e., Indian) thought. Thus, as I read I try to bracket while allowing my thoughts to loop back and appreciate and integrate what I learned from the earlier interviews read. Quite a trick . . . but that is the approach I am attempting. I am taking this approach/these steps (indeed, is not the very idea of "steps" a bit linear?) so as to get a good feel for the data. Frank

I originally thought that I would approach reading and data gathering from the interviews much like I do reading and data gathering for my other academic work. I sat down with a highlighter, notebook and pencil, and prepared to "dissect" the interviews. I ended up reading all of the interviews all the way through without making a single note or highlight. This gave me a better overall perspective to simply get an understanding (and enjoyment) of the interviews.

After reading them through, I reviewed them a second time. I began to take notes in the margins of the interviews, but in doing so, I would recall other interviews that had similar patterns (or themes). Thus I ended up putting all of my notes in my notebook. *I used a two-column approach: on one side, I noted generalized themes of interviewer questions, and on the other I noted themes that the interviewee responded (although not necessarily questioned about)* [italics added]. In some instances, I could draw a line across the column, as to which questioning concept led to which response concept. Yet at other times, I noted that the response concepts developed independently of questioning or as a result of different question concepts. This approach was the easiest for me to use in organizing the data in my mind. Heather

I illustrate here how this information can be used to understand how students process information about qualitative research. You can review the various topics that students suggested, which I have italicized in the transcripts. Paul looked at an initial perspective, Leanne knew about bracketing her thoughts (because she was following a phenomenological tradition), Frank spoke of a forward-leaning spiral (because he knew we were thinking about nonlinear analysis), and Heather got practical with developing a structure. In so many ways, these thoughts are reflective of these students. It is quite uncanny. We would never know these things in a regular classroom discussion because our data would be lost in the air.

The culture of an online classroom is also revealed by the data. Some transcripts might reveal issues about authority and hierarchy, who is in charge, and dynamics of interaction.

Opening up our courses for all to review and comment upon is a very new idea for teachers at any level. Most teachers are used to closing their doors and working with a confined group of students who they see and with whom they come in personal contact. There is something in it for the students and for the teachers as well. Teaching on the Internet poses new challenges, some of which are described by Joy (2004) in her dissertation about online teaching from the point of view of professors. She concludes that a new culture is established in such courses. I believe there is much more to study on this front.

Visual Diaries, Blogs and Vlogs

Blog is short for Web log and vlog is short for visual Web log. Technology, ready availability, and little or no cost have resulted in an enormous quantity of information presented on the Internet. I have read several blogs by individuals who are pursuing degrees in qualitative research. They are like diaries, although open for all to see. Typically, a writer makes daily entries and posts them online. Some blogs permit others to make comments. Group blogs are becoming popular. In these, a number of individuals post on the same blog.

Below are excerpts from several blogs related to qualitative research. Someone who calls herself "Profgrrrl" reveals her frustration with qualitative research in her blog of February 26, 2005:

> I entirely understand why qualitative research is often treated like the redheaded stepchild when people have these beliefs AND even worse act on them. There are a lot of crappy qualitative studies that have been published. But there are some truly wonderful ones as well. . . . *But the bottom line is that it requires a clear, systematic plan that is followed with checks in place at regular intervals.* And all too often I don't see people paying attention. Grrrr. End of rant. For now.

Listen to "Zapisała marysia o godz" in a 2003 blog:

> A friend of mine adviced me not to focus on quantitative researches and results but to switch directly to qualitative studies, especially if I wanted to study the possible psychological profile of the bloggers—"you don't need demography to do it." Is it true? I don't know. My latest observations make me think that bloggers in Poland (I am mainly thinking about those who write diaries online) have some features in common that are related both to the personality and to the sex, age or place of living. Is there a solution that I am not able to notice?

And finally, we learn about visual ethnography with "Flickr" in an April, 2005 blog:

> Last year, when I was offered the opportunity to teach a course on anthropology and photography at Haverford College, I immediately knew I wanted to do something with Flickr.

I have to admit that it was exhausting correcting papers with dozens of hyperlinks to photos on Flickr. But it was also fun. I especially enjoyed seeing the various ways students used Flickr's tags to come up with interesting paper topics. . . . One student looked at how people interact with art on camera. Comparing art in the museum, with public art. Someone looked at the "what's in my bag" meme, comparing it to John Berger's discussion of oil painting as a depiction of wealth. Another student looked at depictions of the disabled, which raged from offensive, to inspiring, to practical. Similarly, another student found offensive pictures of fat people presented as social commentary. She also had interesting things to say about pictures of fat cats.

I am not quite sure what can be done with this information, but I believe it to be useful. It may take the creative mind of a new qualitative researcher to examine how such postings can serve as data in a qualitative research study. "Where else can we learn so much that is so new, so rapidly?" I ask you. Keep your minds open.

Available Data and Communication

Have you considered what to do with the data you have collected and stored in your computer and analyzed with your software? Most of us keep close tabs on our raw data and will release it if pressed to do so, but researchers are beginning to call for placing data online so that others may gain access to it and use it for subsequent analyses. In a recent issues of *FQS* (Lichtman, 2004), transcripts of interviews or the audio version of interviews were made available as part of the journal articles.

Another advantage of the Internet in qualitative research relates to potential for scientific exchange. According to the editors of *FQS,* the Internet provides opportunities for flexible publication times; flexible publication space; and direct interaction among authors, editors, and readers.

SUMMARY

I hope you have been challenged by the new ideas I presented in this chapter. Whether you collect data through observations; using documents, records, or images; or on the Internet, the potential is there for you to learn about people and how they interact. It is your challenge to keep your mind open to new ideas and new ways of doing things.

GROUP ACTIVITY

Purpose: To develop skill in looking more carefully.

Activity: Select video or film clips showing families at mealtimes. I have used different ethnic groups showing different families. An Italian family setting can be seen as Cher plays the starring role in the 1987 movie *Moonstruck.* An excellent example of a Jewish family meal can be found in Barry Levinson's 1990 film *Avalon.* The Amish culture is depicted by Harrison Ford's 1985 movie *Witness.* My last selection shows a Christian family as Mary Tyler Moore and Donald Sutherland depict the standoffish nature of the parents in the 1980 movie *Ordinary People.* I show the videos in class and ask students to take notes on how the members of the family interact with each other. We usually see the entire set and then have a discussion. The discussion serves to simulate others to look and listen more closely.

Evaluation: Explore the ways in which class members focus on certain things and how they are influenced by the discussion.

INDIVIDUAL ACTIVITY

Purpose: To refine observational skills.

Activity: Select a television show that involves a family or members of a group. Pick at least two or three episodes. The class can identify the show they want to watch. Get a class member to videotape the shows so that you can discuss them in class at a later time. Make detailed notes on three aspects of the show. One area to observe is the things that are visible, such as the physical surroundings, how members are dressed, what props are used, and what makes the setting into a home or family setting. A second area to observe is the content of the show and the verbal and nonverbal interactions of the cast. A third area is the underlying meaning of the interactions. What are the dynamics of the interactions? What is the emotional content? Organize your notes into a one-page handout for the entire class.

Evaluation: Examine the extent to which class members are able to move from the concrete to the abstract, from the inductive and immediate nature of the show to a deeper meaning behind the surface.

Writing in your journal should now be part of your regular routine. I hope you make some comments about new technologies.

NOTE

1. This ethnocentric view was modified by Boas, who developed the concept of cultural relativism, which states, among other things, that cultural aspects of human behavior are learned and not biological. It was thought that through immersion in the society over an extended time period, the society's culture could somehow be described and understood.

PART 3

Putting It All Together

There are four chapters in this section. They are grouped together because they deal with organizing the data you have collected and presenting it. Chapter 10 deals with how you can draw meaning from the data you have collected. While I touch on the use of computer programs to assist you, I want you to recognize that you would need to spend a considerable amount of time with such programs.

Ultimately, what you present is what others will know about your research. At the current time, much of what is presented appears in written form. Thus Chapter 11 discusses various ways of communicating your ideas. I urge you, however, to consider alternative ways of communicating, and some ideas are presented for you to consider. You will read about how others grapple with judging the quality of the work in Chapter 12. Chapter 13 concludes with the self. These very important issues regarding reflexivity and subjectivity are fairly new, and I hope you find them challenging.

CHAPTER 10

Making Meaning From Your Data

Qualitative research takes time to constantly review where you are in the research process; what you have accomplished, what you have not accomplished, what challenges you have overcome and what new challenges you may have to deal with in the future. Once I was confident that I had captured my study participant's perceptions, then I organized, analyzed and interpreted my data. I began writing my findings, observations as I went along. I found that presenting the feelings and perceptions of study participants can be difficult, especially when you are trying to be an objective observer and recorder of other people's thoughts, feelings and perceptions. Capturing the experience through the images of your study participants requires good in-depth interviews, accurate transcriptions and unbiased reporting. None of which is an easy task. A well-organized and conducted qualitative research study will enable you to make valuable contributions to the literature like these from my study.

—Warren Snyder

Qualitative research, no matter which tradition you select or type of data, uses an inductive approach. Its purpose is to examine the whole, in a natural setting, to get the ideas from those being interviewed or observed. As a consequence, data analysis in qualitative research is also inductive and iterative. Some people like to collect data and analyze it simultaneously. The analysis leads to further questions that can be asked of subsequent participants. Some people find that they collect the data and then begin the analysis. While this is not advised, it often happens. But you can make the process iterative by proceeding through the steps below with some of the data and then testing it on additional data.

I see data analysis as being about process and interpretation. Whether you analyze your data through statistics or choose some other method, there is a process you follow and interpretations to be made from that process. The process in quantitative research is straightforward—at least once you determine what statistics to run. When I was in graduate school, the process was very difficult. You entered your data on 80-column cards and sorted the cards in the appropriate order. You wrote a program or selected a program to run your data, and you had your university run the program on a behemoth of a computer. How you interpreted the data you ran was also straightforward. Mostly it was a matter of testing hypotheses and rejecting (or failing to reject) these hypotheses.

Analyzing the qualitative data you collect is a daunting enterprise. One of the dilemmas is that qualitative researchers do not agree on how the data should be analyzed. Many approaches or paradigms are silent about what analysis should be performed. It is only grounded theory that makes a particular analytic approach specific.

If you have done any quantitative research, you likely have gathered numerical data, chosen one or several statistical approaches, selected a statistical software program, entered your data, and run a statistic. While you may not have been entirely clear about which statistical approach to use or precisely how to enter your data, or even how to make meaning from your data once it was run, you felt comfortable that the results you obtained were objective and scientific. Once you selected the various statistical tests to run, the process was easy: enter or import your data and run the program. You also expected that those who read your research would be comfortable with your results and find them objective and believable.

I suspect, however, that you were left somewhat dissatisfied when you tried to organize your thoughts and put words to paper. What did those numbers really mean? Why were you rejecting the null hypothesis? Could you even be exactly sure that you understood the null hypothesis? What did it mean to test at the .05 level of significance? But you were usually able to get guidance from a professor or tutor who helped you interpret what you did.

Analyzing qualitative data is an entirely different matter. The data are not numerical. There are not agreed-upon ways of analyzing the data you have. And whether you have a theoretical component to your research or not, you have the practical dilemma of doing something with the data. Most qualitative approaches provide very general information about how to do this. With the exception of grounded theory, you are pretty much left on your own. Thorne (2000) reminds us that "qualitative data analysis is the most complex and mysterious of all of the phases of a qualitative project, and the one that receives the least thoughtful discussion in the literature" (p. 68). There is a lack of standardization and few universal rules. Basit (2003) comments that qualitative data analysis is the most difficult and most crucial aspect of qualitative research (p. 143). I agree completely.

A systematic approach to analysis and interpretation brings order and understanding to your qualitative research project. You will need creativity and discipline as you embark on your data analysis. What is challenging is that the way you do this is flexible and open to discussion and interpretation. Unlike quantitative research, there are no agreed-upon statistical tests. In this chapter, I discuss several key issues.

First, I introduce the idea of data analysis as a process. What constitutes data? When should you do your analysis? How should you get started? What about coding and themes, or would you prefer to focus on the stories and narratives of those you study? How do you know when you are finished? Are you ever finished? I suspect you will find those questions in any discussion of qualitative analysis.

Next I discuss clarification of your philosophical stance. What do you believe qualitative research can do with and for data? What is your belief regarding what I call "who is right?" Do you need to verify what you have done with an expert? After all, who is an expert?

I then introduce a concrete example of what I refer to as the three C's of analysis. This six-step approach should provide you with enough detail to start your own analysis.

Another topic I cover is whether, and in what ways, you should make use of computer software to analyze your data. While most of you will have your data on your laptop computer, this is different from using computer software. If you choose to use software, which program should you choose? And how do you learn the software? Many faculty members are not qualified to assist you. Many of the instructional manuals cannot be used without additional workshops or tutoring. I conclude with new trends, especially in the area of secondary analysis.

THE PROCESS

There are various ways to conceptualize data analysis in qualitative research. I want to discuss two of them: identifying themes and telling stories. Much of the writing about analysis deals with identifying themes. Here is the idea in a nutshell: You gather a large amount of data. It might come from one individual over a long time period; it might come from several individuals; it might come from one or a number of settings; or it might come in a number of ways (chat rooms, interviews, observation notes). All data are gathered in order to answer research questions. Now, the data itself are usually so voluminous that they make no sense without some thought and organization. As a researcher, it is your task to provide that step. I have provided detailed information below on some steps you can follow to move from the data to development of themes. I see this as a process of sorting and sifting. Imagine that you have a large sieve. Some holes are square, some round, and some irregularly shaped. You put into the sieve a number of objects—some round, some square, and some irregularly shaped. You shake the sieve. The round ones drop through the round holes. The square ones drop through the square holes. Some of those irregularly shaped drop through the odd holes, while others stay in the sieve. You have sorted your objects based on a system. Some fit well while others do not. I hope you can see the parallel with the sorting and sifting I describe below. Coffey and Atkinson (1996) write about concept and coding.

One limitation of this type of analysis is that it operates from a reductionist perspective. Do we really believe that we can capture so much of what a person thinks and feels and portray it in five or six simple concepts? Some would argue that by doing this we are trying to move into an analytic mode that is more closely allied to principles of quantitative paradigms. In an alternative approach to analysis, the emphasis is on narrative or stories (Coffey & Atkinson, 1996). The intention is to examine how such stories can be used as structured or formal ways to transmit information. You can read in greater detail Denzin's (1989) account of interpretive biography. More recently, Baumgartner (2000), in her study of HIV-positive adults, sheds light on exploring how stories can be used as a source of data. I must caution you, however, that as with so much of qualitative research, the details are not explicit. I particularly like Coffey and Atkinson's admonition:

There are no formulae or recipes for the "best" way to analyze the stories we elicit and collect. . . . Such approaches also enable us to think beyond our data to the ways in which accounts and stories are socially and culturally managed and constructed. That is, the analysis of narratives can provide a critical way of examining not only key actors and events but also cultural conventions and social norms. (p. 80)

Writing about the process is linear; in contrast, actually doing the analysis is anything but. You will be faced with many questions you need to answer and decisions to make. It is often the case that you know in advance the main types of data you will collect. However, as your project develops, you might discover that additional data become available. You may decide in advance that you will use a computer software program to analyze your data. However, the program you want may not be readily available, or you may think you can learn how to run a program that turns out to be much more complicated than you anticipated. You may decide that you are going to concentrate on one aspect of a problem and then find that the data you collect lend themselves to exploring totally different arenas. You may decide to incorporate images in your data, but you are not really able to determine how best to include the visual data and how to incorporate them into an analysis. The process may appear to be relatively clear and systematic. However, in reality you might find yourself getting bogged down in details you did not expect.

What Is Qualitative Data?

I think most would agree that qualitative data generally take the form of words, not numbers. Modern writers include visual, audio, or graphic data in the definition, as well as verbal or textual data. While some argue that qualitative data can be transformed into quantitative data, I think it is those who practice a traditional or fundamentalist paradigm who take this position. If you support a more inclusive position, then almost any data you gather from, by, or about your study can be seen as qualitative data.

Suppose you are interested in studying single-sex classrooms. Some schools have adopted the practice of segregating classrooms by gender. According to Senator Hutchison, in her speech before Congress in 1999, "study after study has demonstrated that girls and boys in same-gender schools, where they have chosen this route, are academically more successful and ambitious than their coeducation counterparts." You are interested in going beyond the statistical data. You want to determine what is going on in the classrooms and how the experience is seen by various participants. Let's look at the kind of qualitative data you might collect. Here are some likely types: interview data with students, teachers, and parents; observational data recorded in note form of classroom practices and student behaviors; photographs or videos of students interacting; your notes regarding your thoughts about the practice; student work products, either on the computer or in hard copy; student chat line comments regarding their feelings about participating in this type of class; and your observations about the classroom's physical appearance and the appearance of the students. All are legitimate types of data. No one form of data is better or more legitimate or more meaningful than another type. You are limited only by your creativity and the available technology.

I use this example to help you see that the kind of data you might collect can be enormous and take different forms. It is your job when doing your data analysis to organize the data and ultimately draw meaning from it.

As you can imagine, you will have an enormous quantity of data in somewhat different forms. You will most likely transcribe your interviews and observations into a word processing program. You may have some data already on your computer taken from chat room discussions or student work products. All of your verbal data can be organized in a word processing program. You will have to devise a way to organize your visual or graphic data. Some qualitative software programs are beginning to incorporate visual and audio data and provide ways to analyze them.

I want to stress that the data will be collected not at one time but at several times across the life of your research project. In the same way, your analysis should cover the life of the project and should begin as you begin collecting your data. Planning how you will do your analysis might precede actual data collection. Let me emphasize that your plan should represent a general guide and should be modified as necessary depending on the data you collect and the available tools for analysis.

Process and Traditions

I want to comment briefly on how the different traditions you have learned have somewhat different expectations in data analysis. For the most part, the process I will describe can be followed with any of the traditions. However, the emphasis may differ depending on the tradition. I have found it very frustrating to try to determine specifically how to conduct analyses. Almost all of the material you read will leave you with more questions than answers. I know many of you will be looking at a particular tradition, so I provide you with a general sense of what each tradition emphasizes. But by no means are there specifics associated with any of the methods, with the exception of grounded theory.

If you were following an *ethnographic approach,* no specific guideposts are suggested, but you would focus on an understanding of the culture. Often your data will include field notes based on observations. You might also have data from informal interviews.

If you were following a *grounded theory approach,* you would follow a very specific three-part coding approach: open, axial, and synthetic. If you choose this approach, it would be helpful to review Strauss and Corbin's (1990) detailed explanation for this multi-step coding process. If you were following a *phenomenological tradition,* you would be interested in the lived experiences of the individuals. You would need to explore some of the philosophical underpinnings of phenomenology, but your data analysis would be facilitated if you bracketed your own views.

If you were following a *case study approach,* you might use single cases and then multi-cases, where you treated each case separately and then combined them.

If you were following a *feminist tradition,* you would concentrate on examining power disparities.

If you were following a *generic approach,* you would look for general themes or use narratives.

If you were following *narrative analysis, biographical, autobiographical* or *oral history traditions,* you might concentrate on the gathered stories and narratives and look for epiphanies.

If you were following a *postmodernist* or *critical theoretical approach,* you might look at issues of sexuality and gender. Because these approaches are more theoretical than practical, analyses are very general.

If you were using *mixed methods,* you would tend to organize your data and construct tables as well as look for themes.

What About Transcribing?

There is a considerable discussion in the literature and on Listservs about transcribing your interviews. Some equipment on the market that presumably takes audiotapes and transcribes them is not yet perfected. Perhaps by the time you begin your research, better equipment will be available. But for now, you will need to transcribe your interview data—not write a summary. This is, of course, time consuming and quite difficult, especially if you have focus group data. Some will look for individuals to transcribe their data, but, in my view, it is worth the effort for you to do on your own.

When Should You Do Your Analysis?

I see analysis as an ongoing process, not a linear process following the collection of data. A circular model of gathering and analyzing data is proposed. This is referred to as an iterative process. Often a researcher will enter data into a computer program—whether a word processing program or qualitative software program—in concert with collecting additional data. Even when a researcher makes a decision not to conduct analyses using a computer, he or she organizes the data via the computer. Having entered the first piece of data—an interview, some field notes, or the current teaching unit—a researcher begins the process of analysis. Some do this on an informal basis while others proceed in a more formal manner.

Coding and Themes or Concepts

In many traditions, there appears to be general agreement that the goal of analyzing the text and words collected is to arrive at common themes. (In the remainder of this chapter, I use the term "concepts" in place of "themes.") Most procedures involve a process in which the researcher chooses to code words, phrases, segments, or other portions of text. Some people believe that the codes should be determined a priori. However, most take the position that the codes emerge from the data via a process of reading and thinking about the text material. Aside from a specific process identified with grounded theory, most believe that coding is done through a careful reading of the text. I have seen some people read the text and mark large chunks of material with codes. Others work from a micro level and code text chunks or segments. Whatever the process, and I believe it varies by individual and perhaps even by type of data, the goal is to arrive at a manageable number of codes.

I see the process as one of sifting and sorting. You begin with a large amount of material—for example, the text of an interview. That material is dissected and categorized into codes. Next you proceed to a second interview. Again, dissect and categorize into codes. You can use the previous codes or add new codes. This iterative process continues until you have coded all your interviews. By this time you have reviewed many interviews and coded them. You can now review your codes and look for ones that overlap or are redundant. You might find that you will rename some of your codes. In my experience, you will generate many codes. These codes can then be organized into hierarchical categories, in which some codes will be subsets of larger categories. You might have 80 to 100 codes that you then organize into 15 to 20 categories and subcategories. These categories can then be organized into five to seven concepts. As a general rule, even large data sets do not reveal more than this small number of central and meaningful concepts about the topic of interest.

Narratives or Stories

In contrast to the process described above, some researchers believe that the analysis process involves identifying salient stories that either emerge from the data or are constructed as composites from bits and pieces of several data sources. For them, the meaning is in the story and in the interpretation of the story by the researcher. This process works best if you have interview data from a number of individuals, although I have also used it with detailed and extensive interviews from one or two individuals. Those who adopt this stance take the position that coding raw data into concepts is a reductionistic practice and detracts from the meaning of what is said. (See Chase, 2005 and Riessman, 2005 for additional details about the process.)

How Do You Know When You Are Finished?

Unlike statistical analysis, qualitative analysis has no defined end. You do not create statistical tables or statements about hypotheses. Rather, the process you follow seems to reach a logical saturation point. You collect your data and analyze your data at the same time. At some point you complete collecting data. That point is often dictated by time or availability of people to interview or scenes to observe. I believe that you will know when you have sufficient data. Glaser (1978) refers to this as theoretical saturation. You find that you are not learning anything new. Well, your analysis follows the same idea. You read through your text. You code chunks, whether large or small. You reread your data. You change your codes. You combine your codes. You add codes. You delete codes. You combine your codes into categories. Your concepts come out of the categories. You reread your data. You look at new data. And so it goes.

You begin to see some common elements among the various interviews or observation notes. You might also see some inconsistencies, what statisticians often call outliers. Do not discard these; they are important, but they do not discredit the coding and categorizing you have done.

Now it is time to combine these codes into categories and then into concepts. You begin your sifting and sorting process anew, but you are working from the codes, not the raw data. You look to see whether the codes can be combined into categories. You try to winnow the number of codes down to a manageable number of categories. You restructure your codes into major categories and subcategories. Again you work through a distillation from which concepts emerge from your categories.

Your final step is to select supporting evidence for the concepts or themes you have developed. This evidence is often in the form of quotations from the raw data. Once done, you are ready to write.

PHILOSOPHICAL STANCE

I agree with so many writers who say that qualitative analysis is the least understood and most complex of all aspects of conducting qualitative research. I think it is important for you to clarify your own views about the process of analysis, but first I want to reveal mine.

As the researcher, you are the best equipped to make sense of the data. Using others to verify your interpretations assumes that there are "right" themes to find or that some "findings" are better than others. Get rid of that assumption. Unlike statistical analysis, there is nothing that says that one set of interpretations is better than another. Now, that does not mean that you might not make a case for one set of interpretations over another based on your raw data, but "experts" are not needed here. You should be closer to your data than anyone else.

Using computer software makes the process easier; it does not give more reliable or believable results. The hard work of sifting, sorting, coding, organizing, and extracting remains yours.

The analysis is an integral part of the process of qualitative research. As such, it must begin early in your project. You should not wait until all your data are collected before you begin to think about your analysis. There are various procedures that you can choose to follow. Whichever you choose, you need to document how you carried out your analysis.

It is important not to get to the end too quickly. The data need to be looked at several times. Don't jump to conclusions and themes too quickly. That often leads to superficial analyses that don't really add much new information to the literature.

THE THREE C'S OF ANALYSIS

The goal of qualitative analysis is to take a large amount of textual data that may be cumbersome and without any clear meaning and interact with it in such a manner that you can make sense of what you gathered. You should not be surprised that there is no right way to do this. In fact, there is less written about the mechanics of doing such analysis than about any other topic in qualitative research. When authors do write about the process, they are quite vague. I propose here a process that I have used over many years. I suggest you think about it as a starting point rather than a prescription. I hope you will find the ideas useful.

Getting Started

Qualitative research is usually a solo activity. You collect data on your own, analyze it on your own, write it on your own, and are responsible for what you say. But we know that much of research benefits from interacting with others, trying your ideas out on others, and learning about the reaction of others to your ideas.

I know that students learn by doing and practicing. Here are some steps you can follow as you begin to work with your own data. I encourage you to work with small groups of students as you embark on looking for meaning in what you have gathered.

Now, suppose you have a dozen or so interviews and observations on a particular topic that you want to analyze. You have chosen to follow a phenomenological approach, and you know that one of the very first things you need to do is to bracket or make explicit your own views on the topic.

Preparing and Organizing Your Data

Once you have gathered your data, you need to put it into a format that is useful for analysis. In most cases, you will need to find a way to transcribe interviews, capture online discussions, or otherwise put words and text in a useful format. I recommend that you place each item in separate files using a word processing package. It is helpful to insert your comments in brackets in a different font and color.

Make a folder and label it My Qualitative Research Project. You will place several files in this folder, depending on how much data you have collected. These files can be individual interviews and/or your observation notes and your researcher journal. At the very least, you will place your data and your journal files in the folder. It is helpful if you label each file in a systematic manner. For example, suppose you have four interviews: two with the same person and two additional ones. You would create the following four files: DonaldInt1, DonaldInt2, DavidInt1, DanielInt1. By using labels like this you can add files to your project. In a large project you might have observation data as well: DonaldObs1, DavidObs1, and so on. Of course, your choice of file names depends on the type of data you collect. Some researchers like to incorporate a date in the file name.

In addition to these data files, you will want to enter your researcher journal. Make another file and label it Researcher Journal. Some people also put information collected from a literature review in this folder. This folder should be developed when you begin your research, not when you finish it. You should plan to keep adding to it as you move along.

Make sure you save a copy of this folder in a location other than your hard drive. There are too many horror stories of people who have lost everything because of computer glitches. I remember many years ago when data were collected on 80-column IBM cards. I had a friend who had two copies of her data in boxes. Unfortunately, she kept both copies in the trunk of her car. One day, after a hard rain, she discovered the trunk inundated with water. Of course, both copies were ruined. A sad lesson.

Reviewing and Recording Your Thoughts

Most people find it helpful to read through all the material in their folder. First, open a new file and call it My Thoughts. In keeping with the iterative nature of the process, you should begin by reading a transcript. Put your own thoughts and comments in this new file that you have created. It is okay to use informal writing here. Remember to date your notes. Your comments might look something like this:

9/15/2005. Read through the transcript of DanielInt1. Daniel certainly had a lot to say. I wish I had asked him more about why he decided to leave the field of teaching. I will need to remember to do that in my next interview and if I go back with him as well.

9/20/2005. Finished my second interview of DanielInt1. Glad he clarified his thoughts on this topic. Not sure I would have picked this up unless I read what he said.

Coding, Categorizing, and Identifying Concepts

You are now at a point where you can see how to move from raw data to meaningful concepts. I call this the three Cs of analysis: from Coding to Categorizing to Concepts.

Coding conversation and text into meaningful chunks is a challenging task. Whether you work with a word processing program or with other software, you have the responsibility to generate the codes. Do not expect that a computer program will generate codes or organize them; rather, you will need to provide the input. I have broken down this process into six steps.

Figure 10.1   Three C's of Data Analysis: Codes, Categories, Concepts.

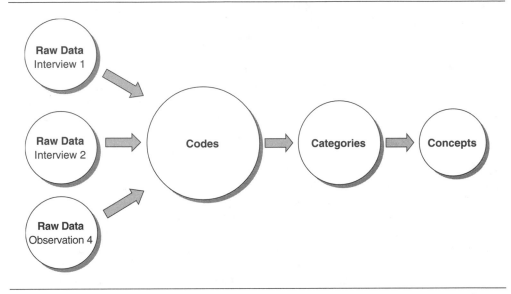

Step 1. Initial coding. Going from the responses to some central idea of the responses.[1]

Step 2. Revisiting initial coding.

Step 3. Developing an initial list of categories or central ideas.

Step 4. Modifying your initial list based on additional rereading

Step 5. Revisiting your categories and subcategories.

Step 6. Moving from categories into concepts (themes).

Step 1. Initial Coding. Even if you have only collected a small amount of data, it is not too early to begin coding. Select any transcript. Read the initial page or two. Use the "comments" function in your word processing program to insert your initial codes (in Microsoft Word, you will find the function on the Insert menu.) Enter your initial codes. Continue reading the transcript while entering different codes. Upon completion of initial coding with one transcript, select another transcript and continue the same process.

Box 10.1 is an example that might help you see this more clearly. The researcher's codes are in brackets.

Step 2. Revisiting Initial Coding. By now you will have developed a large number of codes. Some of them will be redundant and you will need to collapse them and rename codes. I have observed that some people tend to code almost every phrase or sentence while others are more global. You need to choose whatever works best. You may want to modify your codes based on an examination of what you have already collected and new raw data.

Box 10.1   Examples of Initial Coding

Transcript 1. Partial Interview: Cross-Gender Friendship

It was sophomore year in college. We knew each other—or at least who each other were—from freshman year. Sophomore year on the first day of classes, we met during some orientation. She was orientating freshmen. I was probably hanging around, looking for something or other to get into around campus. About four months after that we started hanging out constantly. [Maintenance as friendship only.]

We just—or at least I tried to—stay out of situations where it could have turned, become physical. [physical attraction] And we tried not to talk about it—those kind of things. [Evolution into something more.]After about eight months or so, things shifted. We both realized our feelings had changed. We tried to hold off as long as we could and keep the friendship as long as we could. But we started going to the next step.[potential problems]

One of the main things is that since I'm not actively seeing another person or actively engaged, is that when I meet a girl, any girl, is potentially more than a friend. [tensions/barriers]

Transcript 2. Partial interview: Cross-Gender Friendship

Someone that I can talk to intimately. Someone that I can tell just about anything. [intimacy, talk to] . . . It's just a spark similar to physical attraction [physical attraction] but it's different. You know, when you talk to them that, you know, you may not agree on things necessarily, but you can understand each other. . . . natural progression. [something more]

Step 3. Initial List of Categories. Now that you have modified your codes it is time to organize them into categories. I have found that certain codes become major while others can be grouped under a specific topic and become subsets of that topic. In essence, you have moved from one long list of codes into several lists of categories with related codes as subsets of the categories.

Box 10.2   Example of Initial Categories

(I have added ideas and restated others for the sake of illustration. Subcategories have been omitted.)

Maintenance

Physical attraction

Intimacy

Tensions/barriers

Problems

Issues with boyfriend/girlfriend

Meaning of friendship

Issues of homosexuality

Step 4. Modifying the Initial List. At this point you will need to continue the iterative process. You may decide that some of your categories are less important than others, or you may see that two categories can be combined. What is important for you to remember is that your goal in the Three C's analysis is to move from coding initial data through identification of categories to the recognition of important concepts.

Step 5. Revisiting Categories. I would suggest that at this point you revisit your list of categories and see whether you can remove redundancies and identify critical elements. In my experience, most new researchers tend to see everything as important. They appear reluctant to say that one area might reveal more interesting ideas than another. This is where you can exercise your own judgment about what is important and what is not.

Here is an example taken from an entirely different context. Suppose you have 100 books and you want to arrange them into 5 piles. Well, there are a number of ways you can do this. You can sort by color—all blue-covered books together, all green-covered books together, and so on. You can sort by topic—all books on science together, all books on humor together, and so on. Or you can sort by author—all books by Roth together, all books by Faulkner together, and so on. You could arrange by publication date—all books published after 2000 together, all from 1990 to 2000 together, and so on. Obviously, some categories make more sense than others, depending on your purpose. Further, you could place the books in subsets within each of the major categories. To continue with my example, you could place light blue books together, navy blue together, and so on. If you arranged by author, you could put major works together and minor works together.

Step 6. From Categories to Concepts. The final step in the process is to identify key concepts that reflect the meaning you attach to the data you collect. While there are no definitive rules for the number of concepts you might identify, I believe very strongly that fewer well-developed and supported concepts make for a much richer analysis than many loosely framed ideas. As you read and reread your data, you will see that some ideas appear richer and more powerful than others. It is up to you to determine that. I would suggest, as a rule of thumb, that five to seven concepts should be the maximum number that you can find in a set of data. Some information is unimportant even though it is there.

When organizing your codes into concepts, it is your task to decide what the most informative or logical manner of sorting is. You need to determine from the data what meaning you think can be found. Sometimes your initial thoughts are quite superficial. You will find that reorganizing and rewriting and rethinking often lead to more powerful ideas.

Additional Ideas

By now you will have completed the six steps in the movement from codes through categories to concepts. To add additional texture and depth to your analysis, you may want to return to your documents to look for other things that will enhance your interpretation. One promising area to explore is the use of metaphors. Our language is so rich with metaphorical allusions and they often reveal much about what others mean. To what extent were metaphors used? Are there sufficient metaphors to incorporate as part of your written paper? If so, can you code them according to certain criteria that may emerge? You might look for type of language, metaphor chosen, or gender-related metaphors.

You could also explore the use of stories. To what extent were stories used? Are there stories that might lead to epiphanies? Are some better than others? Other kinds of things to

Figure 10.2

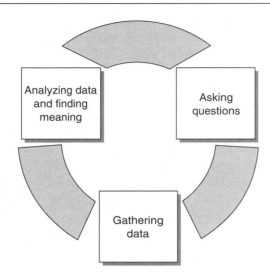

look for in your data might include the richness of detail, conflicting ideas from the same respondent, unusual or unique experiences, or ideas that contradict current thinking on the topic.

I want to reemphasize that making meaning from qualitative data is a process that moves between questions, data, and meaning. Figure 10.2 provides a summary of the data analysis process. Key elements in the model are that it is iterative, circular, and can be entered at any point. You need to try to think of your own work in this way as well.

DATA ANALYSIS WITH COMPUTERS

By now you are probably asking yourself how you can manage all of this. I remember one student telling me that she made 3" × 5" cards with codes and hung them on the wall in her basement. She placed some codes under others, thereby creating categories with subcategories. She could move these around and regroup in order to organize them into themes. Another way to organize into categories is to use markers or pencils of different colors and to sort like colors together. If you have a small amount of data this works pretty well. But even with a small amount of data you lose the links between the raw data you have coded, the codes and categories you have developed, and your concepts. And what happens if you have a large amount of data? This is where computer programs enter the arena.

As I said earlier, I expect that you will have entered your data into a word processing program and that it is located on your computer. This is, of course, valid for data that are in words. At a basic level, you can use a word processing program to find a given word or phrase in the text. For example, Microsoft Word has a "Find" feature that searches text and indicates each instance of a particular word or phrase. You could begin to code your raw data by asking the program to find a given phrase, highlight it, and change the text color. Next you could give each of those phrases the same code. You could do this for each set of raw data you have. Of course, you would have to keep track of the color and coding scheme that you have developed.

Here is an illustration. The text is taken from a student interview. I first searched for the words *love* or *like* because I noticed that they occurred in the text. Next I searched for *money*. My last search was for the term *continue*.

Q: Tell me about your experience as a graduate student.
A: School is a hobby for me. My life is work, home, and school. That's all I do.

Q: If you had the opportunity to do it again, what would you do differently?
A: When I think about it, I wouldn't do anything differently. You really have to have a *love* of school to *continue* at the post-graduate level. You also have to want to do it for yourself and not because someone else thinks it's the right thing to do for your career.

Q.   You said earlier that school is a hobby; what is your motivation?
A: I often hear people say that when they finish graduate school, it will help their career by getting them more *money. Money* or furthering my career has never been motivating factors. I have been motivated by my need to *continue* learning. Some people call me a forever student. For instance, my husband asked me if I will ever finish. I think he has come to the conclusion that I will still continue even after I graduate. I will probably teach and continue to take courses that will continue the learning process. I just choose to learn in a school environment.

Q: Since you are at the end of your program, have you thought about what you would do when you finish?
A: I will probably teach because I *love* school. I *like* learning and the feeling of helping others learn. I don't know what else to say. I am a forever student. Probably because I also *like* to read, research, and write. What a combination. Teaching will also allow me the opportunity to continue the learning process within the education field.

There are several advantages to this simple process: (1) the ability to locate terms in text quickly, (2) the ability to identify text associated with the terms, and (3) the ease of storing and accessing information in comparison to the old way of color coding or sorting on the dining room table.

But several sophisticated computer programs have been developed that permit a more elaborate system of coding, searching, and retrieval of information. QSR International has been the leader in the movement. You can read about several of their programs on their Web site (http://www.qsrinternational.com/).

When I began teaching qualitative research, I was very reluctant to use computers. It seemed to me that by using computers I was buying into a paradigm that valued numbers, tables, and precision, yet I recognized that much of qualitative research took a different approach. What was I to do? In my mind, a qualitative software program might be too structured. In fact, I was not even sure what they did.

Some of the early programs were quite modest in their capabilities. They allowed you either to enter your data directly into a program or import your data from a word processing program. Most of the functions involved word counts. It was believed that by counting the number of occurrences of a given word you would be able to conduct an analysis. Somehow I thought that magically the program would do my analysis for me. I wasn't quite sure how, but I continued to resist because that was not what I wanted.

I began to examine some of the newer programs and discovered a software package called NUD*IST. An unfortunate title, I thought. Were the writers trying to be cute? I did not know. I convinced my university that we should buy several copies and I had them placed in our computer lab. First hurdle accomplished. How was I to learn this program? The user's manual left much to be desired. During the 1990s the only training in the software was based in London. I was fortunate to be able to attend several seminars where we worked on our own data in conjunction with the software. I did incorporate some of the ideas into my courses, but in general did not ask students to use the software.

As of 2005, NUD*IST has been replaced by N6, and soon-to-be-released N7, and another related program has been developed: NVivo. Developed by Lyn and Tom Richards from Australia, NVivo has an enormous capacity to do many things with data. The user's manual is still somewhat daunting, and most students are not able to learn the software without a workshop or course. At this writing, the program is written for a PC only; no Macintosh version is available. But if you are fortunate to have access to NVivo and some training to accompany it, let me tell you what it will do for you and why you might want to explore it further.

Importing Files Into a Project. You can import any text material into the program directly from your word processing program. You can bring in one or many files at the same time. This saves an incredible amount of time. You can also link any other material that is non-textual through a process of External Links. Thus if you have photographs, or audio material that you might have collected and do not want to lose, you can make links directly to your master file. New material can easily be added. You can also bring in results of your literature review. Thus, all of your data—whether interview data, photographs, references, or notes—can be organized and placed in the same project. This is a tremendous advantage, even if the program does nothing else for you.

Coding Information in Your Project. You can begin coding the various files you have in your project. Some simple keystrokes will enable you to mark a word, line, sentence, or section and code that piece of data with whatever term you want. The program begins to make a list of the various codes you have chosen. As your coding progresses, you might find that you have used terms that are similar. The program will let you combine several codes if you wish. New codes can always be added and others deleted. You can also code demographic information and develop tables and charts if you want. If desired, the data can be exported into SPSS or a spreadsheet for display or analysis.

Organizing Codes in Your Project. You can begin organizing the various codes you have developed into a series of nodes with branches. This is the same idea that I discuss when I talk about putting codes into categories and subsets. In a way, this is how you begin to take your raw data, code them, and develop concepts or themes. The program has enormous flexibility with these nodes.

Searching in Your Project. One of the great strengths of this program is that you can conduct complex searches once you have coded your data. There are more than a dozen types of searches that you can conduct. Once you decide what you want to do, the program will locate information from any of your files and bring it into a new file and provide ready access.

Building Models. You can develop models representing your theoretical position either prior to your analysis or subsequent to it. Attractive graphics facilitate this task.

Other Capabilities. You can create a file to write your own personal memos or self-reflections and add these at any time to your project. You can manage an enormous amount of data in a single project. You can work with others on your project and share your ideas. Training has now reached the United States. The developers are readily available to answer your questions. Although based in Australia, they often are in England at workshops and presentations. QSR provides online support and runs a Listserv where most of your questions can be answered.

Limitations. As you can tell, I really like this program. But I will be the first to admit that it is very difficult to learn. I don't think you can learn it on your own, so you need to decide whether it is worth the effort. A student version is available at a reduced cost. If you get it and use it, I believe it will open up many ideas to you that you have not thought of before.

You can read about other computer software programs such as Ethnograph, AtlasTI, and so on. I write about QSR products to illustrate the best of what is out there in 2005.

Now, if you have a small amount of data and a small budget, go for the old-fashioned method. Make use of your computer word processing programs as best as you can.

NEW TRENDS

Secondary analysis of qualitative data is a fairly new idea. Heaton's thoughtful book on reworking qualitative data highlights some important issues (Lichtman, 2005). Kuula (2000) provides information about a project conducted in Finland dealing with archived qualitative data. Mruck (2005) comments on this and issues of data archiving and data protection in her editorial in a special issue of *FQS* on qualitative secondary data analysis.

A number of issues have surfaced recently regarding the use of the Internet and qualitative data. Can you use qualitative data that is found on the Internet for your study? How can you organize and process data you collect on the Internet? Are there available tools to facilitate this process? What about blogs, plogs (photo logs), and vlogs?

A number of online journals make qualitative data available to the marketplace. How can you gain access? How useful is it? Is secondary analysis of qualitative data legitimate?

Should data be archived? What about the quality of the data? Who should have access? Who should maintain the files? The Faculty of Social Sciences Committee on Ethics (FSSCE, n.d.) at Lancaster University has published a paper on the legal aspects of archiving qualitative data that addresses such issues as who holds the copyright, the potentially sensitive nature of some of the data and the potential harm to participants, and the issues of anonymity and privacy. (See also Bryman & Burgess, 1994).

SUMMARY

In this chapter I considered three topics: the process of data analysis, your philosophical position, and the use of computer software. I also illustrated how to move from raw data to meaningful analysis and interpretation. I emphasized an iterative six-step process that enables you to go from coding to categories to concepts. Practical examples and illustrations enable you to practice some of these ideas. Once you have completed analysis of the data, you are ready to consider how best to tell what you learned to others. I address communicating your ideas in Chapter 11.

GROUP ACTIVITY

Purpose: To move from coding to concept development.

Activity: Select a piece of writing from the Internet. You can use a blog, a newspaper article, or other current topic. Have each class member provide codes of the text. Review the codes together as a small group. Work in small teams to categorize the codes into themes. Compare themes from different small teams.

Evaluation: Explore the extent to which individuals are able to move from codes into concepts.

INDIVIDUAL ACTIVITY

Purpose: To practice narrative analysis.

Activity: Write a short paper using metaphors to describe an important event in your life. Share papers with class members. Compare analysis using coding and themes with analysis using narratives.

Evaluation: Determine in what ways class members are able to make meaning from each way of operating.

NOTE

1. An alternative to coding directly from the data is to develop a code structure prior to examining the data. A disadvantage of advanced coding is that it could limit you to placing ideas and statements into a preexisting structure.

CHAPTER 11

Communicating Your Ideas

This life isn't bad for a first draft.

—Joan Konner

I wished I had had more direction as to how I was to write up the results of the dissertation. . . . I found that I really enjoy that sort of research and I can see myself doing more of it. My writing has improved a lot. I learned that I can do a whole lot more than I would have believed five years ago. I found that doing it in simple steps helps a whole lot. I think it's best to focus on small doable steps. Break the dissertation up into goals. Find someone else in the process to pace you with.

—Donna Joy

In this chapter I discuss ways to write your qualitative research projects. I talk about several topics: structure of qualitative writing; the use of first person; integrating literature reviews with your writing; acknowledging the voice of informants; the value of the data; truth and fiction in writing; and alternative forms of presentation such as poetry, theatre, blogs, vlogs, videos, and audios. I also present an illustrative outline and samples from student work.

As a student in college or graduate school, you have been taught a number of characteristics of technical writing. It should be objective. It should be formal. You should not use first person voice; third person voice is preferred. It should be passive. It should be nonjudgmental. You should just report the facts. If you have an opportunity to look at a dissertation or a thesis, you will most likely see a five-chapter account that includes the research problem, the related literature, methods, results, and conclusions or interpretations. Most traditional dissertations will have statistical tables and charts and graphs as well; few will have photographs or other images. With the widespread availability of computers, there is some tendency in the United States to present these works in online formats. Such formats enable the writer to use hyperlinks and other online tools. For the most part, however, the style is formal, cool, and crisp. This style is in keeping with a foundationalist or traditional view of research.

In this book I have presented arguments for alternative research approaches or paradigms. These alternative approaches often use alternative styles of presentation. You may encounter writing that is personal, involves the researcher, and makes use of first person. It is likely to be less formal; a traditional five-chapter account is often abandoned and many structures and formats can be found. Headings are often derived from the voices of the informants. Many readers of this type of writing report being drawn to the accounts they read. Those studied take on a life of their own and are not just "subjects" in a research study. But unlike traditional research, there is no standard form for writing qualitative research.

Chenail (1995) asks us to consider several ideas when writing. Openness is critical because it builds trust between the reader and the researcher. Consequently, the writer should include information that is self-disclosing. I agree with him and recommend a section that I call self-reflection. He suggests that the focus be on the richness and depth of the data. Geertz (1973) used the term "thick description" as an important component of ethnography. Chenail suggests that a detailed and tight description must precede any generalizations. He introduces the idea of juxtaposing the data you collect with your explanations, analysis, and commentaries. I believe that the strength of what you write is revealed in your ability to convince the reader that your interpretations are reasonable and supported by the data. The acceptance of your writing comes down to how you weave your data into concepts. Van Maanen (1988), talking specifically about writing about cultures, suggests that the writer reconstruct in dramatic form an impressionistic tale as a way to crack "open the culture and the fieldworker's way of knowing it" (p. 102). He sees this as a way to "braid" the knower with the known (p. 102). In their award winning study, Ewick and Silbey (2003) use stories of citizen's resistance to authority.

FIRST STEPS

Your task as a writer of qualitative research is, as Liu (2000) suggests, to transform collected words into a piece of writing. Writing is not just putting down the words—it is making meaning of those words (Coffey & Atkinson, 1996; Liu, 2000). It would be a fairly simple task if you just needed to put down the words.

I want you to think about this idea carefully. If you are going to make meaning from the words you have collected, how do you do that? So you see that the writing act is inextricably woven with the task of organizing and making sense of your data. I have written about that extensively in the previous chapter. Here we will focus on the representation or presentation based on your analysis.

Let's first examine the structure of what you write. I suggest that there should be a structure in what you write, but there is no single structure. So you are obliged to develop a structure that fits the data you have collected, the ideas you are trying to convey, and your personal style. It might be easier for me to explain this by telling you what it is not. First, there are no agreed-upon guidelines for the organization or format of what you write. If you were writing a quantitative research article to be published in a journal, or if you were writing a traditional master's thesis or doctoral dissertation, or if you were writing a paper for a research class and the information you were presenting was based on a quantitative or experimental study, you would know just how to proceed. A journal would typically expect you to have headings that would include purpose, related literature, methods, results, and discussion. A thesis or dissertation would usually follow a five-chapter format. A class research paper would generally use similar headings. You would usually include some tables summarizing your statistics. You would write in third person, objective fashion.

I want you to take yourself out of that mindset now and imagine that you are free to develop your own structure and style. You ask yourself: How should I do that? What should I include? How much of myself can or should I include? How much of my participants' voices should be heard? Must my writing be dry and factual? Can I use metaphors and other rhetorical devices? How long should it be? How can I justify my own interpretation of what I learned? Will my work be judged acceptable? Are there clear lines between fact and fiction? Should there be? Must there be?

Before I ask you to suspend your current mindset, let me tell you about what is out there now, as I write this in 2005. I have seen qualitative research representation as theater (Franklin, Attanucci, & Bacon, 2005; Saldana, 2003), as art (Kabel, 2002), as dance (Blumenfeld-Jones, 1995), as blogs (http://www-writing.berkeley.edu/TESL-EJ/ej29/int .html), and as vlogs or video blogs stored online (http://hypertext.rmit .edu.au/vog/). Of course, these approaches are quite extreme for someone just beginning, but you need to know they are out there.

I have seen all manner of written work varying by length, by format, by font, and so on. Variation by content is all too common. I suspect this is somewhat more than the mind can tolerate. People tend to want guidelines; they want some structure; they want authorities to suggest how to do things. With that in mind, accept my guidelines and admonitions. They are meant to serve as guidelines only—they should not be seen as rigid. You are to make the decisions.

GUIDELINES FOR WRITING AND PRESENTING QUALITATIVE RESEARCH

Your Audience—What Do They Expect?

One of the first things you need to think about as you begin to write your research is the audience you are addressing. It might be your professor in a class you are taking. It might be the editors of a journal. It might be the readers of an online journal. It might be your thesis or dissertation committee. It might be a funding agency or the administration of a school system reading a project you completed. Academic journals seem to have the greatest number of rules and regulations and expectations. The best way to determine what they like and expect is to read the guidelines for authors and to examine articles in current issues.

Different audiences and venues also have a different expectation in terms of length. Journal articles might be limited to a dozen pages or less. A final paper for a class might be limited to 25 to 30 pages. A thesis might be about 100 pages and a dissertation even longer.

What Are You Trying to Say?

Do you want to tell a story? Perhaps you are writing a biography or autoethnography. Your goal is to share the life of someone and describe the epiphanies in that life. Maybe you want to describe the lived experiences of individuals who have transferred to a new school. In such a phenomenological study, you might intend to identify a half dozen or so principles regarding such experiences as they make themselves known to you through the details of the many experiences. Maybe you take a feminist perspective and your agenda is to give voice to girls in the sciences. It is up to you to decide and you are the person who knows best. You need to trust yourself and not rely on others to tell you. Other students and professors can help you clarify your thoughts, even make suggestions, but you need to make the final decisions.

So spend some time getting your thoughts together. What is important about what you learned? What adds new insights or clarifies previously poorly understood concepts? What messages are important to share? Most think that you need to go beyond description. To repeat what people have said is interesting, but I don't think it represents research. Research takes you beyond what you heard and involves your putting meanings and interpretations on what you heard. It is necessary but not sufficient to describe; you need to go beyond to give meaning. And you need to think about how what you learned informs us on a topic, takes us further than the prevailing wisdom or research.

The First Person

I urge you to adopt a style of writing that involves yourself, that uses the first person. I have written this book with that in mind. It is engaging, it brings the reader into the story, and it acknowledges your role in doing the research. It becomes more personal. It takes the reader on a journey, and it is generally acceptable by even the most conservative of writers today. (See American Psychological Association, 2001.)

The notion that writing in third person gives what is written greater weight and is more authoritative is an old one and very difficult to overcome. The prevailing wisdom is that keeping the self outside of what is being studied makes representations more believable. Atkinson (1990) posited the idea that a rhetorical device—not using first person in written presentations—would suggest that knowledge claims have greater authority (cited in Amir, 2005). But there is not sufficient evidence to suggest that this idea is really true.

Another reason often cited for not using first person in writing is that the material would be seen as more objective and more scientific. In other words, the researcher has removed himself from the message. But we already acknowledge that in most forms of qualitative research that idea is inconsistent with the fundamental assumptions of a non-foundationalist movement.

Some words of caution. Many of you will be working with advisers and faculty who were trained in traditional methods and writing styles. They will question some of your new ideas. I suggest that rather than becoming combative, you arm yourself with resources and references.

So, to get back to it, use "I." You and your readers will be more attentive and more accepting of what you have to say.

The Voices of Others

We all agree that we want to hear the voices of others. If technology permits, we might actually be able to hear or see them. But for most of us at this point in time, the way we represent the voices of others is through the written word. The people we study are real people. In contrast to traditional experimental research that studies subjects or samples (nameless, faceless individuals who represent a particular category or type), our participants interact with us, and often their stories, thoughts, and feelings capture us in more ways than we can imagine.

I remember a number of years ago sitting in my office in Blacksburg, Virginia. Alice Weiping Lo, a student of mine from Hong Kong, entered my office in tears. "What is wrong?" I asked her. She proceeded to tell me about her encounter with the wives of mainland Chinese graduate students and the difficulties they faced. She remarked that she felt guilty that life had so many hardships for these women and that she was powerless to do anything about it. She had taken on their struggles as part of her doctoral interviews. It became clear that these encounters were more than just data gathering. I encouraged her to consider working with these women after she completed her own doctoral work. I understand that she has remained in Blacksburg and provides a support network for what is now a large Asian population in the town (Lo, 1993).

I relate this example at length because it gives insight into the way in which the lives of a researcher and the people who are studied can become intertwined. Traditionalists would say this is bad and that it brings bias to the study. I need to remind you that you are not conducting traditional research on subjects. You are learning about the lives of individuals—what they think, how they feel, what motivates them, what challenges they face.

It is the goal of qualitative research to acknowledge the individuals studied and to reflect their voices. A parallel goal is to acknowledge that the writer/researcher has a voice that is tied intimately to what and who is studied and the interpretations drawn. Rather than keeping the voice in the distance or hidden, much of qualitative research anticipates and celebrates the voice.

Thus there are dual voices: the writer's and those studied. What is the relationship between the researcher and those studied? What should it be? Holliday (2001) suggests that this interaction creates a third culture: the interaction between the researcher and the participant. Holliday speaks of personal authorship by using first person to relate experience or to explain the author's perspective. This use of the personal reflects the role of the writer in the research. The writer's voice is revealed. This type of writing is associated with postmodern and critical thinking. Gilgun (2005) argues that we need to give voice to informants.

By now you understand that I want you to give voice to those you study. How you do that, how much you say, and how open you are is a matter of some debate. We are used to anonymity in quantitative research. This is not always the case in qualitative research. I can only say it depends. If you interview a public figure or one who chooses to keep his name confidential, that is understandable. But in my experience, many individuals you study like to have their names revealed. That is for discussion between you and those you study.

I find that using direct quotes is a generally accepted practice. I encourage you to do so. I recommend that you leave the language as it is given to you. You should not try to edit it or make it grammatically correct. After all, you are telling a story in the voices of those you studied. Let the voices be their own.

The Use of Metaphors

We use metaphors because they often reveal much about ourselves as writers and our participants as speakers. We use our metaphors and theirs as well. That is why it is so critical that we capture precise words and language from those we study. What is a metaphor? A metaphor is the use of one idea or term to represent another one. It is used to assist with expression and understanding. A metaphor is a rhetorical device in which we compare two seemingly unrelated objects. We can trace the use of metaphors to very early language. Some have said that the stylized cave paintings in southern France are metaphors. You can read extensively about different kinds of metaphors including mixed metaphors, dead metaphors, or extended metaphors. Using metaphors adds variety, clarity, and illumination to your writing. And if you use metaphors spoken by your participants you will extend your own understanding of them and, by implication, our understanding of them.

Koro-Ljungberg (2001) discusses metaphors and how they connect different layers of text even by telling different stories using different fonts. In describing qualitative research, Shank (2002) speaks of the mirror, the window, and the lantern.

I have spoken at length about using your voice and giving the voices of others a dominant place in your writing. In the next sections, I address some of the organizational and stylistic issues you will face.

Structure Is a Good Thing

I don't mean to imply that structure is bad. In fact, I think it is critical for a good piece of writing; it gives order and unity to what you write. I suggest that the structure you choose is one you impose and develop based on the data you have, the audience you plan to address, and the meaning you want to convey. Whichever structure you adopt, here are some suggestions for topics or sections to include. Chenail (1995) offers several alternative structures or formats for writing including "natural, simple to complex, first discovered, theory guided, narrative logic, most to least important, dramatic presentation, no special order." Whatever structure you choose, most pieces of qualitative research include the following sections.

A Beginning Section That Takes the Reader in and Sets the Stage. Traditional research writing often begins with a background, statement of the problem, and research questions. I think it is a good idea to include such topics near the beginning of what you write. I have also seen an opening paragraph that is personal and tells a little bit about who was studied or the data collected. It might relay something one of your participants said. Since much of qualitative research follows an inductive approach, this writing from the particular to the more general is consistent with that format. Here is an example:

> Sure there will be times when "I [find] myself wondering more and more why I [am] in the program." It is all too easy to find myself "feeling overwhelmed by the coursework, the workload." Still all in all, it has proven an experience beyond my wildest imagination. The personal and professional growth alone is amazing. I am actually learning (and unlearning) to "[be] open to opportunities and let the path take me to it." In all honesty and seriousness, "I would not change a thing!"
>
> In many respects, this paper is an ethnographic tribute to the graduate student journey. I have sought to share the cultural behaviors, language, and artifacts of the graduate student through a descriptive storytelling format that presents an "everyday" perspective. Of course, this topic also positions me as the researcher in the somewhat precarious position of "going native," as I am actively engaged in doctoral coursework. Certainly I am "immersed in the day-to-day lives of the people" (Creswell, 1997, p. 58). The bracketing

cautions loom tremulously. Or perhaps my immersion merely positions me for the emic perspective of an insider's view of the graduate student culture (*Ways of approaching research: Qualitative designs,* n.d.). While there are also admitted limitations in the variety of data sources, the nature of the research question, as well as the data itself, suggest the opportunity to provide a holistic portrait of the graduate student experience. Fully realizing that this qualitative effort may not generalize to the larger population, I acted on the opportunity to capture a glimpse of this world.

A Section on Methods and Procedures. While traditional research writing often expects this section to follow next, I have seen authors choose to include such information in an Appendix or at the end of what they write. I believe they do this because they do not want to detract from the personal nature and deep description about the topic. Some qualitative writing is silent about methods and procedures.

Profiles of Participants. Much of qualitative research involves the study of individuals. I often see a description of each participant, including demographic characteristics. These are usually introduced with fictitious names. Sparkes and Smith (2003) introduce one of the three men in their study.

> David is 28 years old and a teaching assistant, living in a large city in Northern England. His father, a headmaster at the local school, was the chairman of the local rugby club, and his mother was involved in the general catering for the club. (p. 302)

Harding (2005) introduces the city girl in her study:

> The 30-year-old national board certified teacher is 5 feet 6 inches tall with a medium build. She has long, red hair that she keeps pulled back in a ponytail meant to harness her curls. She wears glasses when she teaches, and they add to her overall seriousness. She is not a person who starts out smiling—I get the sense that her laughter will have to be earned. Her speech is punctuated with "Ya know what I mean?" I am never sure if she is asking this question of herself or of me. (p. 55)

Concepts and Supporting Evidence. You may see a section that identifies the major concepts that emerged from the study. Usually quotations that come directly from the data are used to support the themes. Most quotations are relatively short and several are used. The themes are often named with quotes directly from the participants.

Self-Reflection. You will often see information about the self disclosed in the writing. Here are some examples.

> While I have attempted qualitative research before, I have never felt myself being drawn into the data as I have with these interviews. The students became very real to me and I visualized them as I delved into the transitions that they experienced in their various graduate programs. Breur, Mruck & Roth (2002) commented "that doing qualitative research makes the impact of the researcher far more obvious than in its quantitative [counterpart] . . . the interactional and constructional nature of epistemological processes become more

than elsewhere evident and can be experienced in existential ways." As a student in adult learning, adult development and individual change are the lenses I use when examining data. As I reviewed the data, it helped me study individual transitions from a new perspective.

I am feeling very anxious about doing the interview this afternoon. I feel like I have a good relationship with the participant. In some ways this causes more stress because I feel like I have to be very "formal" during this process and this is very different from our usual interactions. Also, I am worried about not having a "pre-set" list of questions. What will happen if I run out of things to ask or if she doesn't respond to the questions? For this reason, I have come up with several questions that I would like to ask her. I feel like at this point I am too inexperienced to "wing it."

Conducting this study has allowed me to look back on my life as a graduate student. While working a full-time job, being a wife, mother, daughter, sister, friend, and trying to balance the demands of school are difficult tasks. I have missed, and will miss, many family gatherings and outings with friends. Sometimes it is a lonely experience, one that only another graduate student can relate, but the reward is going to be wonderful!

Research Literature. Very often the related research is integrated in the paper itself and not as a separate section.

ALTERNATIVE FORMS OF PRESENTATION

Most of you will plan to write your results and present them as a class paper or project, as a thesis or dissertation, as a journal article, or as a report to a sponsor. I want you to be aware of some alternative presentation ideas that have surfaced recently.

Schwandt's (2001) *Dictionary of Qualitative Inquiry* notes alternative means of communicating through poetry, film, drama, and dance. Ethnotheatre is an art form that uses theatrical techniques to present real research findings. You can read Boudreau's (2002) account of how Soldana, a professor of theatre, presented Wolcott's *Brad Trilogy.* Kabel (2002) writes about using poems, photos, and people's voices. Butler-Kisber (2002) also uses poetry.

I have seen a great deal of interest in autoethnography (writing emotionally about the self), in which the method and writing are intertwined (Bochner & Ellis, 2001; Holt, 2003).Quite new on the scene is the use of blogs and vlogs. A blog is an account similar to a diary usually written by a single individual and posted to the Internet regularly. A vlog is a video log that can also include words. I expect that these approaches will become increasingly popular because they reach thousands of individuals all across the world almost instantaneously. How their quality is judged remains to be seen.

QUALITATIVE WRITING

Two excellent sources of qualitative writing that reflects current thinking are both journals specifically designed to publish qualitative writing. *Qualitative Research*, from the United Kingdom, issued its first volume in 2000. The November, 2005 issue's table of contents reflects the type of article it publishes. Topics reflect a broad range of interests and cover such areas as researching online populations, a shadowing method for organizational research, and images in daily life and police practices. You can find this journal online at http://qrj.sagepub.com/current.dtl. *Qualitative Inquiry*, from the United States, also includes a wide range of topics. Its December, 2005 table of contents includes such topics as fragmented narrative and bricolage, reflexivity, the need for thin description, and poetry and prose in the story of homeless mentally ill patients. You can find this journal online at http://qix.sagepub.com/current.dtl. I urge you to look at each of these journals to get a sense of how to write your own qualitative study.

I want to leave you with some examples written by students. This first excerpt is from a paper prepared by a student taking an introductory course in qualitative research. Notice how the writer uses a first person, direct style. When she actually begins her story, she writes as a fictionalized journal.

January 15. It's time. Applications are due in a couple of months and if I'm going to go back to school, now is the time. Children are still a few years away. I can't even imagine how I could possibly balance young kids and an advanced degree program, although I'm sure some people do so successfully. And I don't want to wait the additional years until I actually have kids and then they reach school age. I've waited long enough. I mean seriously, how long can I drive around with "PRE PHD" on my license plate before actually taking action to make that a reality?

Do I consider relocating or are there viable options close to home? How to choose? I guess I need to get serious and go to the library (maybe online?) and start to weigh this out.

January 19. Just to make sure I am making an informed decision, I looked at everything—every school where my program is offered. There are very viable options locally, so I will continue to focus on these. Staying here rather than relocating is more attractive to me. Beyond cost and the application logistics of degree type (Ph.D. or Ed.D.), fees, requisites, prerequisites, and program size what else do I consider? What else is *important* to consider? The basic logistics in the Peterson's guide seem somewhat sterile—no real feel of what this will really be like. Maybe the websites offer more.

And later, she incorporates images and music.

December 3. I need help! I can't do this alone. I need additional strategies next semester. Have to make time to reflect on this—after my papers are done! Why am I even stopping to comment in this journal?!?!

December 13. Ta da! Completion and success. Now can I sleep and de-stress??? YES!!!

December 20. Met up with a few folks from my class for coffee and tea. All are weary and we look it. But no pity or despair! We are also amazingly resilient and energized by our efforts. One person, a neophyte like me, commented that she had "rediscovered learning is very energizing to [her] and exciting." What an amazing testimony. I love it! I too love "to learn and have gotten a lot of enjoyment out of the people interaction in the . . . program." ". . . just the relationships with classmates—many of them have turned into friends and that's really enriched my life."

January 1. Ever a day of reflection and planning, at least for me. Here goes.

What worked? I continue to rely on my tried-and-true internal standards of commitment, perseverance, and time management (e.g., prioritization, organization). I expect I will continue to tap these in the many semesters ahead. (C. L. Wells, personal communication, 2002)

I chose this next excerpt to reveal how Talisha described in detail her approach to data analysis. She also used color and inserts to highlight the points she was trying to illustrate. Notice the use of self-reflection.

There was a lot of information collected in each person's interview that I was not quite sure how to tackle everyone's interview. I decided to begin data analysis by thoroughly reading everyone's interview and jotting notes in the margins about statements that I found surprising, interesting, or themes that were common in everyone's interview. After finding these things, I used Microsoft Excel to create a list for everyone in the class and their interview. The list was titled according to the person who conducted the interview and then interesting and similar statements were listed under the title.

I also color coded similar themes in everyone's interviews. If a participant mentioned something about self-discovery or self-awareness, the statement would be colored **green** as in the above example of Heather's interview. Or if someone mentioned the support of family, a spouse, professors, or students, the statement would be colored **yellow**. Or if someone mentioned something about having to balance work and school, or organize or structure in order to participate in a graduate program, the statement would be colored **red**. Coding is a technique used in grounded theory's open coding. It allowed me to identify similarities and differences in the interviews. This project could be related to a grounded theory approach because, in the end, a theory could be derived regarding graduate student life from the data. (T. McAuley, personal communication, December 5, 2002)

SUMMARY

I have tried in this chapter to convey a sense of how to write up your qualitative research project. My examples are chosen to illustrate various principles about style of writing, structure of writing, and sense of self. You see how difficult a task it is. But I trust you and your readers will be rewarded if you adopt the stance I propose.

GROUP ACTIVITY

Purpose: To practice a simple writing task using qualitative data. To learn about sharing with others and revealing about the self.

Activities: Combine a group observation with a simple writing exercise. During a break between classes, choose a location where you will meet or see other students. This could be in a cafeteria, bookstore, lounge, or hallway. You are to take about 30 minutes. You will be focusing on interactions among students. You can choose any aspect of interaction of interest. You will not be taking notes but rather making mental images and practicing your ability to look and listen.

Immediately upon returning to class you will write three paragraphs. One paragraph will focus on your observation. What did you see? What do you think it means? What insights do you have about this human encounter? The second paragraph will describe your own reflections of self. How did you feel? What did you understand about the task and about yourself? The last paragraph will be about the method you used. All writing should be in first person. If possible, you should write on your laptop.

The final part of this task is sharing and getting insights from others. Depending upon the size of your class, you can either share with the entire group or split into smaller groups.

Evaluation: As a first writing task you would be looking for the ease with which you can communicate some ideas to others. Second, you will learn from others how they attend to such an observation and writing experience.

INDIVIDUAL ACTIVITY

Purpose: To reinforce writing ideas by using what you wrote in the group experience and modifying it based on what others did and what you learned about yourself.

Activities: Take your writing assignment that you produced in the above example and rework it. Work on your writing style, your ability to communicate, and your ability to set the tone of what you are trying to say. Send as an attachment to other class members. Choose one or two other examples you receive and examine how they have been changed. Begin to build a portfolio of your own writing.

Evaluation: Continue to assess your own ability to communicate. Judge what other information you need in order to move forward with your own writing.

CHAPTER 12

Judging and Evaluating

The nice thing about standards is that there are so many to choose from.

—Andrew S. Tannenbaum

I recall a number of years ago writing an article with some colleagues about the process of supervision for family therapists. At the time, I believed we used a novel approach. We videotaped several supervisors and students. We then assigned four pairs (composed of a supervisor and a student) to observe each videotape and develop themes independently of each other. The various iterations resulted in common themes based on our individual and joint observations To our chagrin, the editors of a respectable journal in the field, although they liked the article, said it resembled our own reflections and was not sufficiently scholarly or scientific. We subsequently rewrote the article in light of the criticisms. But I believe the reasons it was not accepted were that the reviewers were still developing their own criteria for judging research that did not fit traditional modes. Today, editors of various journals, while still differing on what constitutes acceptable qualitative research, are more open to alternative methods and approaches.

As you read this chapter you will become aware that one of the most controversial areas surrounding qualitative research is how to evaluate what you read. There are currently several schools of thought regarding how qualitative research should be judged, what criteria should be used, and who should determine the criteria. I see these issues along a continuum. Conservative, more traditional views, especially those that emerged prior to 1990, are represented at the right. These people believed that the same criteria used for traditional research methods should be used for qualitative research. I believe this view is now in the minority. Moving along the continuum, there are those who want to make qualitative

Figure 12.1

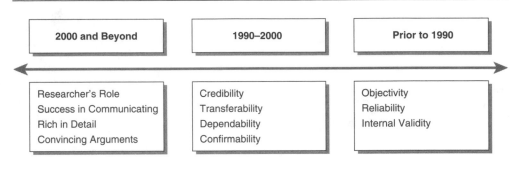

2000 and Beyond	1990–2000	Prior to 1990
Researcher's Role Success in Communicating Rich in Detail Convincing Arguments	Credibility Transferability Dependability Confirmability	Objectivity Reliability Internal Validity

research more scientific. They adopted concepts supposedly parallel to those of the traditionalists. They suggest, for example, the use of triangulation to demonstrate reliability.[1] This faction adopts a postpositivist position, in which the researcher strives for an objective stance. But this point of view, too, is not necessarily one adopted by many qualitative researchers in the new millennium. Another view is one in which such terms as trustworthiness and verifiability come into play. Criteria developed in the 21st century represent differing points of view. They tend to emphasize the role of the researcher, for example. I find the criteria very much influenced by some of the newer ideas of poststructuralism, feminism, and postmodernism.

I have identified a number of important issues. What should the criteria be to decide whether a piece of qualitative work is good, appropriate, or suitable? Who should decide these criteria? How do the criteria become modified as time and views change? Should there be a single set of criteria, or are several sets suitable depending on the type of qualitative research conducted? In what ways do alternative modes of dissemination such as the Internet affect the criteria? Differing audiences may expect different things, so a conservative academic journal might look for one thing while a more avant-garde source may expect something else. There is the academic community, the government community, and the publishing community. At times they overlap, but not always. Should the criteria be published? How specific should they be?

You might understand some of these issues more clearly if you look outside your own field and into the world of art. You might know of Edouard Manet (born 1832), a great painter and one of the precursors of the Impressionists. But if not, I suspect that many of you have heard of Claude Monet (born 1840) and Edgar Degas (born 1834). Both of these artists are considered preeminent in their field of Impressionism. The Impressionist movement was popular in the mid to late 1800s. It is generally considered one of the most popular and well-received artistic movements today. However, these artists were originally seen as outsiders. They departed from their predecessors by using light and color to depict visual reality. They worked outdoors and tried to capture how the light influenced what they saw.

But these artists were not always so well accepted. In fact, in order to show their work, artists had to be accepted in the Paris Salon. This Salon began in 1791 and eventually became a small group of people who determined the criteria for what was good and desirable in art. In 1863, the Salon refused a very important work that Manet had painted:

Déjeuner sur l'herbe (The Picnic). The artistic community of France, supported by Napoleon III, formed an alternative to the traditional Paris Salon and called it the Salon des Refusés. Manet's painting created quite a scandal. Why? Because it didn't meet the criteria that were acceptable to those who ran the traditional Salons. One reason for the scandal was the content of the painting. Manet juxtaposed a female nude with males in modern dress as a gesture of provocation. Further, Manet's painting of *Olympia* (a nude courtesan) also shocked the viewers at the 1865 Salon. People jeered at it. In fact, the first Impressionist exhibition was not held until 1874, although by this time Manet was no longer involved. By 1886, the eighth and last Impressionist exhibition was held, showing the work of 17 artists. Subsequently, the movement fell into a sharp decline. Those who were judging realized that they had to expand their expectations of what was good and beautiful. Of course, this led to many other breaks with artistic tradition, such as Cubism in the early 1900s, Surrealism some years later, and Abstract Expressionism in post–World War II New York. By the next century the artistic world had been knocked completely off its feet and room was made for a vast range of work ranging from video installations to performance art to ready-mades. No longer is it clear what art is, how to judge it, or what it should be like. What is clear is that the world has opened up to new ideas, to new expressions, and to new people who were not previously in the field.

I have gone into detail about the art community because I want you to understand that the issues the Impressionists faced are not so different from what you face. Just as "What is good art?" is a question that cannot easily be answered, "What is good research?" is a question that we consider now. With these ideas in mind, I want to begin with my personal criteria. I stress "personal" and yet want to make clear that the criteria are not presented without considerable thought, reading, and experience.

PERSONAL CRITERIA

You will find many lists of what should be included in a good piece of qualitative research. However, you will find little or no evidence that these criteria are anything more than those generated by people who have worked in the field or who have read about the field. They seem to be based implicitly on the philosophy and assumptions made by the writers. Throughout this book, I have chosen to make my personal philosophy explicit. This is important as you begin to understand personal criteria. I will talk about three intertwined concepts: the self, the other, and the interaction of the self/other. Next, I discuss the importance of setting what was studied and what was found into a larger context. How convincing is the researcher in arguing a case? A third issue is to make explicit the manner in which the study was done. Does the writer include rich detail and explanation so that others may decide its worth? Finally, I look at success in communication.

Researcher's Role: Revealing the Self and Other Connection

Why is the self so important? Shouldn't the self remain outside the research? If the self is involved, can you trust what you read? I believe strongly that the role of the researcher is critical to the work. He or she should not try to remain outside the system. He need not try to achieve objectivity, since that is an assumption of quantitative research and not of qualitative research. He need not try to get "experts" to approve of what he writes, since he is the expert in the situation. He needs to reveal himself through a process of self-reflexivity.

In addition to revealing the self, the researcher should reveal what he learns about "the other." By the other I mean those who are studied. Unlike quantitative research where those who are studied are the subjects or the sample—nameless and faceless individuals who have been chosen at random to represent others with similar characteristics—those studied in qualitative research are real people with real needs, ambitions, and desires. Their stories to ch the researcher and touch the readers. I believe that is why we are so captivated and energized by them.

I argue here that an understanding of the other does not come about without an understanding of the self and how the self and other connect. I believe each is transformed through this research process.

I have chosen to divide my criteria along several dimensions. What was studied? How was the study done? What was found? How does the writer communicate?

Convincing Arguments: What Was Studied and What Was Found

I see this concept as critical in an assessment of the worth of a piece of qualitative research, yet it is very difficult to get at its essence. What is important to one person may have no relevance to someone else. Yet if the researcher does a good job, she convinces the reader that the topic is an important one to consider and fits into a larger context. You can assume that the topic that is studied is important to the researcher. Otherwise, why would she choose to write about it? But the strength of a qualitative study is the extent to which the writer convinces you that what she studied is important, that it fits into a larger context, and that the findings go beyond mere reporting.

Rich in Detail: How the Study Was Done

You can judge what you read by the information provided about how it was done. Can you determine what the researcher did, how she did it, and why it was done? Can you follow a path to how interviews were done or how those studied were selected? Can you determine why the author chose to conduct a phenomenology or ethnography? Does the author provide enough explanation? I think it is important that you are provided sufficient information to determine what was done.

Communication: Are You Convinced by the Presentation?

Finally, we can only judge the worth of research by what we read or hear or see. You need to decide to what extent the writer reaches you by her presentation. Do the words convey a story? Does the play provide insight and meaning? Does the video clip provide a window into understanding a particular issue? Most of what you will encounter is the written word, so I want to say a few more things about what to look for.

Opening. Are you drawn into the context or story immediately? Since qualitative research tends to be inductive in nature, I find that manuscripts that draw me in and take me on a personal journey are those that are most effective. I want to be grabbed when I begin to read. This is not to say that you are just reading a story, but a story is an excellent way to begin.

Engaging Style. Does the writer use a style that is open and engaging while at the same time reflecting thoughtfulness and scholarship?

Reflections. Does the writer incorporate personal reflections and insights, thereby drawing the self into the writing?

Integration. Does the writer clarify and draw connections between the extant research, what has been learned on the journey, and her own insights?

Rich Detail. Does the writer provide sufficient detail regarding methods and findings so the reader can understand the message?

Voices of Others. Does the writer use the voices of others to reach new insights and interpretations?

Justification. If the researcher uses a particular tradition, does he or she provide ample explanation?

New Meanings. Does the writer offer new connections, interpretations, or insights based on her research?

These criteria are meant as a starting point for you as you begin to read what others have written and plan your own research. You might find that you will want to add to or modify what I have written; I hope you will. You should also find it helpful to examine criteria that have evolved over the past 20 years or so. In this next section, I offer a brief history so you can understand the context of the criteria.

WHAT DO OTHERS HAVE TO SAY?

Although I have offered my criteria for evaluating qualitative research, I think it is helpful for you to understand the larger field and what has gone before. I will begin this discussion with what is known already. What are the criteria for reviewing traditional research approaches? Most would agree that they are internal validity (the degree to which the study maps the phenomena in question), external validity (the degree to which the findings can be generalized), reliability (the degree to which the findings can be replicated), and objectivity (the degree to which the findings are free from bias). These are pivotal and expected of those conducting research based on positivist or postpositivist positions. I want you to remember these as you begin your journey to establish new criteria.

I am going to remind you again of some of the underlying assumptions on which these criteria are based. One assumption is that methods associated with the natural sciences are the best and can be used in the social sciences. Second, only observable phenomena are considered. The researcher seeks an objective reality; thus, the researcher's role is to find a way to observe the phenomena. They are not mediated through her eyes. These assumptions underlie the four criteria of traditional research.

Below, I also illustrate some criteria that have emerged as qualitative research has taken a more prominent place in the research domain. I think it will help you to see the historical and chronological evolution of these criteria. Prior to the 1990s, most qualitative researchers operated from a postpositivist perspective. As such, they found themselves in the traditional mindset. But I think some knew that something was amiss; they just weren't sure quite what.

Some criteria are generic and meant to apply to all types of qualitative research paradigms, while others are quite specific. Some take on either explicit or implicit assumptions that qualitative research should be similar to quantitative research, while others take on newer ideas.

Prior to 1990

As qualitative research began to take hold, many were unsure how to judge this type of research. Journal editors tended to rely on traditional criteria, and many journals were reluctant to publish research that did not appear to fit the format of traditional research. There were not any journals that devoted themselves primarily to qualitative research. I recall when several of us submitted a qualitative research study to a marriage and family journal. The reviews came back: We found the study very interesting but did not see it as more than some ramblings from a few people.

Among the earliest to write about evaluating qualitative research studies were Lincoln and Guba (1985), who tried to develop criteria that were parallel to foundationalist criteria. They wrote about credibility, transferability, dependability, and confirmability. Smith and Heshusius (1986) criticized Lincoln and Guba and commented that Lincoln and Guba adopted the assumption that there is an external reality independent of the researcher. I think in these early days many were left wondering whether they should adopt criteria from the traditional scientific perspective even though what they were doing did not necessarily fit this traditional mode.

By the next decade, the winds of change were in the air and we began to see alternative criteria based on different assumptions.

1990 and Beyond

During this period we see alternative attempts to define criteria emerging. One camp develops criteria that are meant to be comparable to traditional criteria. Trochim (2001), using Guba and Lincoln's four terms, compares them to traditional criteria. Thus, internal validity is replaced by credibility, external validity by transferability, reliability by dependability, and objectivity by confirmability. In my view, on closer examination these criteria are somewhat limited and limiting.

Credibility suggests that the results should be evaluated from the point of view of the participants, and thus they are the only ones capable of judging the credibility of results. I think this seems simplistic. The research is not written for the benefit of the participants. It should be set in a larger context and the interpretation of the term credibility expanded. I would agree that they may be the only ones to judge the extent to which the researcher explained or captured meaning in what he saw. However, they are not the only ones to determine the extent to which the researcher's interpretations make sense in a larger context. (See Choudhuri, Glauser, & Peregoy, 2004, who speak to credibility.)

Transferability, akin to generalizability, is the extent to which the results can be transferred to other settings. Here Trochim (2001) suggests that the reader needs to decide whether the results transfer. But he offers no guidance as to how the reader should make such a judgment.

Dependability emphasizes the need for the researcher to account for the ever-changing context within which research occurs. The researcher is responsible for describing the changes that occur in the setting and how these changes affected the way the researcher approached the study. I am not clear what Trochim means when he speaks to the ever-changing context. Does he mean the context in which the research is conducted? Does he mean the larger social context?

Confirmability looks at the degree to which results could be confirmed or corroborated by others. I have the most difficulty with this criterion since it implies an attempt to describe an objective reality.

These four criteria are typical of some of the earlier attempts to establish criteria comparable to those used in traditional research. Glaringly omitted are comments about the researcher's role and self-acknowledgment. You will see these emerge as you read criteria established more recently.

In the 1990s, many peer reviewers' assessment of qualitative research also followed criteria often used to judge experimental research (Taylor, Beck, & Ainsworth, 2001). Taylor et al. looked at how peer reviewers judged qualitative research and, not surprisingly, found six themes to be essential to the publication of qualitative research: What is the purpose of the study? How does the purpose build on previous research? How thorough is the methodology? How are the findings presented? What are the contributions, implications, and significance of the study? Is the manuscript organized, edited, and well-formatted? If you think these criteria sound familiar and represent a traditionalist stance, you are correct. The trend continues even in the new century. Writers discuss such traditional criteria as study design, sampling and data collection, analysis, findings, interpretations, trustworthiness, and implications (Bromley et al., 2002; Choudhuri et al., 2004). Morse (2003) acknowledges what she calls the "uncertain exploratory nature" of qualitative research using a flexible design and emerging findings. Yet she suggests that evaluators look for relevance (the worthiness of the question and its value), rigor (the adequacy and appropriateness of the method used to answer the questions), and feasibility (the ability of the researcher to conduct the research) (p. 833).

Other approaches ask us to consider rigor by looking at five fundamental considerations: Does the researcher convey reflexivity or the ability to stay open to the participant's experience? Does the researcher show credibility or validity and accuracy (a concept of traditional research)? Is transferability observed or the ability to generalize (again a concept from traditional research)? Is there an audit trail? And is there confirmability or objectivity?

Some traditionalists use the concept of triangulation. In general, triangulation refers to the idea that multiple sources bring more credibility to an investigation. Guion (2002) offers an elaboration of the idea in that she identifies five kinds of triangulation: data triangulation, investigator triangulation, theory triangulation, methodological triangulation, and environmental triangulation. Most writers think about data triangulation, in which data from different sources are collected. Investigator triangulation involves the use of different investigators, while theory triangulation involves the use of multiple perspectives. Multiple methods is the mainstay of methodological triangulation. Finally, using different locations or settings is the key element of environmental triangulation. I believe that triangulation was adopted as a way to make qualitative research more objective and less subjective—in other words, more scientific. In other words, if one view of something led to one interpretation, looking at that thing from two different vantage points, where all led to the same interpretation, made the interpretation more acceptable or more legitimate. Guion's concept that there can be triangulation of different kinds of things besides data is an elaboration of the same idea. In contrast to criteria that build on fairly traditional notions of what makes for good research, others take a somewhat different view.

As mentioned earlier (p. 24), Parker (2003, pp. 5–6) poses four questions regarding criteria that address issues relating to what is good, who is the audience, what is analysis, and role of theory. Rather than answering these questions in a predictable manner, he suggests that there are no clear answers. Instead he suggests that we explore three additional issues as well as their exceptions.

1. How is the study related to existing research? We know that a study does not exist in a vacuum and that we need to relate our research to existing research. But isn't it possible that there is no existing research out there and the absence of research may be equally important?

2. Does the narrative move in a linear fashion to reach its conclusion? In general, we expect this to happen. Parker suggests that may be times when a fragmented form is more appropriate and a traditional format may inhibit innovation.

3. To whom is the research accessible? He suggests that at times issues are complex and arguments difficult to write, thus making writing less accessible.

I find it particularly interesting the he suggests "the study should make clear by what criteria it should be evaluated"(Parker, 2004, p. 6) and when the rules should be followed or broken. In encouraging innovation and flexibility, Parker suggests that criteria typically associated with quantitative research are not necessarily appropriate in qualitative research.

Devers (1999) and Hoepfl (1997) agree that clear criteria are critical, but express the concern (as I have) that we have been relying on traditional criteria based on positivism. Devers wants criteria to address the voice of the researcher and alternative means of reporting. Denzin and Lincoln (2000) add the ideas of verisimilitude,[2] emotionality, personal responsibility, caring, political praxis, multivoiced texts, and dialogues with subjects. I know you will agree that these ideas bear little resemblance to the criteria I mentioned earlier.

But Parker (2003) warns that using fixed criteria might limit innovation as it has done with traditional psychological research and risks making legitimate certain types of qualitative research at the expense of others (see also Elliott, Fischer, & Rennie, 1999). He continues that there really are no overriding criteria that fit a particular situation. He suggests that new research questions call for a new combination of research methods.

Barbour and Barbour (2002) caution against using checklists that appeal to credibility and rigor and suggest that some of the most influential papers would not have been published if traditional criteria had been used. They conclude their thoughtful article with the suggestion that qualitative researchers and reviewers should look for suggestions from their own modes of collaboration and look for new ways of collaborating.

Other new ideas are emerging. For example, you will see such criteria as including thick description, prolonged engagement (this is primarily appropriate for ethnography), reflexivity (consideration of subjectivity and bias—an idea from traditional research), member checking (using respondents to check language—an idea that the researcher is trying to "get it right"), theoretical richness (incorporation of appropriate theory, which only works if theory is an issue), alternative structure for writing, and expressiveness (data and analysis should be interesting).

Morrow (2003) speaks to credibility/trustworthiness/rigor and validity in a recent syllabus for a qualitative course in psychology:

> If necessary in your field, give rationale and educate a bit. DON'T do this if your program is accustomed to qualitative research, as you will bore them to tears. The 10th time one reads about Guba and Lincoln's parallel criteria they will want to cry. If using critical or feminist or other ideological theory, describe authenticity criteria and how you will accomplish them.
>
> Briefly summarize components of rigor that you have already described (self-reflective journal, multiple data sources, immersion in the data, peer research team, etc.).

One final take on criteria for judging qualitative research comes from the United Kingdom. The list below reflects some of the thinking that has emerged as the new century is upon us.

- Owning one's own perspective, and reflecting on subjectivity and bias
- Producing coherent connection between theory and method
- Focusing on meaning
- Accounting for, and being sensitive to, context
- Open-ended stance on data collection and analysis
- Collection of, and in-depth engagement with, "rich" data
- Balancing description of data with interpretation of data
- Offering transparent analysis (e.g., grounded in example)
- Offering plausible/credible/meaningful (to reader or others) analysis
- Offering sense of what is distinct within account of what is shared
- Drawing out "resonant"/accessible conclusions (Larkin, 2002)

What is clear is that criteria in the 21st century are not one-dimensional. Patton (2002) has suggested different criteria depending on the type of qualitative research being conducted. He suggests that a traditional, scientific type of qualitative research would involve the expected ideas of objectivity, rigor, generalizability, and triangulation. On the other hand, a study that used social constructivism would look at trustworthiness, reflexivity, particularity, subjectivity, and multiple perspectives, and a study based on critical change would identify the nature of injustice and inequality and issues of power and of taking action. Despite the diversity of views on the feasibility or desirability of criteria, many believe that several criteria need to be developed. However, it is clear that more discussion and debate should be conducted.

So you can see that during the last decade of the 20th century, scholars and researchers were struggling with how to evaluate these new products. Almost all accepted the idea that the traditional criteria of objectivity, reliability, validity, and generalizability were not appropriate. Some looked for parallel ideas, while others recognized that alternative criteria needed to be developed. Some hold to the view that qualitative research should not be evaluated in the traditional manner but rather should be judged by the user. By the time you read this I think you will find that the field is still in a state of evolution.

JOURNALS AND EDITORIAL BOARD CRITERIA

I think you might find it interesting to read about the criteria that qualitative journals use in evaluating studies. You can find a comprehensive list of journals that publish articles of a qualitative nature at http://www.slu.edu/organizations/qrc/QRjournals.html.

I e-mailed the editors of several journals specifically aimed at publishing qualitative research studies. All agreed that their journals did not publish specific criteria. Paul Atkinson (editor of *Qualitative Research*) commented that he was not convinced that "codification of such criteria" was particularly helpful (P. Atkinson, personal communication, 2005). Norman Denzin (editor of *Qualitative Inquiry*) suggested I read the chapter in his book *Performance Ethnography* on reading and writing interpretation (N. Denzin, personal communication, 2005). Jude Spier from the *International Journal of Qualitative Methodology* sent their editorial review form. The six review criteria included: relevance to journal's purpose; quality of information, writing, and documentation; and adherence to ethical standards. Ronald Chenail (editor of *The Qualitative Report*) indicated they did not have a set of written criteria. He referred me to several journal articles with guidelines for publication (R. J. Chenail, personal communication, 2005).

SUMMARY

Just as the field of qualitative research has undergone major changes over the past 20 years or so, how we judge what is good and worthy has also undergone changes. There is by no means agreement as I write. One group continues to hold on to traditional criteria. Although they try to adapt them to fit many of the characteristics of qualitative research (e.g., small numbers of people studied, unstructured interviewing, and the role of the researcher), attempts are made to develop parallel criteria to those associated with experimental, traditional research.

At the same time, others have moved far away from those traditional criteria and identify new areas that we should look at. Many ask us to address the role of the researcher in ways other than apologizing for the researcher showing his own point of view. They value it rather than see it as a limitation. The richness of the story and the detail with which it is told offer us insight into a clearer understanding of the lives of humans.

GROUP ACTIVITY

Purpose: To compare my criteria with Lincoln and Guba's four criteria—credibility, transferability, dependability, confirmability.

Activity: Select a qualitative research study that has been published in either *The Qualitative Report* or *FQS,* two journals that are devoted exclusively to qualitative studies and that are in the forefront of thinking in this area. Make sure the study represents a completed piece of research. Together with two other students, read the study, then discuss the two sets of criteria and decide how they are alike and how they differ. Now evaluate to what extent the study does or does not meet my criteria and the others I describe above. Comment on what the authors might have done differently.

Evaluation: Gauge how students are able to select specific elements from a study to illustrate the extent to which it is judged "good."

INDIVIDUAL ACTIVITY

Purpose: To learn how to add your own voice to what you are doing. By this time, you have begun to think about the field and have some of your own ideas. I would like you to work on developing your own checklist.

Activity: Working from my checklist, react to each item and indicate what you like and what you would change. Share with the class, if time permits.

Evaluation: Here you will begin to see how students are evolving and thinking on their own. You should get a range of comments and hopefully some that you can use as you develop new criteria or adapt what is out there.

Journal entries should continue even if I haven't reminded you to do so.

NOTES

1. Triangulation is a concept coming from trigonometry and geometry. It is the process of finding a distance to a point by calculating the angles to it from two fixed points a known distance apart. It is used in surveying, navigation, and the aiming of weapons.

2. This concept refers to the appearance of truth.

CHAPTER 13

Self-Reflexivity and Subjectivity

He who knows others is wise. He who knows himself is enlightened.

—Lao Tzu

The process of doing your dissertation is not given to you in a neat packet of information. After all self-direction is a big part of the process. Therefore, learning how to work through problems and difficult situations is part of the process. Being able and having the drive and determination to complete the process was probably the most important thing I learned about myself. Writing was a struggle. I found that writing in a scholarly manner while maintaining a readable document for the audience of parents and teachers at the Center was difficult to achieve. Do not take long breaks from your work, stick to it! Have your research advisor and your chair read and monitor your work along the way. Find support through classmates and obtain your family's support. Stay focused and get it done!

—Paul Glass

Working on my dissertation has been very helpful in teaching all of my classes, in observing student teachers, in working with doctoral students, and in conducting my own research. It also helped me to develop keen observation skills, to analyze data and write about my research. I am able to perceive my life differently as a teacher, as a researcher, and as a woman. I am told that I have keen observational skills, and these skills help me to open up to a whole different world in which I am more analytical, critical, and insightful. I have also noticed that by working on my dissertation, I can see things in contextual ways, and I also pay more attention to detail now.

—Satomi Izumi Taylor

Writing the dissertation was one of the most challenging and rewarding experiences of my life. I see myself as a lifelong learner with a long interest in research. The dissertation gave me valuable skills as a researcher while also forming valuable connections with faculty at Virginia Tech. I believe the whole dissertation is a process as well as a product (yes, a copy does sit as a featured book on my coffee table!). It was in the process rather than the product that true learning took place. It was transformation from a neophyte doctoral student to a confident researcher that evolved during this endeavor.

—Judy Smith

Throughout this book I have tried to expose you to some of the most recent thinking on topics of interest to qualitative researchers. At the same time, I have tried to provide you with sufficient background to understand these issues. I think this challenge has influenced me to clarify my own thoughts so I can explain to you more clearly.

One of the foundations of traditional research, and one that has been ingrained in many of us, is objectivity. Objectivity is considered to be a fundamental assumption of traditional research. You can think about objectivity in this way: In traditional research, the researcher designs an experiment in such a way that he remains outside of the system and keeps his own biases external to the system. For example, in collecting data about how students performed in reading, a researcher might give a standardized test following a set of prescribed guidelines. Each student would have the same input in terms of how to take the test. Ostensibly, then, the results would not be influenced by the test administrator and thus would be "actual" or "true" results. In terms of judging how good a piece of research is, the scholarly community would look for safeguards that would keep the researcher outside the system. By using such standardized procedures, the research would be more acceptable and credible to the scientific community. You may have heard of double blind studies in medical research, in which different groups are unaware of which group they are in (whether treatment or control-placebo group) and researchers, too, are unaware of which group receives the treatment and which does not. It follows, then, that a hallmark of good traditional research is to strive for objectivity.

Now, some have said that there are at least two problems with this scenario. Breur et al. (2002) speak about the "fiction of objectivity." So they make the case that objectivity cannot really be attained.

In their everyday scientific life almost all (experienced) researchers nevertheless "know" about the impact of personal and situational influences on their research work and its results. "Officially" and in publications these influences are usually covered up—they are treated as defaults that are to be avoided. (¶ 1)

A second point is that much of qualitative research, whatever the tradition or approach used, acknowledges the role of the researcher as a filter through which data are collected, organized, and interpreted. As such, looking for objectivity is not only foolish, it is impossible. Researchers should not strive to be objective and look for ways to reduce bias. Rather, they need to face head on the subjective nature of their role. They need to consider effects on the research process and effects on themselves.

I am going to write about some of these issues in this chapter. Before I do that, I want you to consider yourself. Here is an exercise you might try. Take out one piece of paper. Fold it in half lengthwise to make two columns. In one column, write down three characteristics about yourself that you think will make you a good qualitative researcher. Put the heading "good researcher" at the top. In the other column, write down three characteristics that you think you will need to work on to improve your ability to do this kind of research. Put the heading "work on" at the top. This should take you about 10 minutes. Since part of this exercise is about revealing yourself to yourself and to others, you will be sharing your ideas. Hand the paper to someone else in your class and ask him or her to read it. The final part of this exercise is for you to go to your journal, enter the date, and write about how you felt making your strengths and weaknesses explicit and how you felt sharing them with others. You have just finished an important exercise in self-reflection. Hopefully you will have learned a little bit about yourself and why revealing and reflecting on the self is so powerful. You should now read Day's (2002) article "Me, My*self and I: Personal and Professional Re-Constructions in Ethnographic Research." After I take you on a personal journey, I will talk about the role of the self in qualitative research, reflexivity, and self-awareness and growth.

PERSONAL JOURNEY

Most of your professors remain impersonal and remote. They share very little about themselves. Yet my students tell me that they looked forward to being in class with me and to see what I was wearing. Did I have new earrings? What sort of odd clothes was I wearing? At first glance, wondering what clothes your professor is going to wear may seem trivial, but it reveals how we connect with others. Our first impressions are lasting and reveal so much of ourselves and what we react to in others. So while I have not ever read a textbook in which the author shared anything except acknowledgments to those who helped her or thanks to family members, I have decided, as I wrap up my writing of this text, to share my journey into this field of qualitative research. If you find it irrelevant or boring, feel free to skip ahead.

I began my professional career late in the 1960s, having received my doctorate in educational research. After working as a public school teacher and reading teacher, I decided that teaching at the college level would provide me with maximum flexibility to raise my three small children and juggle the demands of work and family. I was sure that I knew what was right about doing research and for many years taught statistics and research methods. I thought I knew what others should do and valued statistics and experimental research more than anything else. I remember that even in college I was attracted to the positivist Auguste Comte and wrote a paper on his ideas for a senior project.

My transformation began during the mid-1980s, when I relocated to the main campus of my university and availed myself of the opportunity to take courses. I chose a course in marriage and family therapy. One course followed another, and soon I was interning at a family therapy clinic. I was exposed to professional writing far different from what I normally read. "Multiple realities" was a term I often encountered. In couples therapy, for example, a husband might see things one way while his wife interpreted the same situation in quite a different way. Who was right? I decided that neither was right and that personal experiences and viewpoints shaped their realities. Some of my students at this time were pursuing degrees in family therapy and welcomed alternative approaches to answering questions. I became the research adviser or "designated hitter" for students who were both in my classes and with whom I attended class. A strange place to find myself, I thought.

I remember thinking about the inappropriateness of conducting multiple regressions to analyze data they collected. All students had to learn how to do them, but they demanded predicting a single outcome based on several isolated variables. They used a linear approach and looked for cause and effect. Yet the questions I found myself asking about family therapy did not seem to be explicable using this kind of statistic. I did read a number of studies comparing various approaches to family therapy and asking which one was better. I was not interested in questions like that. I recall Scott Johnson, a student who wanted to study the Laocoan sculpture in the Vatican. This sculpture shows the interrelatedness of family members. He traveled to Rome and spent time with this work of art. We encouraged him to think outside the box as he completed his dissertation on the topic, and in 2005 Johnson is the president-elect of the American Association of Marriage and Family Therapy. I wonder where he would have been if we had insisted he follow a traditional research path rather than his muse.

At the same time, my colleagues in our traditional educational research department thought something had happened to me. "What about objectivity and science?" they asked. How could you do a dissertation on such a small number of individuals? Were these methods legitimate? One colleague asked me whether I had lost my mind. Another remarked that he thought we might teach students about this emerging field, but that it could not replace the real way to do research.

My classical training in behavioral science methods and statistics had served me in good stead for close to 20 years. Was I to throw over everything I knew and believed in? I had no one to talk to and worse yet had colleagues who, behind my back I suspect, laughed at me or at least thought I was getting careless. I had always been somewhat of an outsider, so this role for me was not new. The more I read in family therapy, the more I questioned why we were doing certain things. Why would we impose an experimental design and hypothesis testing on questions that were somewhat vague and unclear? Why would we expect linear thinking when so much of family therapy came in many directions?

I religiously attended meetings of my professional association—The American Educational Research Association—but felt that my thinking was disparate from the mainstream of the community. Instead, a chance meeting of the American Association of Marriage and Family Therapy put me in contact with Ron Chenail, Tony Heath, and others. We seemed to be talking the same language. I was drawn to their ideas and welcomed the opportunity to contribute to the new journal that Ron was developing. While my professional life seemed to be on a new course, my personal life took many twists and turns. My first husband and I divorced after many years of marriage, and I found myself needing to address my personal and family life. I married a colleague. My time and attention seemed to be drawn more to taking care of my new husband and family, and my quest for new ideas in my professional life took something of a back seat.

During this time, I developed several courses in qualitative research, worked diligently to develop courses to be taught online, and devoured all there was to read on this new topic. I worked in isolation much of the time, not finding colleagues with whom I had a sense of camaraderie and cohesion. I questioned my own ideas and training, was challenged by the new ideas, and continued to believe that other ways of doing research were legitimate and appropriate.

My growing interest in art also influenced me. Many movements in art had paralleled these times in research methods. I was especially drawn to the Cubist movement and developed a paper and presentation on how Picasso and Braque were seen as outsiders and were rejected because of new ways of doing things. The Old Guard was judging, but perhaps their criteria were not appropriate for the new way of doing things. This seemed to me a mirror of what I was finding in qualitative research. What was right? In fact, I asked myself, was there a "right" at all? And who were the guardians of the criteria?

I should say a word or two about being female. In 1974, when I answered an ad for a position in educational research that a colleague of mine called to my attention, I received a phone call from the chairman of the search committee. Unfortunately, he is no longer with us today. He remarked that he liked my credentials and he was especially pleased that I was female. I was offended. How dare he. Little did I realize that the department of 11 faculty members I joined was all white men. I actually was subconsciously pleased with myself. I was good enough to join the men, I thought. Although a decade earlier Betty Friedan's *The Feminine Mystique* (1963) made a profound impact on my decision to return to graduate school, I still thought that somehow being in this profession dominated by men was to be valued and that I would be thought of more highly than if I were pursuing a "soft" discipline like anthropology or sociology.

My department expected that students would adopt the scientific method and pursue statistics; they looked with disdain on anything other than that. All our courses were aimed at teaching about experimental design and hypothesis testing. I went along with the tribe. I was sure I was doing right.

I am not quite sure when this notion of "doing right" left me, but it certainly has. Rather, I would like to think of "doing" and not "doing right," for I question whether there is a "right" or a "best." And if there is, who is to be the judge of that? After all, the scientific community had been established by men, white men at that, and men from Europe or the United States. There was no place for the voices of women. While I can't find a reference to it, I remember that early versions of the American Psychological Association's Manual of Style cited men and women differently in a reference list. Women were cited with their first names, while citations for men included only initials. Professional associations were dominated by men. There was no place for the voices of people of color. There was no place for the voices of people from South America or Asia or Africa. In 2005, things are different, but in those early years that was not true.

Life-threatening illnesses have a profound effect on our lives. We worry that we might not be here tomorrow. We worry that we won't have accomplished what we set out to do. We worry that we won't have made a contribution. We worry that our time will come before we are ready. In 1999, I was diagnosed with breast cancer. I could hardly believe it. I was young and healthy and vibrant. I am here today and feel better than ever. In 2002, my husband was diagnosed with cancer; sadly, he lived only one year longer. I am truly sorry he is not here, but I have learned to go on and to value our time each day. I share with others this philosophy.

So here I am in 2005, writing a book for education students about qualitative research. I do not claim to know everything. I do not say that one way is better than another. I do not have all the answers. But I offer many questions and some solutions. I urge you to be creative and bold. I urge you to take a risk and follow your own muse. I urge you to disclose who you are to others and especially to yourself. We are always in a place of becoming.

Perhaps you wonder why I tell you all this information. I hope you will see that by disclosing my personal story I will get you to reveal yours. And by modeling yours, you will get your participants to open up and reveal the fabric of their lives in ways you could not expect. You need to explore why you are in school, what you hope to accomplish, and how you plan to get there. And as you examine doing research, you need to think about what works for you and how best to accomplish your personal goals. I wish you luck.

ROLE OF SELF

Let's begin our discussion with this premise: Qualitative researchers involve themselves in every aspect of their work. Through their eyes, data are developed and interpreted. Through their eyes, meaning is brought from an amalgam of words, images, and interpretations. Through their eyes, a creative work comes into fruition. We are not static humans who maintain an aloof posture as we pursue our thoughts, dreams, and desires and the thoughts, dreams, and desires of those from whom we learn. Rather, our work is an expression of who we are and who we are becoming. In fact, Haskell, Linds, and Ippolito (2002) see this expression as making the research more meaningful as we appreciate our own role in it. Consider this question: In what ways are the researcher, the participants, and the setting shaping each other?

I cannot emphasize enough that the researcher is critical in all forms of qualitative research. It is through her senses that information flows. It is through her senses that meaning is constructed from available data. It is through her senses that ideas are generated. Since it is the researcher who is the conduit through which all information flows, we need to recognize that the researcher shapes the research and, in fact, is shaped by the research. As a dynamic force, she constantly adapts and modifies her position with regard to the research topic, the manner in which questions are formulated, and the interpretations she gives to the data.

I often find that students apologize for not being objective. They think they should strive to be objective even if they recognize that they cannot. I believe this comes from some misunderstood assumptions. Let me reiterate. The researcher plays a critical role in all aspects of the research process. As such, she cannot and should not take the position that she wants to remain objective. It is really not desirable or expected.

REFLEXIVITY

One definition of reflexivity is a bending back on oneself. I think about a reflex action when the doctor hits your knee with a little mallet. According to Russell and Kelly (2002), reflexivity is a process of self-examination primarily informed by the thoughts and actions of the researcher. Ahern (1999) says we can put this into operation by using diaries, by reflecting on our own assumptions, and by clarifying our own belief systems.

Although you can find many meanings for the term reflexivity, it is usually associated with a critical reflection on the practice and process of research and the role of the researcher. It concerns itself with the impact of the researcher on the system and the system on the researcher. It acknowledges the mutual relationships between the researcher and who and what is studied. It is often associated with postmodernism.

You need to ask yourself what is meant by the term reflexivity. Much has been written about this topic in the last 10 years or so. I want you to think about reflexivity in at least two ways. One idea is that by acknowledging the role of the self in qualitative research, the researcher is able to sort through biases and think about how they affect various aspects of the research, especially interpretation of meanings. Creswell's view reflects this idea. The qualitative researcher is aware of and sensitive to the way his or her own history shapes a study (Creswell, 1997; Nightingale & Cromby, 1999).

An alternative is to acknowledge that the researcher is the instrument through which all meaning comes and that she shapes the research and is shaped by it. Rather than seeing this as a drawback or limitation, self-reflection can be seen as an asset. Fook (1996) speaks about celebrating the self in qualitative research. Reflexivity is also connected to power (Adkins, 2004; Pillow, 2003; Reinharz, 1997). For example, Pillow (2003) suggests that through reflexivity qualitative researchers can question certain practices, especially those related to postmodern ideologies. She highlights the idea that not only is reflexivity a recognition of the self, it is also recognition of the other. She urges us to move away from the comfortable uses of reflexivity toward uncomfortable practices that enable us to recognize the complexities and intricacies of the qualitative.

Pyett (2003) reminds us that especially in data analysis, constant reflexivity and self-scrutiny is needed. She talks about a balance between creativity and rigor. Tinelli (2000) revealed much about himself in his dissertation on how leaders lead.

Lest you think that qualitative research or anthropology or sociology are the only domains in which self-reflection has become popular, I want to remind you to look at Chuck Jones's 1953 "Duck Amuck" cartoon for Warner Brothers. This masterpiece is now being recognized as *the* self-reflexive film. Polan (2004) uses it as his example of self-reflexivity in "Brecht and the Politics of Self Reflexive Cinema," and Bordwell and Thompson (2004) use it as their example of Hollywood animation in "Film Art." Self-referentiality has been explored in many other fields, including quantum mechanics, mathematics, computer programming, evolution, computer-based writing such as hypertext, and the visual arts.

SELF-AWARENESS AND GROWTH

Arvay (1998) reflects on her struggle with the issue when she comments on self-disclosure and vulnerability in a narrative research project. Researcher self-disclosure, when carefully and appropriately offered, initiates authentic dialogue. It is a way of sharing the self of the researcher, exposing beliefs and feelings, and contributing to the construction of the research narrative. As a feminist practice, it supports the notion of nonhierarchical research (Josselson, 1996; Reinharz, 1992). These presuppositions about researcher self-disclosure influenced the communicative interactions between my self and the participants.

Reinharz (1992) states that "researchers who self-disclose are reformulating the researcher's role in a way that maximizes engagement of the self but also increases the researcher's vulnerability to criticism, both for what is revealed and for the very act of self-disclosure" (p. 34). What this criticism suggests is the traditional positivist paradigm's insistence on being "objective." I am not alone in my approach to research as conversation. There are many human science scholars who are taking a holistic, reflexive approach to science and who are investigating the moral and emotional aspects of their work (Behar, 1996; Denzin, 1997; Josselson, 1996; Richardson, 1997). As researchers, we are "situated actors" (DeVault, 1990), and we need to understand the nature of our participation in what we know. We need to include ourselves in our research texts in visible ways in order for the reader to discern our interpretations. Also, there needs to be a place in research for somatic and emotive ways of knowing in the construction of knowledge. Reflecting on the process of self-disclosure and its impact on knowledge production during the research encounter is a starting place.

I hope you will see how revealing aspects of yourself will serve you well as you begin to study the lives of others. Thinking about how you serve as the instrument of research is critical as you gather data, analyze it, and construct meaning.

SUMMARY

In this chapter I shared my personal journey through the world of quantitative research and then to qualitative research. I discussed how self-disclosure and reflecting on the self assist in your interpretation of information. I also talked about how modeling reflexive behavior facilitates openness in your respondents.

FINAL ACTIVITY

Purpose: To examine how you have changed as a result of learning different ways of doing research.

Activity: Post a blog or vlog on the Internet regarding yourself as a student and your growth and thinking about research. At the time of this writing, I have read a few blogs that speak of a student's growth. Post a blog for at least one week. Comment on other blogs posted by students in your class and others.

Evaluation: Judge to what extent your knowledge and experience reflect new ideas and your ability to communicate them to others.

EPILOGUE:
KEEPING ABREAST
OF AN EVOLVING FIELD

Some set great value on method, while others pride themselves on dispensing with method. To be without method is deplorable, but to depend on method entirely is worse. You must first learn to observe the rules faithfully; afterwards, modify them according to your intelligence and capacity.

—Lu Ch'ai, *The Tao of Painting,* 1701

Reality is merely an illusion, albeit a very persistent one.

—Albert Einstein

This chapter will be brief. It is possible that by the time you read it, these ideas will have entered the mainstream of the qualitative research field or may have disappeared entirely. What I found in my journey with this book is that what I thought I knew when I started has been enlarged, transformed, modified, and enhanced. It could only be so because our lives make it so.

What else is out there? What is on the cutting edge? What ideas will challenge you to think about and rethink qualitative research and your role in doing it and changing it? How can you possibly stay current? What strategies do I use? What do I wish would happen?

THE INTERNET

I believe that more than anything else to date, the Internet has changed the way we access information, communicate with people, and learn about new things. It has also challenged qualitative researchers to rethink some of their tried and true methods.

Access to Information

Let me address access to information first. Of course, you all know that search engines provide the capability to access print, audio, and visual information in ways that we never dreamed of just a few years ago. At the time of this writing, Google has become the preeminent search engine. The company is contemplating scanning in texts from major libraries. This is mind boggling. It could give equal access to information to anyone around the world; all you need is a computer and a connection to the Internet. In the United States, most public libraries provide free Internet access. Wireless access is readily available in airports, coffee houses, and malls. College students in many areas are required to have computers and to be linked to the Internet. Access is almost instantaneous. Many elementary and high schools teach students to get online and to access information. You can post something on the Internet today and it will become available immediately to anyone who locates it. This has revolutionized how information is sent and received worldwide; no longer do we have to wait for material to be written, edited, and published in hard copy.

But there are several problems associated with this instant access. Access is also transitory. "Here today and gone tomorrow" may be quite common; some information that you locate today may not be there tomorrow. Other information might be old and never updated. There is no central clearing house that maintains what is on the Internet; rather, it is up to the Web site owner to keep files current and accessible. As a user, you must be ever diligent in locating and judging what is there and how useful it is to you.

But I want to offer a word of caution: More information does not necessarily mean good information. In the past, we used to rely on information in journals because it was reviewed by a panel of peers. So a student might rely on a published journal article being sound because others had reviewed it. But this is less true with material online; anyone can publish anything online and it may or not be reviewed or even suitable. But I would not want to limit information just because it is not reviewed by one's peers. As you read in Chapter 12, how qualitative information is judged is subject to question.

Communication With Everyone

Communication with and among people has also changed. Instant messaging, blogs and vlogs, chat rooms, and other devices have facilitated discussions and interchanges among colleagues. No longer is the United States the primary force in communication. The art of letter writing is in the dim past for all but the few stalwarts. People post their ideas and wait for others to respond. Sometimes discussions occur among people who would never before have come in contact with each other. And communication is not limited to written words alone: pictures are posted, videos are available, audio discussions are presented. Some communication becomes interactive.

As a result of this new kind of communication, I find myself challenged by ideas that I would not ever have encountered previously. I find many offering comments who would not have had a venue in the past. By opening up communication, the playing field has been leveled. Power issues seem less important. Voices can be heard from those who otherwise were silenced.

New Ideas

Learning about new things has also changed. Online journals demonstrate how the old process of lengthy peer reviews and delayed publication dates can be shortened. An individual can submit a paper, have it reviewed online, and publish it in the time it takes for the readers to react. And as an aside, enormous numbers of trees have been saved, use of storage space in homes and offices is reduced, and information can be organized and accessed on one small flash drive or DVD.

New ideas for doing and promoting qualitative research can also be found. Online focus groups are being conducted with opportunities for interaction between participants who might never have seen or heard each other before. For example, you can set up your own chat room for free by going to Parachat (www.parachat.com), Anexa (www.anexa.com), or Talk City (www.talkcity.com). You can set up your own Listserv for free by going to Yahoo groups (groups.yahoo.com), Tight Circle (www.tightcircle.com), or Topica (www.topica.com). These sites I mention are free, but include paid advertising; if you want to avoid that, you can set up a Listserv for a small cost at Listhost (www.listhost.com), Sparklist (www.sparklist .com), or Lyris (lyris.net).

Online cultures are being studied, and the traditional issues of gaining access and the role of the researcher are only some of the things to consider. Blogs are being posted with ideas about qualitative research and what writers think. Presentation of research can be only as challenging as the skill of the writer in using the new technology. I have seen writers use pictures and audio, link to other sites on the Web, and take the reader in new directions not possible with traditional writing in journals or term papers. Some universities are now requiring students to post their theses and dissertations online rather than in a traditional format. So what we study and how we study things are changing as a result of the new technology.

The voices of all can be heard. No longer is the field dominated by the culture of Western Europe and the United States. Influences from Asia, South America, and Africa are beginning to be felt. Qualitative research in education has reached beyond the purview of departments of educational research and ethnography; other voices are being heard. Nurses are among the forefront of those voices as I write, but perhaps others will emerge as well.

Greater Acceptance by the Field

In 1990, *The Qualitative Report* was launched as a traditional paper journal. By 1994, it went online and reached a worldwide audience. According to Chenail, St. George, and Wulff (2004), there has been a much greater acceptance of qualitative research in a variety of disciplines. In fact, this journal has even shifted its approach from peer review to a process where authors are aided in developing their research into acceptable articles. In 2005 I finished this type of review and found myself contemplating the value in what the authors had to say rather than being critical of what they omitted. This process is facilitated in part by the availability of technologies that permit multiple reviewers to comment directly on the manuscript.

I see traditional disciplines such as psychology, sociology, family studies, nursing, and education being more accepting of qualitative research than in the past. More journals offer opportunities for publishing and have modified or revised criteria for submissions. More universities offer courses in qualitative research than ever before. More publishers are publishing books directly related to qualitative research.

I anticipate that this trend will continue as researchers and readers see the benefits and rewards of conducting qualitative research.

ABOUT THEORY

Many qualitative researchers believe that holding a particular theory about something before we gather data is severely limiting. Thomas Jefferson reminds us that "the moment a person forms a theory, his imagination sees in every object only the traits which favor that theory."

You might be interested in some of what I learned about linking theory and practice. The Jones and Barlett Nursing Theory Art Gallery (http://nursing.jbpub.com/sitzman/artGallery .cfm) exhibits students' artistic impressions of nursing theory. In this series, students create art works to illustrate a particular theory.

As you know by now, I have a very strong interest in art. I believe many artists operate without a clear theory. Here is some evidence to support this idea. Brancusi says, "Theories are patterns without value. What counts is action." Kazantzakis supports this notion: "The ultimate most holy form of theory is action." Felix Cohen says, "Generally the theories we believe we call facts, and the facts we disbelieve we call theories" (The Painter's Keys, n.d.).

For a very long time I have seen theory and practice as separate. It seems as though it is university people who consider theoretical issues; out in the field, it is another thing. Many of the articles I read continue to stress practice and pay little attention to theory. I don't mean to suggest that we can or should have practice devoid of theory, but I do not see much evidence that theoretical issues regarding practice are evident in published research. How to bridge the gap? I am not really sure.

ABOUT PRACTICE

In terms of practice, I see some compromise. A number of researchers have adopted a mixed methods approach rather than choosing either qualitative or quantitative exclusively. Although supposedly both approaches are treated evenly, I often find that qualitative takes a back seat to quantitative. I believe that those interested in mixed methods focus on the means of gathering data and do not always address different assumptions.

Increasingly, I see researchers taking risks with new methods of gathering and analyzing data. Fueled in part by the Internet, researchers find themselves in chat rooms, using blogs, and looking for alternative ways to display data and make meaning from what they have found.

As the field develops, greater opportunities are available for researchers to experiment with alternative ways of gathering and presenting information. Live performances at national conferences, creating information on the Web, and the use of visual representations will no doubt become more common.

New technologies, demands on students, and costs have led to an increase in online teaching. I have taught online classes in qualitative research for several years. For a transcript from one section of an online class, see the resource "Teaching Qualitative Research Online," which can be found at www.sagepub.com/lichtman

There are a number of ways qualitative researchers use computers. Here are some ideas for you to ponder. Use computers to store and retrieve raw or original data from other projects for additional data analysis or to conduct meta-analyses. Use computers to access chat rooms or Listservs to study online cultures. Use computers to post blogs recording a diary of postings regarding doing qualitative research. Use computers to conduct online focus groups.

Use computers to join discussion groups regarding issues of qualitative research or answer questions regarding using software. Use computers to gain access to databases, online journals, or other sources of qualitative information.

JOURNALS WITH A QUALITATIVE FOCUS

I have seen a number of lists of qualitatively oriented journals. I want to call your attention to the following journals.

International Journal of Qualitative Studies in Education (QSE). ISSN 0951–8398. Publisher: Taylor & Francis, Ltd. First volume: 1988. Originally four issues annually, but now six issues annually. Editors: James Scheurich and M. Carolyn Clark, Texas A&M University, USA. Beginning with Volume 10 (1997), Table of Contents available online. Topics in 2005 include faith-based leadership, hope without illusion, and stories about learning in narrative biographical research. The authors are international. My impression is that this journal publishes fairly nontraditional articles on a wide range of topics.

Qualitative Research. ISSN 1468–7941. Publisher: Sage Publications. First volume: 2001. Three issues annually. Editor: Paul Atkinson. Topics in 2005 include Indians in the park; studying schools: issues around attempts to create a sense of feel and place in narrative research writing; gazing with intent: ethnographic practice in classrooms; and fear of offending: disclosing researcher discomfort when engaging in analysis.

Qualitative Inquiry. ISSN 1077–8004. Publisher: Sage Publications. First volume: 1995. Six issues annually. Editor: Norman Denzin. Topics in 2005 include reflections on portraiture: a dialogue between art and science, expressions of voice in "portraiture," and "city girl": a portrait of a successful white urban teacher.

The Qualitative Report. ISSN 1052–0147. Publisher: Nova Southeastern University. First volume: 1990. Four issues annually. Online since 1994. Editors: Ron Chenail, Sally St. George, and Dan Wulff. Topics in 2004 include qualitative evaluation of emotional intelligence, using NVivo to analyze qualitative classroom data, qualitative look at leisure benefits, and perceptions on school-based English teacher education.

Forum Qualitative Social Research. ISSN: 1438–5627. Publisher: Freie Universität Berlin. First volume: 1999. Editor: Katja Mruck. Peer-reviewed multilingual online journal. Aim is to promote discussion and cooperation among researchers from different countries and different disciplines. Most issues are special topics. Topics in 2005 include reanalyzing qualitative interviews from different angles, revisiting classic studies, and secondary analysis of audio data.

International Journal of Qualitative Methods. ISSN: 16094069. Publisher: International Institute for Qualitative Methodology at the University of Alberta, Canada. First issue: 2002. Four issues annually. Founding Editor: Janice Morse. Aim is to heighten the awareness of qualitative research; to advance the development of qualitative methods in varying fields of study; and to help disseminate knowledge to the broadest possible community of academics, students, and professionals who undertake scholarly research. By keeping the journal free of charge, they hope to reach an audience who, for whatever reason, do not read traditional, subscription-based journals.

Qualitative Research in Psychology. ISSN: 1478–0887. Publisher: Hodder Arnold Journals, UK. First issue: 2004. Editor: David Giles. Topics in 2005 include genealogy; discourse; "effective history": Foucault and the work of critique; the understanding and experiences of children affected by parental mental health problems: a qualitative study; and doing Q methodology: theory, method, and interpretation. This is a new journal and I believe it is still making its way.

Of course, many other journals publish articles either about qualitative research or of a qualitative research nature. You will find many that address topics of education in nursing journals, health journals, business journals, and others as well.

Perhaps the most challenging, yet frustrating, part of writing this book has been to keep on top of what is out there. When I began teaching qualitative courses in the early 1990s, I could not find an appropriate book to use; my students used articles I located and put into a study packet. Few of my colleagues were talking about qualitative research, and even fewer were willing to encourage students to embark on such an endeavor. Education faculty in many universities were trained in traditional modes of experimental research and were often reluctant or too busy to learn alternative ways of doing research. For some, it meant a challenge to their own basic tenets of what is good and right. For others, qualitative research methods were the ramblings of those who were "touchy-feely" and not real scientists. This has now changed. Qualitative research is a discipline that has reached its legitimate place in the research hierarchy. It is no longer second best. It no longer needs apologists. It no longer is a step-child.

I stay current by belonging to discussion groups and chat rooms online, by reading online journals, by being on the editorial boards of two prestigious online journals, and by using search engines to see what else is out there.

FOR THE FUTURE

In an ideal world, qualitative research will continue to grow and challenge those who find it exciting. Questions will be posed and insight gained that takes us in directions not yet conceived. Legitimacy and acceptance by the larger scientific community and scholars worldwide will not lead to conservatism and complacency. The voices of all who want to study and those from whom we gain knowledge and understanding will be heard.

You, as students, are on the forefront of this movement. I know some of you will make meaningful contributions in your chosen fields. Perhaps you may even make contributions to how we learn about others and ourselves.

APPENDIX: CHECKLIST FOR INDIVIDUAL AND FOCUS GROUP INTERVIEWS

I have conducted many interviews. Sometimes I have been on a tight schedule and have had to complete three to five interviews or focus groups in a single day. This takes careful planning and coordination. This checklist contains specific suggestions that will make your interviews or focus groups go more smoothly.

Goal: Get the Story in the Participant's Own Words

Before You Go

- Schedule appointments. Make sure you have a suitable location. I recall having to conduct focus groups of school children in a library. We did not have any privacy. Even though I had requested a private space in advance, the school did not really have one.
- For interviews: audio recording equipment, including microphones, extra batteries, tapes. I was with a colleague and we were conducting focus groups in Panama. It was fortunate we had brought two sets of equipment because one of our tape recorders died and we did not have access to anything but our other recorder.
- For focus groups: video recording equipment. If you are fortunate to have a proper room in which to conduct focus groups, this will make things go more smoothly. But unless you work for a large company or have a grant, this is not likely to be the case. If possible, enlist the assistance of a colleague to help with videotaping. Sometimes permission is difficult to obtain and you may have to resort to audio equipment only. If this is the case, make a diagram of the seating arrangement and number the speakers 1, 2, etc.
- A one-page handout indicating the purpose of your study and how the participants can contact you. You will leave this with the participants, so if you are doing multiple interviews be sure to bring sufficient copies.
- Prepare two forms in advance:
  - Supplementary sheet with topic areas;
  - Record form with participant's name, location, date of interview, and other pertinent information.
- Bring paper, pens, and a watch or clock.

- Bring your journal for making memos and notes.
- Check yourself to make sure you are prepared.

When You Arrive

- Confirm appointments. This is especially important with focus groups. If you are doing several focus groups in one day, arrange for a waiting area.
- Set up and check your equipment before you begin.
- Review your own tasks. Make sure you feel ready. Review major areas you plan to cover that are on the supplementary topic sheet.

During the Interview

- Record the time you start.
- Check recording equipment after two or three minutes to make sure everything is working. Be prepared with extra batteries or additional tapes.
- Watch your time and gauge what you are doing.
- Be prepared to deal with interruptions.
- Maintain a high level of interest in the participants even if you find what they say boring.

When You Complete the Interview

- Record the time you completed the interview. Label the tape with a number so you will be able to locate it later. Put the same number on your supplementary sheet.
- Make notes or observations that you have learned from this interview that you want to remember. Record your thoughts in your journal. It is always easier to do this right after the interview than later; our memories can really play tricks on us.
- Pat yourself on the back. Conducting successful interviews without detailed questions is very difficult. Each successive one will be easier.
- Give yourself a 10-minute break if you are conducting multiple interviews. Interviewing of this type is quite intense, and you need some time to recover and unwind.
- Prepare for the next interview. Have your materials ready and check your equipment.

GLOSSARY

Action research: A type of qualitative research that focuses on a solution to a specific local problem.

Anthropology: The systematic study of cultures and groups of people.

Axiology: A branch of philosophy related to values and judgments. See also epistemology, ontology.

Bias: In quantitative research, a researcher attempts to minimize bias by remaining objective and outside of the system. In qualitative research, researcher bias and subjectivity are accepted and inevitable— it is not seen as negative.

Blog: Short term for Web log, a personal journal published on the Internet.

Bracketing: A process used by phenomenologists to identify the researcher's preconceived beliefs.

Case study: A type of qualitative research focusing on the study of a single individual or organization.

Coding, codes: A technique of data analysis in which text is sorted and organized to identify recurrent themes and concepts. Coding is the process; codes are the terms used to describe portions of data.

Concept: In qualitative data analysis, an idea that builds on coding and categorizing of raw data. See also themes.

Constructivism: A theory or philosophical doctrine that says that knowledge is constructed by the researcher and is affected by the context. It is a belief in multiple truths and a belief that the interaction of the researcher with what is being studied affects the determination of truth. It was originally associated with Kant, and more recently associated with Lincoln, Guba, and Denzin.

Content analysis: A technique of data analysis in which detailed review of text content leads to themes.

Co-researcher: An individual who provides information about the research and sometimes participates in analysis of data. See also informant, participant.

Critical theory: A philosophical movement that began in 1923 and was associated with the Institute of Social Research, part of the Frankfurt School. It combined psychoanalysis and Marxism. Prior to World War II, it was connected with Columbia University and subsequently moved to California.

Culture: Attitudes and behaviors associated with a particular social group or organization.

Deductive reasoning, approach: A type of reasoning that moves from the general to the specific or from the abstract to the concrete (see also inductive reasoning). It is associated with quantitative research.

Discourse analysis: A technique of data analysis dealing with naturally occurring written discourse.

Emic perspective: A term associated with ethnography to refer to an insider's view. See also etic perspective.

EndNote: Computer software published by Thomson with three purposes: online search tool, reference and image database, and bibliography and manuscript maker.

Epistemology: A branch of philosophy dealing with the theory of knowledge, the nature of knowledge, or how we know what we know. See also ontology, axiology.

Ethnography, ethnographic approach: A type of qualitative research emanating from anthropology and focusing on the study of the culture of groups.

Ethnomethodology: The study of how group members make sense of their surroundings. See also ethnography.

Etic perspective: A term associated with ethnography to refer to an outsider's view (see emic).

Feminist theory, perspective, feminist researchers: A philosophical movement related to postmodernism that emphasizes power disparities and inequalities between the genders. Some feminists see bias in both quantitative and qualitative research approaches.

Field notes: Notes, often informal, made by a researcher during and after observations or visits to a setting.

Focus group interviewing: A technique of data collection that relies on group interaction and discussion.

Foundationalist: A synonym for traditional experimental research.

Generic approach: An approach to qualitative research that does not rely on any particular tradition but utilizes elements of many.

Grounded theory: A type of qualitative research from which theories may emerge. It relies on observations in real-world settings and uses open, axial, and selective coding. It is associated with Strauss, Glaser, and Corbin.

Hermeneutics: A technique or discipline of data analysis involving detailed analysis of transcripts and textual material. It is associated with phenomenology.

Hypothesis: A formal statement about the relationship between variables. It is commonly associated with quantitative research.

In-depth interview: A technique of data collection that relies on long and probing questions and does not use formal questionnaires. It is also called a depth interview.

Inductive reasoning, approach: A type of reasoning that moves from the specific to the general or from the concrete to the abstract (see also deductive reasoning). It is associated with qualitative research.

Informant: An individual who provides information relative to the research. See also participant, co-researcher.

Insider: An informant with special status based on greater access and membership in a group.

Interpretivism: A theory or philosophical doctrine that emphasizes analyzing meanings people confer on their own actions.

Journal: A researcher's written thoughts during the life of a project. Journals tend to be self-reflexive, as distinguished from field notes or memos, which are usually about the content.

Listserv: A program that sends e-mail to a group of people and lets people respond to everyone or to an individual.

Literature review: An integration and interpretation of research on one's topic of interest.

Memo, memoing: Comments and notes written by the researcher, usually after reading a transcript. It may be a separate document or interspersed in the transcript.

Metaphor: A figure of speech in which a word or phrase that means one thing is applied to another in order to suggest an analogy. It is often used in qualitative writing to vividly describe ideas.

Methodology: The various techniques, methods, and procedures used in conducting research.

Mixed methods: A type of qualitative research that combines both quantitative and qualitative methods.

Naturalistic inquiry, natural settings: A type of qualitative research or a method of studying phenomena as they exist in the world.

NVivo: A powerful computer software program available from QSR. Useful for storing, organizing, and managing complex qualitative data.

Objectivity: A goal of quantitative research in which a researcher attempts to remain outside of the system.

Observation: A technique of data collection in which the researcher observes the interaction of individuals in natural settings.

Online interviewing: A technique of data collection in which the researcher "talks" to informants online. Data may be collected from a pre-identified informant or from one who appears by chance. It can include individuals or groups in chat rooms or Listservs.

Ontology: A branch of metaphysics concerned with the nature of reality. See also epistemology, axiology.

Paradigm: A way of seeing the world. In education, the term was popularized by Thomas Kuhn. It is also a set of interrelated assumptions about the world that provides a philosophical and conceptual framework.

Participant: An individual who provides information for the research. See also informant, co-researcher.

Participant observation, observer: A type of observation in which the researcher is either already part of the group being studied or becomes part of the group.

Phenomenology: A type of qualitative research with philosophical roots that emphasizes the study of lived experiences.

Positivism: A theory or philosophical doctrine in which science deals only with observable entities and objective reality. It involves belief in one truth and was originally associated with Comte.

Postfeminism: A term coined in 1982 that signifies a shift from feminism, in which women sought equality, to a stance where differences are valued. Postfeminists see feminism as irrelevant.

Postmodernism, poststructuralism: A philosophical movement popularized in the 1990s. Postmodernists question institutional authority and seek greater power. Poststructuralists (associated with Derrida) react to structuralism and suggest that meaning is constantly in motion and resistant to closure. Defines present cultural climate and differentiates from positivism. Researchers take activist stance.

Postpositivism: A philosophical doctrine that acknowledges the shortcomings of positivism but strives to attain objective reality. It includes belief in the approximation of one truth.

Psychology: The study of the mind and behavior of individuals.

Qualitative interviewing: A technique of data collection that ranges from semi-structured to unstructured formats. Interviewing is seen as a conversation in which an informant and a researcher interact so that the informant's thoughts are revealed and interpreted by a researcher.

Qualitative research, qualitative inquiry: An umbrella term that includes many traditions whose focus is to study individuals in their natural settings in order to understand and interpret.

Quantitative research: A term describing traditional methods of hypothesis testing, determining cause and effect, and generalizing.

Queer theory: Grew out of gay/lesbian studies of the 1980s. Suggests that sexual and gender identity are socially constructed. Deals with understanding sexuality in terms of shifting boundaries, ambivalences, and cultural constructions.

Random sample: A sample drawn from a population in such a way that each population element has a chance of being selected. Useful for generalizing.

Reflexivity: A researcher's capacity to reflect on his or her own values both during and after the research.

Research: A systematic investigation of phenomena.

Research approach: A design or plan to conduct research, for example, using case study, phenomenology, or grounded theory.

Science, scientific approach, method, research: A systematic way of testing hypotheses and determining cause and effect. It is presumed to be objective, but some new critics question its assumptions.

Self-reflection: Originally associated with phenomenology, self-reflection is now seen as awareness of self and one's influence on the research process as well as the influence of the process on the self.

Snowball sampling: A technique for identifying informants in which the original group of informants is asked to identify additional individuals with similar characteristics. Lillian Rubin suggests that you ask informants to identify acquaintances rather than close friends.

Sociology: The study of social lives and behaviors.

Subject: An individual who is studied in an experiment. The term is associated with quantitative research; participant, informant, or co-researcher replaces this term in qualitative research.

Symbolic interactionism: A sociological term which examines how individuals and groups interact as process of symbolic communications.

Themes: Central issues or concepts that a researcher identifies based on coding original data. Most research data can be organized in five or six themes. See also concept.

Theory: A substantiated explanation of some aspect of the world. A proposed explanation of a phenomenon. Not a fact, but an attempt to explain facts.

Thick description: Used by ethnographers to emphasize providing a detailed description of a culture. A term associated with Clifford Geertz.

Triangulation: The use of several methods or strategies to gather data with the purpose of increasing the credibility of findings or of obtaining a more substantive view of reality.

Unobtrusive observation, observer: A type of observation in which the observer is not known to those being studied.

Vlog: A blog using videos, also called v-log, video blogging, or vog.

Voice: A term related to privileged position and self-disclosure. With self-disclosure comes potential vulnerability of the researcher.

REFERENCES

Adkins, L. (2004). Passing on feminism: From consciousness to reflexivity. *European Journal of Women's Studies, 11*(4), 427–444. Retrieved November 21, 2005, from http://ejw.sagepub.com/cgi/content/refs/11/4/427

Adler, P. (1993). *Wheeling and dealing: An ethnography of an upper-level drug dealing and smuggling community.* New York: Columbia University Press.

Agar, M. (1973). *Ripping and running: A formal ethnography of urban heroin addicts.* New York: Seminar Press.

Aggleton, P. (1987). *Rebels without a cause: Middle class youth and the transition from school to work.* London: Falmer Press.

Ahern, K. (1999). Ten tips for reflexive bracketing. *Qualitative Health Research, 9*(3), 407–411.

Aldridge, M. (1995). Scholarly practice—ethnographic film and anthropology. Beyond ethnographic film: Hypermedia and scholarship. *Visual Anthropology, 7*(3), 233–235.

Allen, S. (1998). *Toward a grounded theory of parent education: A qualitative analysis of parenting classes, parenting practices, and adult education.* Unpublished doctoral dissertation, University of South Dakota, Vermilion.

American Psychological Association. (2001). *Publication manual of the American Psychological Association* (5th ed.). Washington, DC: Author.

Amir, D. (2005). The use of "first person" writing style in academic writing. An open letter to journals, reviewers, and readers. Voices: A World Forum for Music Therapy. Retrieved November 21, 2005, from http://www.voices.no/columnist/colamir140305.html

Angrosino, M. V. (1994). On the bus with Vonnie Lee: Explorations in life history and metaphor. *Journal of Contemporary Ethnography, 23*(1), 14–28.

Aparicio, F. R. (1999). Through my lens: A video project about women of color faculty at the University of Michigan. *Feminist Studies, 25*(1), 119–130.

Armstrong, G. (1998). *Football hooligans: Knowing the score.* New York: Berg.

Arvay, M. (1998). *Struggling with re-presentation, voice and self in narrative research.* Retrieved November 3, 2005, from http://www.educ.uvic.ca/connections/Conn98/arvay.html

Askew, J. W. (1983). *Some thoughts on the value of grounded theory for the study and practice of higher education.* Paper presented at the Annual Meeting of the Association for the Study of Higher Education, Washington, DC.

Atkinson, R., & Flint, J. (2001). *Accessing hidden and hard-to-reach populations: Snowball research strategies.* Retrieved November 3, 2005, from http://www.soc.surrey.ac.uk/sru/SRU33.html

Babchuck, W. A. (1997). *Glaser or Strauss? Grounded theory in adult education.* Paper presented at the Midwest Research-to-Practice Conference, Michigan State University.

Barbour, R., & Barbour, M. (2002). Evaluating and synthesizing qualitative research: The need to develop a distinctive approach. *Journal of Evaluation in Clinical Practice, 9*(2), 176–186.

Barnacle, R. (2001). *Phenomenology and education research.* Paper presented at the Australian Association for Research in Education, Fremantle, Australia.

Barrett, S. (1996). *Anthropology: A student's guide to theory and method.* Toronto, ON: University of Toronto Press.

Basit, T. (2003, Summer). Manual or electronic? The role of coding in qualitative data analysis. *Educational Researcher, 45*(2), 143–154.

Baumgartner, L. (2000). *Narrative analysis: Uncovering the truth of stories.* Adult Education Research Conference Proceedings, Vancouver, B. C. Retrieved November 21, 2005, from http://www.edst.educ.ubc.ca/aerc/2000/baumgartnerl-web.htm

Becker, H. (1976). *Boys in white: Student culture in medical school.* New Brunswick, NJ: Transaction Books.

Behar, R. (1996). *The vulnerable observer: Anthropology that breaks your heart.* Boston: Beacon Press.

Berger, R. (2004). Pushing forward: Disability, basketball, and me. *Qualitative Inquiry, 10*(5), 794–810.

Bergman, M. (2005). *Mixed methods: Keynote abstract.* Retrieved November 28, 2005, from http://www.health-homerton.ac.uk/research/files/ka_03.pdf

Bertaux, D. (1981). *Biography and society: The life history approach in the social sciences.* Beverly Hills, CA: Sage.

Bertaux, D., & Delacroix, C. (2000). Case histories of families and social processes. In P. Chamberlayne, J. Bornat, & T. Wengraf (Eds.), *The turn to biographical methods in social sciences: Comparative issues and examples* (pp. 71–89). London: Routledge.

Bissell, M. (2001). 1938: B. F. Skinner publishes The Behavior of Organisms: An Experimental Analysis. In D. Schugurensky (Ed.), *History of education: Selected moments of the 20th century.* Retrieved November 7, 2005, from http://fcis.oise.utoronto.ca/~daniel_schugurensky/assignment1/1938skinner.html

Blumenfeld-Jones, D. S. (1995). Dance as a mode of research representation. *Qualitative Inquiry, 1*(4), 391–401.

Blumer, H. (1969). *Symbolic interactionism: Perspective and method.* Englewood Cliffs, NJ: Prentice Hall.

Bochner, A., & Ellis, C. (Eds). (2001). *Ethnographically speaking: Autoethnography, literature, and aesthetics.* Walnut Creek, CA: AltaMira Press.

Boeree, G. (1998). *Qualitative methods.* Retrieved November 9, 2005, from http://www.ship.edu/~cgboeree/qualmethone.html

Bogdan, R., & Biklen, S. (1992). *Foundations of qualitative research for education.* Boston: Allyn & Bacon.

Bordwell, D., & Thompson, K. (2004). *Film art: An introduction.* New York: McGraw-Hill.

Bottorff, J. (2003). *Workshop on qualitative research.* Retrieved November 3, 2005, from http://www.vchri.ca/i/presentations/QualitativeResearch/

Boudreau, D. (2002). *The drama of data.* Retrieved November 3, 2005, from http://research-mag.asu.edu/stories/ethnotheatre.html

Brayton, J. (1997). *What makes feminist research feminist? The structure of feminist research within the social sciences.* Retrieved November 3, 2005, from http://www.unb.ca/web/PAR-L/win/feminmethod.htm

Breuer, F., Mruck, K., & Roth, W.-M. (2002, September). Subjectivity and reflexivity: An introduction [10 paragraphs]. *Forum Qualitative Sozialforschung/Forum: Qualitative Social Research, 3*(3). Retrieved July 4, 2004, from http://www.qualitative-research.net/fqs-texte/3-02/3-02hrsg-e.htm

Breuer, F., & Roth, W.-M. (2003, May). Subjectivity and reflexivity in the social sciences: Epistemic windows and methodical consequences [30 paragraphs]. *Forum Qualitative Sozialforschung/Forum: Qualitative Social Research, 4*(2). Retrieved November 3, 2005, from http://www.qualitative-research.net/fqs-texte/2-03/2-03intro-3-e.htm

Bromley, H., Dockery, G., Fenton, C., Nhlema, B., Smith, H., Tolhurst, R., et al. (2002). *Criteria for evaluating qualitative studies.* Retrieved November 3, 2005, from http://www.liv.ac.uk/lstm/download/guidelines.pdf

Brown, S., Stevens, R., Troino, P., Schneider, M. (2002). Exploring complex phenomena: Grounded theory in student affairs research. *Journal of College Student Development, 43*(2), 1–11. Retrieved November 3, 2005, from http://www.mtholyoke.edu/offices/careers/cdcintro/staff/grounded.pdf

Bryman, A., & Burgess, R. G. (1994). Reflections on qualitative data analysis. In A. Bryman & R. G. Burgess (Eds.), *Analysing qualitative data* (pp. 216–226). London: Routledge.

Butler-Kisber, L. (2002). Artful portrayals in qualitative research: The road to found poetry and beyond. *The Alberta Journal of Educational Research, XLVIII*(3), 229–239.

Byers, D. (2003). *Intentionality and transcendence: Closure and openness in Husserl's phenomenology.* Madison: University of Wisconsin Press.

Byrne, M. (1998). *Hermeneutics 101.* Paper presented at the QUIG98, Athens, GA. Retrieved November 3, 2005, from http://www.coe.uga.edu/quig/proceedings/Quig98_Proceedings/byrne.html

Byrne, M. (2001, May). Hermeneutics as a methodology for textual analysis—nursing applications. *AORN Journal.* Retrieved November 3, 2005, from http://www.aorn.org/journal/2001/mayrc.htm

Caelli, K., Ray, L., & Mill, J. (2003). "Clear as mud": Toward greater clarity in generic qualitative research. *International Journal of Qualitative Methods, 2*(2). Retrieved November 3, 2005, from http://www.ualberta.ca/~iiqm/backissues/2_2/html/caellietal.htm

Camic, P., Rhodes, J., & Yardley, L. (Eds.). (2003). *Qualitative research in psychology: Expanding perspectives in methodology and design.* Washington, DC: American Psychological Association.

Campbell, A. (1984). *The girls in the gang: A report from New York City.* Oxford: Clarendon Press.

Campbell, B. (n.d.). *Phenomenology as research method.* Retrieved November 7, 2005, from http://www.staff.vu.edu.au/syed/alrnnv/papers/bev.html

Campbell, D., & Stanley, J. (1963). *Experimental and quasi-experimental designs for research.* Boston: Houghton Mifflin.

Chamberlayne, P., Bornat, J., & Wengraf, T. (Eds.). (2000). *The turn to biographical methods in social science: Comparative issues and examples.* London: Routledge.

Chase, S. E. (2005). Narrative inquiry: Multiple lenses, approaches, voices. In N. K. Denzin & Y. S. Lincoln (Eds.), *Handbook of qualitative research* (pp. 651–679). Thousand Oaks, CA: Sage.

Chenail, R. (1995, December). Presenting qualitative data. *The Qualitative Report, 2*(3). Retrieved November 21, 2005, from http://www.nova.edu/ssss/QR/QR2-3/presenting.html

Chenail, R., St. George, S., & Wulff, D. (2004). A new beginning. Editorial statement. *The Qualitative Report*. Retrieved November 27, 2005, from http://www.nova.edu/ssss/ QR/Editorial/editstm.html

Choudhuri, D., Glauser, A., & Peregoy, J. (2004). Guidelines for writing a qualitative manuscript for the *Journal of Counseling and Development*. *Journal of Counseling and Development, 82*(4), 443–446.

Clark, A. M. (1998). The qualitative-quantitative debate: Moving from positivism and confrontation to post-positivism and reconciliation. *Journal of Advanced Nursing, 27*(6), 1242–1250.

Clayton, P. (1997). Philosophy of science: What one needs to know. *Zygon: Journal of Religion and Science, 32*(1), 95–105.

Clinchy, B. (n.d.). *Tales told out of school: Women's reflections on their undergraduate experience*. Retrieved November 3, 2005, from http://www.lcc.edu/cte/resources/ teachingexcellence/

Coffey, A., & Atkinson, P. (1996). *Making sense of qualitative data: Complementary research strategies*. Thousand Oaks, CA: Sage.

Conrad, C. E. (1982). Grounded theory: An alternative approach to research in higher education. *Review of Higher Education, 5*(4), 239–249.

Conteh, J. (2003). *Succeeding in diversity: Culture, language and learning in primary classrooms*. Stoke-on-Trent, UK: Trentham Books.

Cook, T. D., & Campbell, D. (1979). *Quasi-experimentation: Design and analysis issues for field settings*. Boston: Houghton Mifflin.

Correll, S. (1995). The ethnography of an electronic bar: The lesbian café. *Journal of Contemporary Ethnography, 24*(3), 270–298.

Cox, G. (1994, January). Ready-aim-fire: Balancing the team for quality results. *Management Scotland*. Retrieved November 3, 2005, from http://www.newdirections.uk.com/ article6.htm

Crabtree, B., & Miller, W. (Eds). (1992). *Doing qualitative research*. Newbury Park, CA: Sage.

Creswell, J. (1997). *Qualitative inquiry and research design: Choosing among five traditions*. Thousand Oaks, CA: Sage.

Creswell, J. (2003). *Research design: Qualitative, quantitative, and mixed methods approaches* (2nd ed.). Thousand Oaks, CA: Sage.

Crotty, M. (2003). *The foundations of social research: Meaning and perspective in the research process*. Thousand Oaks, CA: Sage.

Crump, R. E. (1928). *Correspondence and class extension work in Oklahoma*. New York: Columbia University, Teachers College.

Custer, R. L. (1996). Qualitative research methodologies. *Journal of Industrial Teacher Education, 34*(2), 3–6.

Davey, N. (1999). The hermeneutics of seeing. In I. Heywood & B. Sandywell (Eds.), *Interpreting visual culture: Explorations in the hermeneutics of the visual* (pp. 3–29). London: Routledge.

Davidson, A. L. (2002). *Grounded theory*. Retrieved November 3, 2005, from http://az .essortment.com/groundedtheory_rmnf.htm

Davis, O. L. (2002). Editorial: Educational research in the foreseeable future. *The Journal of Curriculum and Supervision, 17*(4), 277–282.

Day, E. (2002, September). Me, my*self and I: Personal and professional re-constructions in ethnographic research [59 paragraphs]. *Forum Qualitative Sozialforschung/Forum:*

Qualitative Social Research, 3(3). Retrieved November 2, 2005, from http://www .qualitative-research.net/fqs-texte/3-02/3-02day-e.htm

Denny, T. (1978). *Story telling and educational understanding.* Retrieved November 7, 2005, from http://www.wmich.edu/evalctr/pubs/ops/ops12.html

Denzin, N. (1989). *Interpretive interactionism.* Newbury Park, CA: Sage.

Denzin, N. K. (1997). *Interpretive ethnography: Ethnographic practices for the 21st century.* Thousand Oaks, CA: Sage.

Denzin, N., & Lincoln, Y. (Eds.). (1994). *Handbook of qualitative research.* Thousand Oaks, CA: Sage.

Denzin, N., & Lincoln, Y. (Eds.). (2000). *Handbook of qualitative research* (2nd ed.). Thousand Oaks, CA: Sage.

Denzin, N., & Lincoln, Y. (Eds.). (2005). *Handbook of qualitative research* (3rd ed.). Thousand Oaks, CA: Sage.

Dermot, M. (2000). *Introduction to phenomenology.* London: Routledge.

Deutsch, N. (2004). Positionality and the pen: Reflections on the process of becoming a feminist researcher and writer. *Qualitative Inquiry, 10*(6), 885–902.

DeVault, M. (1990). Talking and listening from women's standpoint: Feminist strategies for interviewing and analysis. *Social Problems, 37*(1), 96–116.

Devers, K. (1999, December). How will we know "good" qualitative research when we see it? Beginning the dialogue in health services research. *Health Services Research,* 1–12.

De Welde, K. (2003). The brouhaha of ethnography: Not for the fainthearted. *Journal of Contemporary Ethnography, 32*(2), 233–244.

Dholakia, N., & Zhang, D. (2004, May). Online qualitative research in the age of e-commerce: Data sources and approaches [27 paragraphs]. *Forum Qualitative Sozialforschung/ Forum: Qualitative Social Research, 5*(2). Retrieved November 17, 2005, from http:// www.qualitative-research.net/fqs-texte/2-04/2-04dholakiazhang-e.htm

Dick, B. (2002). *Grounded theory: A thumbnail sketch.* Retrieved November 3, 2005, from http://www.scu.edu.au/schools/gcm/ar/arp/grounded.html

Diekelmann, N. (2002). *Interpretive research: Postmodernism.* Retrieved November 7, 2005, from http://www.son.wisc.edu/diekelmann/courses/701/schedule6.htm

di Gregorio, S. (2000, September). *Using NVivo for your literature review.* Paper presented at the Strategies in Qualitative Research: Conference, Institute of Education, London.

Dillman, D. (1978). *Mail and telephone surveys.* New York: Wiley.

Dillon, M. (1997). *Merleau-Ponty's ontology.* Evanston, IL: Northwestern University Press.

Donmoyer, R. (1990). Generalizability and the single-case study. In E. Eisner & A. Peshkin (Eds.), *Qualitative inquiry in education: The continuing debate* (pp. 175–200). New York: Teachers College Press.

Efinger, J., Maldonado, N., & McArdle, G. (2004). PhD students' perceptions of the relationship between philosophy and research: A qualitative investigation. *The Qualitative Report, 9*(4), 732–759. Retrieved November 17, 2005, from http://www.nova.edu/ssss/ QR/QR9-4/efinger.pdf

Eisner, E., & Peshkin, A. (1990). *Qualitative inquiry in education: The continuing debate.* New York: Teachers College Press.

Ellingson, L. J. (2001). *Communicating across disciplines: A feminist ethnography collaboration on a geriatric oncology team.* Unpublished doctoral dissertation, University of South Florida, Tampa.

Elliott, R., Fischer, C. T., & Rennie, D. L. (1999). Evolving guidelines for publication of qualitative research studies in psychology and related fields. *British Journal of Clinical Psychology, 38,* 215–229.

Ellis, C. (1995). *Final negotiations: A story of love, and chronic illness.* Philadelphia: Temple University Press.

Ellis, C., & Bochner, A. (2000). Autoethnography, personal narrative, reflexivity: Researcher as subject. In N. Denzin & Y. Lincoln (Eds.), *Handbook of qualitative research* (pp. 733–768). Thousand Oaks, CA: Sage.

Embree, L. (2003). General impressions of our tradition today. In C.-F. Cheung, I. Chvatik, I. Copoeru, L. Embree, J. Iribarne, & H. Sepp (Eds.), *Essays in celebration of the founding of the Organization of Phenomenological Organizations* (pp. 1–4). Retrieved November 4, 2005, from http://www.o-p-o.net/essays/lesterintroduction.pdf

Estroff, S. (1985). *Making it crazy: An ethnography of psychiatric clients in an American community.* Berkeley: University of California Press.

Ewick, P., & Silbey, S. (2003). Narrating social structures: Stories of resistance to legal authority. *American Journal of Sociology, 108*(6), 1328–1372. Retrieved November 26, 2005, from http://web.mit.edu/anthropology/faculty_staff/silbey/pdf/%208narrate_.pdf

Faculty of Social Sciences Committee on Ethics. (n.d.). *Collection, storage, and archiving of qualitative data.* Retrieved November 21, 2005, from http://www.lancs.ac.uk/fss/resources/ethics/storage.htm

Falk, E., & Mills, J. (1996). Why sexist language affects persuasion: The role of homophily, intended audience, and offense. *Women and Language, 19*(2), 36–44.

Faux, R. B. (2005, February). To reveal thy heart perchance to reveal the world. *Forum Qualitative Sozialforschung/Forum: Qualitative Social Research, 6*(2). Retrieved November 2, 2005, from http://www.qualitative-research.net/fqs-texte/2-05/05-2-7-e.htm

Fetterman, D. M. (1998). *Ethnography: Step by step* (2nd ed.). Thousand Oaks, CA: Sage.

Fine, M. (1992). *Disruptive voices: The possibilities of feminist research.* Ann Arbor: University of Michigan.

Flowers, L., & Moore, J. (2003, Winter). Conducting qualitative research on-line in student affairs. *Student Affairs On-Line, 4*(1). Retrieved November 17, 2005, from http://www.studentaffairs.com/ejournal/Winter_2003/research.html

Fook, J. (1996) *The reflective researcher.* St. Leonards, NSW: Allen & Unwin.

Fordham, S. (1988). Racelessness as a factor in black student school success: Pragmatic strategy or Pyrrhic victory? *Harvard Educational Review, 58*(1), 54–84.

Franklin, B., Attanucci, J., & Bacon, E. (2005). *Seeing the narrative: An esthetic of knowing—a boal theater workshop.* Retrieved November 21, 2005, from http://www.coe.uga.edu/quig/preconf2005.html

Freeman, M. (2000). Knocking on doors: On constructing culture. *Qualitative Inquiry, 6*(3), 359–369.

Friedan, B. (1963). *The feminine mystique.* New York: Dell.

Garson, G. D. (n.d.). *Case studies.* Retrieved November 9, 2005, from http://www2.chass.ncsu.edu/garson/pa765/cases.htm

Geertz, C. (1973). *The interpretation of cultures.* New York: Basic Books.

Geiger, S. N. (1986). Women's life histories: Method and content. *Journal of Women in Culture and Society, 11,* 334–351.

Genzuk, M. (2003). *A synthesis of ethnographic research.* Retrieved November 5, 2005, from http://www-rcf.usc.edu/~genzuk/Ethnographic_Research.html

Gilgun, J. (2005). "Grab" and good science: Writing up the results of qualitative research. *Qualitative Health Research, 15*(2), 256–262. Retrieved November 21, 2005, from http://qhr.sagepub.com/cgi/content/abstract/15/2/256

Giorgi, A. (1989). One type of analysis of descriptive data: Procedures involved in following a scientific phenomenological method. *Methods: A Journal of Human Science, Annual Edition, 1,* 39–61.

Glaser, B. G. (1978). *Theoretical sensitivity: Advances in the methodology of grounded theory.* Mill Valley, CA: Sociology Press.

Glaser, B. G. (1992). *Basics of grounded theory analysis: Emergence vs. forcing.* Mill Valley, CA: Sociology Press.

Glaser, B. G. (1998). *Doing grounded theory: Issues and discussion.* Mill Valley, CA: Sociology Press.

Glaser, B G., & Holton, J. (2004, March). Remodeling grounded theory [80 paragraphs]. *Forum Qualitative Sozialforschung/Forum: Qualitative Social Research, 5*(2). Retrieved November 3, 2005, from http://www.qualitative-research.net/fqstexte/2-04/2-04glaser-e.htm

Glaser, B. G., & Strauss, A. (1967). *The discovery of grounded theory: Strategies for qualitative research.* Chicago: Aldine.

Glass, P. (2001). *Autism and the family.* Unpublished doctoral dissertation, Virginia Polytechnic Institute and State University, Falls Church.

Goldman, R., (2004). *Digital video design ethnography in the learning sciences.* Paper presented at The American Educational Research Association Annual Meeting, San Diego, CA.

Goode, D. (1994). *A world without words: The social construction of children born deaf and blind.* Philadelphia: Temple University Press.

Goodson, I. (Ed.). (1992). *Studying teachers' lives.* London and New York: Routledge.

Guion, L. (2002). *Triangulation: Establishing the validity of qualitative studies.* Retrieved November 3, 2005, from http://edis.ifas.ufl.edu/pdffiles/FY/FY39400.pdf

Gültekin, N., Inowlocki, L., & Lutz, H. (2003, September). Quest and query: Interpreting a biographical interview with a Turkish woman laborer in Germany [55 paragraphs]. *Forum Qualitative Sozialforschung/Forum: Qualitative Social Research, 4*(3). Retrieved November 17, 2005, from http://www.qualitative-research.net/fqs-texte/3-03/3-03gueltekinetal-e.htm

Haig, B. (1995). *Grounded theory as scientific method.* Retrieved November 3, 2005, from http://www.ed.uiuc.edu/EPS/PES-yearbook/95_docs/haig.html

Hamill, C. (1999). Academic essay writing in the first person: A guide for undergraduates. *Nursing Standard, 13*(44), 38–40.

Harding, S. (1987). *Feminism and methodology.* Bloomington: Indiana University Press.

Harding, S. (1998). *Is science multicultural? Postcolonialism, feminism & epistemologies.* Bloomington: Indiana University Press.

Harding, S. (2005). *Science and social inequality: Feminist and postcolonial issues.* Champaign: University of Illinois Press.

Harré, R. (2004). Qualitative research as science. *Qualitative Research in Psychology, 1*(1), 3–14.

Haskell, J., Linds, W., & Ippolito, J. (2002, September). Opening spaces of possibility: The enactive as a qualitative research approach [96 paragraphs]. *Forum Qualitative Sozialforschung/Forum: Qualitative Social Research, 3*(3). Retrieved November 4, 2005, from http://www.qualitative-research.net/fqs-texte/3-02/3-02haskelletal-e.htm

Hébert, T. (2001). *Jermaine: A gifted black child living in rural poverty.* Paper presented at the QUIG-Qualitative Interest Group Conference, Athens, GA.

Hempel, C. (1965). *Aspects of scientific explanation and other essays in the philosophy of science.* New York: Macmillan/Free Press.

Henson, M. (2001). Cultural imperialism: A case study of football in Bath in the late-Victorian era. *The Sports Historian. The Journal of the British Society of Sports History, 21*(2), 20–34.

Hey, V. (1997). *The company she keeps: An ethnography of girls' friendships.* Philadelphia: Open University Press.

Hoepfl, M. (1997, Fall). Choosing qualitative research: A primer for technology education researchers. *Journal of Technology Education, 9*(1). Retrieved November 3, 2005, from http://scholar.lib.vt.edu/ejournals/JTE/v9n1/hoepfl.html

Holliday, A. (2001). *Doing and writing qualitative research.* London: Sage.

Hollway, W., & Jefferson, T. (2000). *Doing qualitative research differently.* London: Sage.

Holt, N. L. (2003). Representation, legitimation, and autoethnography: An autoethnographic writing story. *International Journal of Qualitative Methods, 2*(1). Retrieved November 21, 2005, from http://www.ualberta.ca/~iiqm/backissues/2_1/html/holt.html

Hopkins, B., & Crowell, S. (Eds.). (2003). *The new yearbook for phenomenology and phenomenological philosophy.* Madison: University of Wisconsin.

Humphreys, L. (1970). *Tearoom trade: Impersonal sex in public places.* New York: Aldine.

Husserl, E. (1981). Pure phenomenology, its methods and its field of investigation (R. W. Jordan, Trans.). In P. McCormick & F. Elliston (Eds.), *Husserl: Shorter works* (pp. 9–17). Notre Dame, IN: University of Notre Dame Press. (Original work published 1917)

Hutchison, K. B. (1999). Single sex classrooms amendment. 106th Cong., 1st sess. *Congressional Record* (6 October).

Ihde, D. (1995). *Postphenomenology: Essays in the postmodern context.* Evanston, IL: Northwestern University Press.

Imel, S. (1998). *Race and gender in adult education.* ERIC Clearinghouse Trends Alert. Retrieved November 7, 2005, from http://www-tcall.tamu.edu/erica/docs/race-gen .htm

Imel, S., Kerka, S., & Wonacott, M. (2002). *Qualitative research in adult, career, and career-technical education. Practitioner file.* Columbus, OH: ERIC Clearinghouse on Adult, Career, and Vocational Education. (ERIC Document Reproduction Service No. ED472366)

Intrator, S. (2000). *Eight text devices useful in writing qualitative research.* Paper presented at the American Educational Research Association, New Orleans, LA.

Janetius, T. (2003, June). *Phenomenological approach to human condition in counseling and psychotherapy.* Paper presented at the Phenomenology of Human Condition Conference, Dharmaram Vidya Kshetram, Bangalore, India.

Jensen, J. L., & Rodgers, R. (2001). Cumulating the intellectual gold of case study research. *Public Administration Review, 61*(2), 236–246.

Jewett, L. (2004). *A delicate dance: Autobiography, ethnography and the pedagogical lie of autoethnography*. Paper presented at the American Educational Research Association, San Diego, CA.

Josselson, R. (Ed.). (1996). *Ethics and process in the narrative study of lives* (Vol. 4). Thousand Oaks, CA: Sage.

Joy, D. (2004). *Instructors transitioning to online education*. Unpublished doctoral dissertation, Virginia Polytechnic Institute and State University, Blacksburg.

Kabel, C. J. (2002). *Qualitative research, now there are choices: My study used photos, poems, and people's voices*. Retrieved November 3, 2005, from http://www.coe.uga .edu/quig/proceedings/Quig02_Proceedings/choices.pdf

Katsulis, Y. (2003). Mixed methods: Theory and practice. *CIRA Methodology and Biostatistics Seminar Series*. Retrieved November 6, 2005, from http://cira.med.yale.edu/events/ Mixed%20Methods%20Presentation.pdf

Kearney, C. (2003). *The monkey's mask: Identity, memory, narrative and voice*. Stoke-on-Trent, UK: Trentham Books.

Kearney, K., & Hyle, A. (2004). Drawing out emotions: The use of participant-produced drawings in qualitative inquiry. *Qualitative Research, 4*, 361–382.

Kearsley, G. (2002). MEPP: A case study in online education. *The Technology Source*. Retrieved November 3, 2005, from http://ts.mivu.org/default.asp?show=article&id=935

Kelly, A., & Kerner, A. (2004). The scent of positive lives: (Re)memorializing our loved ones. *Qualitative Inquiry, 10*(5), 767–787.

Kidder, T. (1989). *Among schoolchildren*. New York: Avon Books.

Kitzinger J. (1994). The methodology of focus groups: The importance of interaction between research participants. *Sociology of Health, 16*(1), 103–121.

Koro-Ljungberg, M. (2001). Metaphors as a way to explore qualitative data. *International Journal of Qualitative Studies in Education, 14*(3), 367–379.

Kozinets, R. (2002). The field behind the screen: Using netnography for marketing research in online communities. *Journal of Marketing Research, 39*(1), 61–72.

Krueger, R. A. (1988). *Focus groups: A practical guide for applied research*. London: Sage.

Kuula, A. (2000). *In pursuit of qualitative data*. Retrieved November 3, 2005, from http:// www.fsd.uta.fi/tietoarkistolehti/english/03/quali.html

Kvale, S. (1996). *InterViews: An introduction to qualitative research interviewing*. Thousand Oaks, CA: Sage.

Lagemann, E. C. (2000). *An elusive science: The troubling history of education research*. Chicago: University of Chicago Press

Larkin, M. (2002). *Features of a good qualitative project*. Retrieved November 21, 2005, from http://www.psy.dmu.ac.uk/michael/qual_good_project.htm

Lather, P. (1991). *Feminist research in education:Within/against*. Geelong, Victoria, Australia: Deakin University Press.

LeCompte, M. (2002). The transformation of ethnographic practices. *Qualitative Research, 2*(3), 283–299.

Lemke, J. L. (1994). Semiotics and the deconstruction of conceptual learning. *Journal of Accelerative Learning and Teaching, 19*(1), 67–110.

Lemke, J. L. (2003). Analysing verbal data: Principles, methods, problems. In K. Tobin, & B. Fraser (Eds.), *International handbook of science education*. Retrieved November 6, 2005, from http://academic.brooklyn.cuny.edu/education/jlemke/papers/handbook.htm

LePage-Lees, P. (1997). Struggling with a nontraditional past: Academically successful women from disadvantaged backgrounds discuss their relationship with 'disadvantage'. *Psychology of Women Quarterly, 21*(3), 365–385.

Lester, P. (n.d.). *A picture's worth a thousand words.* Retrieved November 26, 2005, from http://commfaculty.fullerton.edu/lester/writings/letters.html

Lester, S. (1999). *An introduction to phenomenological research.* Retrieved November 5, 2005, from http://www.devmts.demon.co.uk/resmethy.htm

Lévi-Strauss, C. (1968). *Structural anthropology* (M. Layton, Trans.). New York: Penguin Press. (Original work published 1958)

Lewis, M. (1995). *Focus group interviews in qualitative research: A review of the literature.* Retrieved November 3, 2005, from http://www.scu.edu.au/schools/gcm/ar/arr/arow/rlewis.html

Lichtman, M. (2004, September). "The future is here; it is just not widely distributed yet"—Adapted from William Gibson. Ron Chenail in conversation with Marilyn Lichtman [19 paragraphs]. *Forum Qualitative Sozialforschung/Forum: Qualitative Social Research 5*(3). Retrieved November 7, 2005, from http://www.qualitative-research.net/fqs-texte/3-04/04-3-11-e.htm

Lichtman, M. (2005, August). Review: Mechthild Kiegelmann and Leo Gürtler (Eds.) (2003). Research questions and matching methods of analysis [22 paragraphs]. *Forum Qualitative Sozialforschung/Forum: Qualitative Social Research, 6*(3), Retrieved November 28, 2005, from http://www.qualitative-research.net/fqs-texte/3-05/05-3-16-e.htm

Lichtman, M., & Taylor, S. I. (1993). *Conducting and reporting case studies* (Report No. TM 019 965). Paper presented at the annual meeting of the American Educational Research Association, Atlanta, GA. (ERIC Document Reproduction Service No. ED 358 157)

Liebow, E., (1967). *Tally's corner: A study of Negro street corner men.* London: Routledge.

Liebow, E. (1993). *Tell them who I am: The lives of homeless women.* New York: Penguin Books.

Lincoln, Y. S., & Guba, E. (1985). *Naturalistic inquiry.* Beverly Hills, CA: Sage.

Lincoln, Y. S., & Guba, E. (2000). Paradigmatic controversies, contradictions, and emerging confluences. In N. Denzin & Y. S. Lincoln (Eds.), *Handbook of qualitative research* (pp. 163–188). Thousand Oaks, CA: Sage.

Lindwall, L., von Post, I., & Bergbom, I. (2003). Patients' and nurses' experiences of perioperative dialogues. *Journal of Advanced Nursing, 43*(3), 246–253.

Liu, Y. (2000, May). How to write qualitative research? A book review [9 paragraphs]. *The Qualitative Report, 5*(1/2). Retrieved November 21, 2005, from http://www.nova.edu/ssss/QR/QR5-1/liu.html

Lo, A. (1993). *Sojourner adjustment: The experience of wives of mainland Chinese graduate students.* Unpublished doctoral dissertation, Virginia Polytechnic Institute and State University, Blacksburg.

Lye, J. (1996). *Some principles of phenomenological hermeneutics.* Retrieved November 9, 2005, from http://www.brocku.ca/english/courses/4F70/ph.html

Maguire, P. (1987). *Doing participatory research: A feminist approach.* Amherst: University of Massachusetts.

Mann, C., & Stewart, F. (2000). *Internet communication and qualitative research: A handbook for research online.* London: Sage.

Markham, A. (1998). *Life online: Researching real experience in virtual space.* Walnut Creek, CA: AltaMira Press.

Markham, A. (2004). Reconsidering self and other: The methods, politics, and ethics of representation in online ethnography (Draft of chapter). In N. K. Denzin & Y. Lincoln (Eds.), *Handbook of qualitative research.* Retrieved November 17, 2005, from http://faculty.uvi.edu/users/amarkha/writing/denzinlincoln.htm

Maxwell, J. (2004). Causal explanation, qualitative research, and scientific inquiry in education. *Educational Researcher, 33*(2), 3–11.

McCarthy, A. (1999). *Getting serious about grounded theory.* Paper presented at the Western Australian Educational Research Forum.

McCarthy, A. (2001). *Educational choice: A grounded theory study.* Paper presented at the Western Australian Institute for Educational Research.

McCracken, G. (1988). *The long interview.* Newbury Park, CA: Sage.

McGinn, M., & Bosacki, S. (2004, March). Research ethics and practitioners: Concerns and strategies for novice researchers engaged in graduate education [52 paragraphs]. *Forum Qualitative Sozialforschung/Forum: Qualitative Social Research.* Retrieved November 4, 2005, from http://www.qualitative-research.net/fqs-texte/2-04/2-04mcginnbosacki-e.htm

McIntyre, A. (2002). Women researching their lives: Exploring violence and identity in Belfast, the north of Ireland. *Qualitative Research, 2*(3), 387–409.

McLeod, J. (2000). *Qualitative research as bricolate.* Paper presented at the Society for Psychotherapy Research Annual Conference, Chicago, IL.

McPhail, J. (1995). Phenomenology as philosophy and method. *Remedial and Special Education, 16,* 156–165, 177.

Merriam, S. (1988). *Case study research in education: A qualitative approach.* San Francisco: Jossey-Bass.

Merriam, S. (2002). *Qualitative research in practice: Examples for discussion and analysis.* San Francisco: Jossey-Bass.

Merton, R. K., & Kendall, P. L. (1946). The focused interview. *American Journal of Sociology, 51,* 541–557.

Mitchell, G. J., & Cody, W. K. (1993). The role of theory in qualitative research. *Nursing Science Quarterly, 6*(4), 170–178.

Morgan, D. (1988). *Focus groups as qualitative research.* Newbury Park, CA: Sage.

Morrow, S. (2003). *Qualitative research in psychology syllabus.* Retrieved November 4, 2005, from http://www.ed.utah.edu/psych/coursematerials/7420MorrowS03.pdf

Morse, J. (2003). A review committee's guide for evaluating qualitative proposals. *Qualitative Health Research, 13*(6), 833–851.

Moustakis, C. (1994). *Phenomenological research methods.* Thousand Oaks, CA: Sage.

Mruck, K. (2005, January). Editorial: The *FQS* issue on "secondary analysis of qualitative data" [6 paragraphs]. *Forum Qualitative Sozialforschung/Forum: Qualitative Social Research, 6*(1). Retrieved November 21, 2005, from http://www.qualitative-research.net/fqs-texte/1-05/05-1-48-e.htm

Nakamura, K. (2003). *Visual anthropology.* Retrieved November 7, 2005, from http://www.deaflibrary.org/nakamura/courses/visualanthro/index.shtml

Nettles, S., & Robinson, F. (1998). *Exploring the dynamics of resilience in an elementary school. Report No. 26.* Baltimore, MD: Center for Research on the Education of Students Placed At Risk (CRESPAR).

Neuman, W. L. (2003). *Social work research methods: Qualitative and quantitative approaches.* Boston: Allyn & Bacon.

Nielsen, T. (2000). Hermeneutic phenomenological data representation: Portraying the ineffable. *Australian Art Education, 23*(1), 9–14.

Nightingale, D., & Cromby, J. (Eds.). (1999). *Social constructionist psychology,* Buckingham: Open University Press. Retrieved November 21, 2005, from http://www .psy.dmu.ac.uk/michael/qual_reflexivity.htm

O'Loughlin-Brooks, J. (n.d.). *Literature review for human sexuality.* Retrieved November 17, 2005, from http://iws.ccccd.edu/jbrooks/chapter1.htm

Olson, L. (1995, April 12). Standards times 50. *Education Week,* pp. 14–20.

Online Writing Lab. (2004). Retrieved November 17, 2005, from http://owl.english.purdue .edu/workshops/hypertext/apa/interact/lit/index.html

The Painter's Keys. (n.d.). *Resource of art quotations.* Retrieved November 27, 2005, from http://www.painterskeys.com/getquotes.asp?fname=sw&ID=307

Parker, I. (2003). *Qualitative research in psychology: Criteria.* Retrieved November 5, 2005, from http://www.uel.ac.uk/cnr/documents/Parker.doc

Patton, M. Q. (2002). *Qualitative evaluation and research methods.* London: Sage.

Perttula, J. (2000). Transforming experience into knowledge: The phenomenological method revisited. *The Finnish Journal of Education, Kasvatus 31*(5), 428–442.

Petrie, G. (2003). ESL teachers' views on visual language: A grounded theory. *The Reading Matrix, 3*(3),137–168.

Pillow, W. (2003). Confession, catharsis, or cure? Rethinking the uses of reflexivity as methodological power in qualitative research. *International Journal of Qualitative Studies in Education, 16*(2), 175–196.

Piper, C. (n.d.). *Case study of a multimedia CD-ROM dissertation web.* Retrieved November 7, 2005, from http://www1.chapman.edu/soe/faculty/piper/casestudy.htm

Polan, D. (2004). *Brecht and the politics of self-reflexive cinema.* Retrieved November 21, 2005, from http://www.ejumpcut.org/archive/onlinessays/JC17folder/BrechtPolan.html

Priest, H. (2002, December). An approach to the phenomenological analysis of data (Issues in research). *Nurse Researcher,* 50–63.

Pyett, P. (2003). Validation of qualitative research in the "real world." *Qualitative Health Research, 13*(8), 1170–1179.

Ratcliff, D. (2003). Video methods in qualitative research. In P. Camic, J. Rhodes, & L. Yardley (Eds.), *Qualitative research in psychology: Expanding perspectives in methodology and design* (pp. 113–131). Washington, DC: American Psychological Association.

Ratner, C. (2002, September). Subjectivity and objectivity in qualitative methodology [29 paragraphs]. *Forum Qualitative Sozialforschun/Forum: Qualitative Social Research 3*(3). Retrieved November 7, 2005, from http://www.qualitative-research.net/fqs-texte/3-02/ 3-02ratner-e.htm

Reinharz, S. (1992). *Feminist methods in social research.* London: Oxford University Press.

Reinharz, S. (1997). Who am I? The need for a variety of selves in the field. In R. Hertz (Ed.), *Reflexivity & voice* (pp. 3–20). Thousand Oaks, CA: Sage.

Repass, M. (2002). *The professional woman's desire to retire: The process of transition.* Unpublished doctoral dissertation, Virginia Polytechnic Institute and State University, Falls Church.

Rezabek, R. (2000, January). Online focus groups: Electronic discussions for research [67 paragraphs]. *Forum Qualitative Sozialforschung/Forum: Qualitative Social Research, 1*(1). Retrieved November 4, 2005, from http://www.qualitative-research .net/fqs-texte/1-00/1-00rezabek-e.htm

Richardson, L. (1997). *Fields of play: Constructing an academic life.* New Brunswick, NJ: Rutgers University Press.

Riessman, C. K. (2005). Narrative in social work: A critical review. *Qualitative Social Work, 4*(4), 383–404.

Rist, R. (1980). Blitzkrieg ethnography: On the transformation of a method into a movement. *Educational Researcher, 9*(2), 8–10.

Robbins, J. (2001). *Making connections: Adolescent girls' use of the Internet.* Unpublished doctoral dissertation, Virginia Polytechnic Institute and State University, Falls Church.

Robertson, J. (2003). Listening to the heartbeat of New York: Writings on the wall. *Qualitative Inquiry, 9*(1), 129–152.

Robinson, P. (2000). The body matrix: A phenomenological exploration of student bodies on-line. *Educational Technology & Society 3*(3). Retrieved November 4, 2005, from http://ifets.ieee.org/periodical/vol_3_2000/c05.html

Roman, L., & Apple, M. (1990). Is naturalism a move away from positivism? Materialist and feminist approaches to subjectivity in ethnographic research. In E. Eisner & A. Peshkin (Eds.), *Qualitative inquiry in education* (pp. 38–73). New York: Teachers College Press.

Rose, G. (1993). *Feminism and geography: The limits of geographical knowledge.* St. Paul: University of Minnesota Press.

Rosenberg, D. (1999). *Action for prevention: Feminist practices in transformative learning in women's health and the environment (with a focus on breast cancer).* Retrieved November 9, 2005, from http://www.oise.utoronto.ca/CASAE/cnf99/drosenb.htm

Roth, W.-M. (2004, February). Qualitative research and ethics [15 paragraphs]. *Forum Qualitative Sozialforschung/Forum: Qualitative Social Research.* Retrieved November 7, 2005, from http://www.qualitative-research.net/fqs-texte/2-04/2-04roth2-e.htm

Rubin, H., & Rubin, I. (1995). *Qualitative interviewing: The art of hearing data.* Thousand Oaks, CA: Sage.

Rufi, J. (1926). *The small high school.* Unpublished doctoral dissertation, Teachers College, Columbia University, New York

Russell, G. M., & Kelly, N. H. (2002, September). Research as interacting dialogic processes: Implications for reflexivity [47 paragraphs]. *Forum Qualitative Sozialforschung/Forum: Qualitative Social Research, 3*(3). Retrieved November 4, 2005, from http://www .qualitative-research.net/fqs-texte/3-02/3-02russellkelly-e.htm

Rusu-Toderean, O. (n.d.). *In between positivism and post-positivism. A personal defence of empirical approaches to social sciences.* Retrieved November 4, 2005, from http://www .polito.ubbcluj.ro/EAST/East6/toderean.htm

Ryle, G. (1949). *The concept of mind.* Chicago: University of Chicago Press.

Saldana, J. (2003). Dramatizing data: A primer. *Qualitative Inquiry, 9*(2), 218–236.

Sandelowski, M. (1995). Sample size in qualitative research. *Research in Nursing & Health, 18,* 179–183.

San Filippo, D. (1992). *An educational program for death education.* Retrieved November 5, 2005, from http://www.lutz-sanfilippo.com/library/education/lsfeducationdeath.html

Santopinto, M. (1989). The relentless drive to be ever thinner: A study using the phenomenological method. *Nursing Science Quarterly, 2,* 29–36.

Schalet, A., Hunt, G., & Joe-Laidler, K. (2003). Respectability and autonomy: The articulation and meaning of sexuality among the girls in the gang. *Journal of Contemporary Ethnography, 32*(1), 108–143.

Scheurich, J. (1997). *Research method in the postmodern.* London: Falmer.

Schrage, M. (1999). *Serious play: How the world's best companies simulate to innovate.* Boston: Harvard Business School Press.

Schwandt, T. (2001). *Dictionary of qualitative inquiry.* Thousand Oaks, CA: Sage.

Scown, A. (2003). *The academic as knowledge worker: The voices of experience.* Paper presented at the Third International Conference on Knowledge, Culture and Change in Organisations, Penang, Malaysia. Retrieved November 4, 2005, from http://2003 .managementconference.com/ProposalSystem/Presentations/P000217.

Secretan, L. H. K. (1997). *Reclaiming higher ground: Creating organizations that inspire the soul.* New York: McGraw Hill.

Shank, G. (2002). *Qualitative research: A personal skills approach.* Columbus: Merrill Prentice-Hall.

Shepherd, N. (2003). Interviewing online: Qualitative research in the network(ed) society. *Association of Qualitative Research Sydney, Australia, 17*–19.

Simmons-Mackie, N., & Damico, J. (2003). Contributions of qualitative research to the knowledge base of normal communication. *American Journal of Speech-Language Pathology, 12*(2), 144–154.

Skinner, B. F. (1938). *The behavior of organisms: An experimental analysis.* Englewood Cliffs, NJ: Prentice Hall.

Smith, J. K., & Heshusius, L. (1986). Closing down the conversation: The end of the quantitative-qualitative debate among educational inquirers. *Educational Researcher, 15*(1), 4–12.

Snyder, W. (2003). *Perceptions on the diffusion and adoption of Skillsoft, an e-learning program: A case study.* Unpublished doctoral dissertation, Virginia Polytechnic Institute and State University, Blacksburg.

Sokolowski, R. (2000). *Introduction to phenomenology.* Cambridge: Cambridge University Press.

Soy, S. (1997). *The case study as a research method.* Retrieved November 9, 2005, from http://www.gslis.utexas.edu/~ssoy/usesusers/l391d1b.htm

Sparkes, A., & Smith, B. (2003). Men, sport, spinal cord injury and narrative time. *Qualitative Research, 3*(3), 295–320.

Spradley, J. P. (1979). *The ethnographic interview.* New York: Holt, Rinehart & Winston.

Stake, R. (1995). *The art of case study research.* Thousand Oaks, CA: Sage.

Stanage, S. M. (1995). Lifelong learning: A phenomenology of meaning and value transformation in postmodern adult education. In S. B. Merriam (Ed.), *Selected writings on philosophy and adult education* (pp. 269–280). Malabar, FL: Krieger.

Starbuck, H. M. (2003). *Clashing and converging: Effects of the Internet on the correspondence art network.* Austin: University of Texas.

Steinberg, S. (2000). The post-modernist wonderland [Review of the book *Intellectual impostures*]. Retrieved November 7, 2005, from http://www.wsws.org/articles/2000/jul2000/ post-j01.shtml

Stevenson, H., & Nerison-Low, R. (1998). *To sum it up: Case studies of education in Germany, Japan, and the United States.* Retrieved November 9, 2005, from http://www.ed.gov/pubs/SumItUp/title.html

Stewart, D. W., & Shamdasani, P. N. (1990). *Focus groups: Theory and practice.* London: Sage.

Strauss, A., & Corbin, J. (1990). *Basics of qualitative research: Grounded theory procedures and techniques* (2nd ed.). Newbury Park, CA: Sage.

Sweet, C. (1999). *Designing and conducting virtual focus groups.* Retrieved November 4, 2005, from http://www.sysurvey.com/tips/designing_and_conducting.htm

Tashakkori, A., & Teddlie, C. (Eds.). (2003). *Handbook on mixed methods in the behavioral and social sciences.* Thousand Oaks, CA: Sage.

Taylor, E. B. (1871). *Primitive culture.* London: John Murray.

Taylor, E., Beck, J., & Ainsworth, E. (2001). Publishing qualitative adult education research: A peer review perspective. *Studies in the Education of Adults, 33*(2), 163–179.

Tellis, W. (1997, July). Introduction to case study [68 paragraphs]. *The Qualitative Report, 3*(2). Retrieved November 4, 2005, from http://www.nova.edu/ssss/QR/QR3-2/tellis1.html

Thorne, B. (1993). *Gender play: Girls and boys in school.* Buckingham: Open University Press.

Thorne, S. (2000). Data analysis in qualitative research. *Evidence-Based Nursing, 3,* 68–70.

Tinelli, A. (2000). *Leaders and their learnings: What and how leaders learn as they transform organizations.* Unpublished doctoral dissertation, Virginia Polytechnic Institute and State University, Blacksburg.

Tripp, D. (1992). Critical theory and educational research. *Issues in Educational Research, 2*(1), 13–23.

Trochim, W. (2001). *Research methods knowledge base.* Cincinnati, OH: Atomic Dog Publishing. Retrieved January 3, 2006, from http://www.socialresearchmethods.net/kb/

Vandenberg, D. (1996). *Phenomenology and educational discourse.* Durban: Heinemann Higher and Further Education.

Van Den Hoonaard, W. C., & Schouten, J. (2004). From road to labyrinth: The state, fate, or hope of ethnography. *Journal of Contemporary Ethnography, 33*(4), 488–496.

Van der Mescht, H. (2004). Phenomenology in education: A case study in educational leadership. *Indo-Pacific Journal of Phenomenology, 4*(1), 1–16.

Van Maanen, J. (1988). *Tales of the field: On writing ethnography.* Chicago: University of Chicago Press.

van Manen, M. (1997). *Researching lived experiences: Human science for action sensitive pedagogy.* London, ON: Althouse Press.

Wallace, T. (2003). *N. C. State ethnographic field school.* Retrieved November 4, 2005, from from http://www4.ncsu.edu:8030/~twallace/Guate-Syllabus%202003.htm

Weems, M. (2003). Poetry. *Qualitative Inquiry, 9*(1), 13–14.

Wolcott, H. F. (1973). *The man in the principal's office: An ethnography.* New York: Holt, Rinehart & Winston.

Wolcott, H. F. (1990). *Writing up qualitative research.* Thousand Oaks, CA: Sage.

Wolcott, H. F. (2002). The *sneaky kid and its aftermath: Ethics and intimacy in fieldwork.* Walnut Creek, CA: AltaMira Press.

Wooden, H. Z., & Mort, P. (1929). Supervised correspondence study for high school pupils. *Teachers College Record, 30*(4), 447–452.

Wright, R. L. (2004). You were hired to teach! Ideological struggle, education, and teacher burnout at the new prison for women. *The Qualitative Report, 9*(4), 630–651. Retrieved November 21, 2005, from http://www.nova.edu/ssss/QR/QR9-4/wright.pdf

Yin, R. (2002). *Case study research: Design and methods.* Thousand Oaks, CA: Sage.

Yon, D. (2003). Highlights and overview of the history of educational ethnography. *Annual Review of Anthropology, 32,* 411–429.

Zucker, A. (1996). *Introduction to the philosophy of science.* Upper Saddle River, NJ: Prentice Hall.

Index

ABOUT THE AUTHOR

Marilyn Lichtman is a retired professor of educational research and evaluation from Virginia Tech at both the main campus in Blacksburg, Virginia, and at the graduate campus in Falls Church, Virginia. After attending The University of Chicago as an undergraduate, she moved to Washington, D.C. She completed all her degrees at The George Washington University, receiving her doctorate in educational research. She taught both qualitative and quantitative research courses while at The Catholic University of America and Virginia Tech. She is a regular user of the Internet for teaching and was an early contributor to teaching qualitative courses online. She is currently on the editorial boards of *The Qualitative Report* and *Forum: Qualitative Social Research (FQS),* both online journals devoted to qualitative issues. She has served as a consultant to many school systems, private companies, and government agencies. She has been a docent of the Corcoran Gallery of Art in Washington, D.C., for more than a dozen years.